THE SCHOOLS HISTORY PROJECT

S·H·P

OFFICIAL TEXT

ELIZABETHAN ENGLAND

a study in depth

**CORE TEXTS
FOR GCSE**

**ANDY
HARMSWORTH**

**Series Editors:
Ian Dawson
Chris Culpin**

JOHN MURRAY

The Schools History Project

This project was set up by the Schools Council in 1972. Its main aim was to suggest suitable objectives for history teachers, and to promote the use of appropriate materials and teaching methods for their realisation. This involved a reconsideration of the nature of history and its relevance in secondary schools, the design of a syllabus framework which shows the uses of history in the education of adolescents, and the setting up of appropriate examinations.

Since 1978 the project has been based at Trinity and All Saints' College, Leeds. It is now self-funding and with the advent of the National Curriculum it has expanded its publications to provide courses for Key Stage 3, and for a range of GCSE and A level syllabuses. The project provides INSET for all aspects of National Curriculum, GCSE and A level history.

Series consultants
Terry Fiehn
Tim Lomas
Martin and Jenny Tucker

Note: The wording and sentence structure of some written sources have been adapted and simplified to make them accessible to all students, while faithfully preserving the sense of the original.

Words printed in SMALL CAPITALS are defined in the Glossary on page 163.

© Andy Harmsworth 1999

First published in 1999 by
John Murray (Publishers) Ltd
50 Albemarle Street
London W1X 4BD

Layouts by Liz Rowe
Artwork by Mike Humphries, Oxford Illustrators, Tony Randell, Steve Smith
Typeset in 10.5/12pt Walbaum Book by Wearset, Boldon, Tyne and Wear
Colour separations by Colourscript
Printed and bound by G. Canale, Torino, Italy

A catalogue entry for this title is available from the British Library.

ISBN 0 7195 7474 9
Teachers' Resource Book ISBN 0 7195 7475 7

Contents

INTRODUCTION

A *traitor in the Tower?*

IT IS MARCH 1554. A young princess, just twenty years old, is being held as a prisoner in the Tower of London. She is suspected of TREASON and the penalty is death. Both of her parents and her younger brother are dead. She walks sadly across her room to the window and gazes across the buildings outside. She notices the site of the executioner's block on Tower Green. Her mother had been beheaded there eighteen years earlier. The princess touches the back of her neck. She can almost feel the blade of the executioner's axe. Then her thoughts turn to the events which have shaped her troubled life. She becomes lost in her memories . . .

Who was the princess?

The sad princess gazing out of the window was Elizabeth Tudor. She was the daughter of King Henry VIII and his second wife, Anne Boleyn. In March 1554 she was facing the most dangerous moment of her short life …

■ ACTIVITY

You are Princess Elizabeth's doctor. You are the only person who is allowed to visit her in the Tower of London. When you visit her she talks to you about her life. Study the information on the next three pages. Then write an account of what Elizabeth tells you in your diary, under the following headings:

- how the country has changed since her grandfather became king
- the good times in Elizabeth's life
- the bad times in her life
- what lessons Elizabeth has learned from her life.

■ TASK

Draw a timeline covering the years 1485 to 1558. Use the information on the next four pages to mark along it:

- the reigns of the Tudor kings and queens
- the religion of the country during their reigns
- the main national events during their reigns
- the main events in Elizabeth's personal life.

The Tudors

1485

England was torn apart by CIVIL WARS for 30 years in the fifteenth century. The wars were called the Wars of the Roses. Two rival families, Lancaster and York, fought each other to gain the throne. Several kings were overthrown and murdered. In 1485 Henry Tudor, a Welsh nobleman and leader of the Lancastrians, invaded England. He defeated and killed King Richard III at the Battle of Bosworth.

Henry Tudor became King Henry VII. He married Elizabeth of York and peace was restored to the country. Henry VII was Elizabeth's grandfather.

1509

Henry VII died in 1509. Elizabeth's father became King Henry VIII. He married Catherine of Aragon, a Spanish princess. They had one daughter, Mary.

1527

Henry met Anne Boleyn, a young noblewoman. He soon fell in love with her.

1529

Henry VIII wanted to marry Anne Boleyn. He needed the Pope's permission to divorce Catherine of Aragon. The Pope was the Head of the ROMAN CATHOLIC Church. Divorce was against the teachings of the Church. The Pope would not allow Henry's divorce.

1533

In 1533 Anne Boleyn became pregnant. Henry decided to break away from the Roman Catholic Church, so that he could marry Anne quickly. He became Head of the new Church of England. The Archbishop of Canterbury declared that Henry's marriage to Catherine of Aragon was ended. Anyone who refused to accept Henry as Head of the Church could be put to death as a TRAITOR.

1533

Henry and Anne quickly got married. On 7 September 1533 Anne Boleyn gave birth to a baby daughter. She was named Elizabeth, after Henry's mother.

1536–40

In 1536 Henry VIII was worried. He thought that Roman Catholic countries were planning to attack England. Many monks and nuns still supported the Pope. Henry had no money. He decided to close all the monasteries and nunneries. Over the next four years he seized all their wealth. In the north of England 30,000 people protested against these changes. Henry sent an army to defeat them. 200 protesters were executed.

1536

In 1536 Anne Boleyn, Elizabeth's mother, gave birth to a boy but the baby was born dead. Henry was furious. He accused his wife of being unfaithful and plotting to overthrow him. Anne Boleyn was executed at the Tower of London for treason. Elizabeth was declared ILLEGITIMATE. She was two years old.

1537

Henry VIII quickly remarried. His third wife was Jane Seymour. In October 1537 she gave birth to a son, Prince Edward. Henry was delighted but Jane died a few days later. Henry married three more times but he had no more children.

1543

The young Princess Elizabeth was sent away. She lived in various houses. Several governesses looked after her. Sometimes her half-sister, Mary, lived with her. Mary hated her younger sister. Elizabeth loved her father but she only saw him on special occasions.

1543–47

In 1543 Henry married his sixth wife, Catherine Parr. Elizabeth was now ten years old. She went to live with her father, his new wife and her young half-brother for most of the year. Elizabeth liked her new stepmother. Edward's teachers taught Elizabeth too, and she was a bright, hardworking student. She was brought up as a Protestant. She learnt to speak Greek, Latin, French and Italian. She was also taught stories from the Bible, dancing, riding, archery and needlework. Most of all, she loved music.

continued on next page

The Tudors — continued

The King's will says that Edward should be king after him. Until Edward has children, Mary will be next in line to the throne. Elizabeth will be last.

EDWARD VI
1547–1553

1547
Henry VIII died in 1547. Prince Edward became King Edward VI. He was only nine years old. Before Henry died, he arranged for wealthy lords to rule the country until Edward was eighteen.

1548
Princess Elizabeth was now fifteen years old. She went to live with her stepmother, Catherine Parr. Catherine married Thomas Seymour, a wealthy nobleman. When Catherine died in 1548, Thomas began to flirt with Elizabeth. He wanted to marry her. At first she was flattered by his attention. One day, Seymour burst into Elizabeth's bedroom. She was shocked. She suddenly realised that he only wanted to use her to make himself more powerful. In 1549 Seymour was executed for trying to overthrow the government.

We should get rid of Mary Tudor.

Yes, Elizabeth would be better – at least she's a Protestant.

1554
In 1554 a rebellion broke out in Kent. Led by Sir Thomas Wyatt, 4000 protesters marched to London. They were defeated and forced to surrender. Most of the rebels were pardoned but 90 of them, including Wyatt, were executed.

1548–49
Edward's advisers made the Church of England more PROTESTANT. Colourful wall paintings were whitewashed. Stained-glass windows and statues were removed from churches. In 1549 Roman Catholics in Devon and Cornwall protested against these changes. An army was sent to defeat them. The leaders of the protests were executed.

MARY
1553–1558

1553
Edward VI died in 1553. He was only fifteen. Elizabeth's older half-sister, Mary, became Queen of England. Elizabeth was now HEIR to the throne. Mary made England a Roman Catholic country again. She soon began to punish Protestants; some of them were burnt to death. She announced plans to marry Philip, heir to the Spanish throne.

I am innocent!

1554
Queen Mary suspected that her sister was involved in the rebellion. Elizabeth was arrested and taken to the Tower of London. She was accused of treason. If she was found guilty she would be executed . . .

■ ACTIVITY

Queen Mary cannot decide what to do with her sister. She has appointed you to investigate whether Princess Elizabeth is guilty of treason. Elizabeth will be put on trial if you think there is evidence to show that she:

■ knew about the rebellion before it happened
■ approved of the rebellion
■ wanted to overthrow Mary so that she could become Queen.

If she is found guilty she will be executed. However, if you think the evidence does not prove these three things you should advise Queen Mary that Elizabeth is not guilty. Queen Mary will have to set her free. Study the evidence below and write a report to the Queen to explain your decision.

Evidence against Elizabeth	Evidence in Elizabeth's favour
During the rebellion, Mary ordered Elizabeth to meet her in London. Elizabeth said she was too ill to travel.	Two doctors examined Elizabeth and said that her body was badly swollen.
Thomas Wyatt, the leader of the rebels, said that he had written a letter to Elizabeth about the rebellion.	Elizabeth said that she had never received Wyatt's letter.
Wyatt said that Elizabeth had approved of the rebellion.	Wyatt made this comment when he was a prisoner and was being tortured. Immediately before he was executed, Wyatt said that Elizabeth had not been involved in the rebellion.
	Elizabeth wrote a long letter to Queen Mary. In it, she protested that she was innocent.

What happened to Elizabeth?

Princess Elizabeth stayed in the Tower as a prisoner for two long months. Queen Mary was advised that there was not enough evidence to put her sister on trial. Eventually, she decided to send Elizabeth to Woodstock House in Oxfordshire, far away from London. Elizabeth was guarded at all times. Later, she was moved to a small palace at Hatfield in Hertfordshire.

Four years later, on 17 November 1558, Queen Mary died. All over the country church bells rang out to announce that there was a new monarch.

The young princess was now Queen. She was 25 years old. The country was in turmoil. Would Elizabeth become a successful queen of England? Most people did not think so.

> Your Majesty, Queen Mary is dead. You are now Queen of England!

> This is the Lord's doing, and it is marvellous in our eyes.

Elizabeth receives the news that she has become Queen

> Not another queen! Everyone knows that women are too weak to rule a country like England. I bet she doesn't last long.

> Yes. What about the other queens we've had? When Matilda was Queen in the Middle Ages there was a civil war. And then Mary Tudor – marrying the King of Spain, bringing back the Pope, burning good Protestants and losing a war to the French. No good, the lot of them!

Many people did not expect Elizabeth to become a successful queen

Investigating Elizabethan England

THIS BOOK IS a Study in Depth. You will be studying in detail a period of about 50 years, in order to investigate the reign of Queen Elizabeth I. She reigned for 45 years, from 1558 to 1603. You will be finding out about important events, the achievements of famous personalities, the lives of different kinds of people and England's relations with other countries. You will be working like a real historian investigating important historical questions about Elizabeth's reign. You will improve your historical skills by using different kinds of source to help you reach your conclusions. Some of the sources will be from Elizabeth's reign, others will be interpretations which were produced in later times. Most of all, you will be finding out about the woman who was the ruler of this country for nearly half a century – Queen Elizabeth I.
Your investigation will go through several stages – starting now!

Stage 1: do you know anything about Elizabeth I already?

Usually when historians begin an investigation, they already know something about the period or individual they are going to study. This helps them to decide what exactly they want to find out more about. Even today, 400 years later, Elizabeth I is one of the most famous of England's kings and queens. You must know something about her already, even if it is not much! You have probably studied her reign before – in your primary school and in Year 8 in your secondary school. You might have read books or seen films and television programmes that were set in Elizabeth's reign.

SOURCE 1 Miranda Richardson playing the part of Elizabeth I in the BBC comedy series, *Blackadder II*. Richardson portrays Elizabeth as a rather silly young woman, who enjoyed practical jokes and had people's heads cut off at a whim

Surely the real Elizabeth I wasn't anything like the crazy character in *Blackadder?*

■ TALKING POINTS

1. What do you already know about Elizabeth I and her reign?
2. Is there anything more that you would like to find out?
3. If you already know something about Elizabeth I, is there any point in spending a whole term or more studying her reign?

Stage 2: choosing a question to investigate

The next stage for historians is to choose a 'big' question to which they want to find an answer. There are many 'small' questions about Elizabeth I which you might have already chosen. For example:

- what colour was her hair?
- what did she look like?
- where did she live?

If you think about it, these are not very important questions to ask about a ruler of England. 'Was Elizabeth I a successful ruler?' is a much bigger and more important question to ask. This book has been written to help you investigate this question.

■ **TALKING POINT**

Why is 'Was Elizabeth I a successful ruler?' a 'big' historical question? What sort of information will you need in order to answer it?

What do I really want to find out about Elizabeth I?

Stage 3: forming a hypothesis

You have probably heard the word 'hypothesis' before in your science lessons. It means a theory or idea which you go on to test to find out if it is correct. Before historians begin an investigation, they think of a hypothesis – it contains their first thoughts about the question they are going to investigate. It does not matter if it eventually turns out to be wrong – it often does!

■ **TASK 1**

1. From what you already know about Elizabeth I, do you think that she was a successful ruler? Briefly explain the reasons for your answer.
2. Write this down in the form of a hypothesis. For example, 'I think that Elizabeth I was ... because ...'.

■ **TASK 2**

1. a) From what she has studied so far, what conclusions should Student A (on page 12) reach about Elizabeth I?
   b) Do you think that her conclusions are based on good evidence? Explain the reasons for your answer.
2. a) From what she has studied so far, what conclusions should Student B (on page 13) reach about Elizabeth I?
   b) Do you think that her conclusions are based on good evidence? Explain the reasons for your answer.

3. Who do you think has studied the better evidence about Elizabeth I's reign – Student A or Student B? Explain the reasons for your answer.
4. Using ALL the material you have studied in this chapter, including the sources which the two students studied, write a short paragraph explaining how successful you now think Elizabeth I was as a ruler.
5. How different is your answer to Question 4 from the answer you gave to Question 2 in Task 1? Why do you think this is?

Stage 4: investigating the past

Scientists test a hypothesis by carrying out experiments. Historians cannot do this. They can only study the available sources and see what evidence they contain. Like scientists, however, they have to be prepared to change or even abandon their hypothesis if it does not match the results of their investigation. After all, a hypothesis only consists of their first thoughts.

Here and on the next page are two history students who have just started their investigation into Elizabeth I's reign.

TALKING POINTS

1. Why can't historians carry out experiments to test their ideas?
2. What are the differences between the way you work in history and in the sciences you study? What are the similarities?

Student A

I have started my investigation by finding out what historians have said about Elizabeth I. This is what I have found so far.

SOURCE 2 'Elizabeth I: Gloriana!'

66 *Elizabeth I's reign was a glorious period in English History. When she became Queen in 1558 the country faced many dangers, but Elizabeth solved them all under her wise rule. Her people became united and enjoyed nearly half a century of peace and prosperity. England became a very powerful country, not just in Europe, but across the whole world. It was also a time of brilliant cultural achievement in poetry, art and drama. Elizabeth's reign was a Golden Age. Elizabeth was more than just a queen – she deserves to be remembered as a goddess, Gloriana.* 99

SOURCE 3 'Elizabeth I: a reassessment'

66 *Elizabeth I's success has been greatly exaggerated. When she died hardly anyone was sad at the death of this bad-tempered old woman. She preferred to leave serious problems to her successor instead of solving them herself; the monarchy was in debt, Parliament was becoming more powerful and the country faced dangerous religious divisions. Her people were paying high taxes for an expensive, unsuccessful war. Poverty and unemployment were widespread. Forty years later these problems helped to cause the English Civil War. Elizabeth I was not a successful ruler.* 99

Student B

I've started my investigation by looking at what people who lived during Elizabeth I's reign said about her. I've looked at the way they painted her, too. This is what I have found out so far . . .

SOURCE 4 *Elizabeth and the Goddesses*, painted in 1569. The goddesses of wisdom, beauty and women look worried as Elizabeth walks towards them

SOURCE 5 An extract from a ballad written in 1600

S

66 *The noblest queen,*
That ever was seen,
In England doth reign this day. 99

SOURCE 6 Sir John Harington, a godson of Queen Elizabeth, wrote this in 1606, three years after she died

66 *When she smiled it was pure sunshine that everyone did choose to bask in if they could. I never did find greater show of understanding and learning, than she was blessed with.* 99

SOURCE 7 Sir John Hayward wrote this in his book about Elizabeth's reign in 1612

66 *If ever any person had either the gift or style to win the hearts of the people it was this Queen. She was religious, magnanimous [generous], merciful and just. She was lovely and loving. She maintained justice at home and arms abroad, with great wisdom and authority. Excellent queen!* 99

These two students are just beginning their investigation. The rest of this book will help you to carry out your own detailed investigation into Elizabeth I's reign. Keep your answer to Question 4 in Task 2. Call it your initial hypothesis. Keep it in your mind as you work through the book. You should look at it again at the end of each chapter. At the end of the book you will be asked to give your final answer to the question 'Was Elizabeth I a successful ruler?'

chapter 1

WAS ELIZABETH LIKELY TO BE A SUCCESSFUL RULER?

THE FIRST PART of your investigation will be to work out whether Elizabeth I faced an easy or difficult situation when she became Queen in 1558. Were her chances of becoming a successful ruler good or bad? What did her people expect of her?

You must not assume that monarchs who ruled over 400 years ago were identical to our rulers today. Your views about Elizabeth I should be based upon an understanding of how monarchs ruled the country in the sixteenth century, the powers they had, the problems they faced and what their people expected of them. Pages 14–18 will help you to understand these issues. Then you will investigate how successful the Tudor monarchs who ruled before Elizabeth had been. This will provide you with a basis for assessing Elizabeth's success later on in the book. In the final pages of the chapter you will find out about the country in 1558, the problems Elizabeth faced when she became Queen and whether she was the right kind of person to deal with them.

> What problems are facing the country?

> Will I be a successful ruler?

> What powers do I have now I am Queen?

> What do my people expect of me?

> Am I the right sort of person to be a successful ruler? Will my past experiences help me to rule well, or not?

> Do the reigns of my father, brother and sister make my task easier, or more difficult?

How to be a successful ruler in the sixteenth century!

How similar were sixteenth-century rulers to our rulers today?

TODAY, BRITAIN IS not ruled by kings and queens. Queen Elizabeth II is said to reign but not to rule. This means that, although she is the Queen, she does not make the important decisions that affect our everyday lives. Instead, we choose our rulers. At least once every five years we have a general election to elect Members of Parliament. The leader of the political party that wins the election becomes Prime Minister. The Prime Minister governs the country, but he or she can only pass laws if Parliament agrees to them.

Things were very different 450 years ago when Elizabeth I became Queen. She was expected to govern the country. There were no political parties, no general elections, no Prime Minister – and Parliament was not as important as it is today.

So, should we think of sixteenth-century monarchs as being like modern Prime Ministers? Or were they very different?

■ ACTIVITY

1. Study the responsibilities and powers on the opposite page. Which of them do you think apply to:
   a) sixteenth-century kings or queens
   b) modern Prime Ministers?
2. Draw up a list of what you think a Prime Minister should do in order to govern the country successfully.
3. Which of the items in your list do you think people in 1558 would have also expected Elizabeth I to do in order to be a success as queen?

A. The ruler is crowned.

B. Meeting with advisers to make important decisions.

C. Appointing people to be government ministers, judges and bishops.

D. Meeting and entertaining rulers and important guests from other countries.

E. Sacking government ministers and advisers.

F. Having a child who will rule the country after the ruler dies.

G. Granting honours and rewards to people by giving them medals or making them knights, lords, or ladies.

H. Being interviewed by journalists from the television, radio and newspapers.

I. Leading a political party in Parliament.

J. Making public appearances around the country to win support.

K. Gaining the support of the people to win elections.

L. Being in charge of the Church.

M. Deciding how much tax people should pay to meet the costs of governing the country.

N. Deciding how to spend taxes on public services.

O. Deciding whether someone should be executed.

P. People believe that the ruler is appointed by God.

Q. Leading an army into battle.

R. Paying the costs of governing the country out of his/her own money.

S. Meeting with world leaders to make decisions about global issues such as pollution.

T. Using good publicity to win the support of the people.

How powerful were sixteenth-century rulers?

In the sixteenth century most people believed that God appointed monarchs to reign over them. Monarchs expected complete obedience from their people and anyone who did not obey them could be found guilty of treason and executed. Most sixteenth-century monarchs were men, because, when a king died, it was usually his eldest son who took over the throne. A woman was allowed to inherit the throne and become queen only if there were no male relatives who could claim it.

■ ACTIVITY

Draw up a list of the personal qualities, education and experience a sixteenth-century monarch would have needed in order to be a success. Add to your list as you work through the rest of this chapter.

SOURCE 1 The powers of sixteenth-century monarchs

Job description for a sixteenth-century monarch

The monarch is appointed by God to rule the country. The monarch has complete power to:

- *make important decisions for the people*
- *appoint ministers to give advice*
- *be Head of the English Church (after 1534)*
- *appoint bishops, judges, generals and admirals*
- *decide whether to declare war on other countries*
- *command the army and navy*
- *decide how to make peace after a war*
- *make laws*
- *call meetings of Parliament and decide how long they should last*
- *control the country's coinage.*

What counted as success for sixteenth-century rulers?

It must have been fantastic to be a king or queen in the sixteenth century. Just sitting on a throne and everyone obeying your every word. Being worshipped like a god or goddess. Wow!

Wrong! You have already seen that life as a sixteenth-century monarch could be very dangerous. Ruling the country was sometimes difficult and monarchs needed the support of their people, especially the wealthy nobles. They were often short of money and could not afford a permanent army to make everyone obey them.

Sixteenth-century rulers did not have to provide the same things for their people as governments do today. For example, they did not have to run schools, hospitals or a police force – or find money to care for the old, the sick and the needy. So what were sixteenth-century kings and queens expected to do? What would make the difference between a successful monarch and a miserable failure?

Imagine that you are a sixteenth-century monarch. You have just come to the throne. Opposite you can see the sort of advice that one of your father's most experienced advisers would probably have given you.

1. Survival

Your first aim is to stay alive! You must rule for a long enough period of time to make the country stable and secure. Plots to overthrow you are a great danger. In earlier centuries several rulers were overthrown or killed by rivals. So you must prevent rebellions inside the country and protect the country from invasion. Illness is another threat to your survival. Your doctors have different ideas about what causes disease, and their treatments rarely work.

2. Strong leadership

You must show your people that you are in charge! Listen to advice, especially from your wealthy nobles, but do not allow yourself to be controlled by anybody, even your closest advisers. There are plenty of ambitious nobles and foreign rulers who will take advantage if they think you are weak and easily controlled. Make yourself wealthy – a ruler who is short of money is a weak ruler.

3. Unity, law and order

You must try to keep the country united. If your people become divided they might begin fighting amongst themselves and this could lead to rebellions or even civil war. Protect your people from crime and violence. They want you to provide them with fair laws and see that criminals are punished.

4. Prosperity

Do all you can to help your people become better off. A stable country, good harvests and peace abroad will help landowners, traders and manufacturers to sell their goods. Then they will become wealthy and provide more jobs for the lower classes. Poverty and unemployment, however, will create discontent and this could lead to protests and rebellions.

5. Defending the country

Your people expect you to protect them from foreign attacks. The biggest dangers come from France and Spain, the most powerful countries in Europe. Scotland, which is friendly with France, is also a threat. If a foreign ruler gains influence over you or defeats you in war, you will become unpopular. There will probably be protests and revolts. If you are unable to defeat an invasion you will almost certainly lose your throne! But if you make the country powerful, win wars or defeat an invasion you will be seen as a great success.

6. A settled succession

There is one more essential job for you to do. You must continue the rule of your family by getting married and having children, especially sons. Then everyone will know who is going to be the next king or queen when you eventually die. If you have no children, or have only one child who might die young, the future will be much more uncertain. Ambitious nobles or foreign rulers might start planning to overthrow you and seize power.

SOURCE 2 Advice on how to achieve a long and successful reign

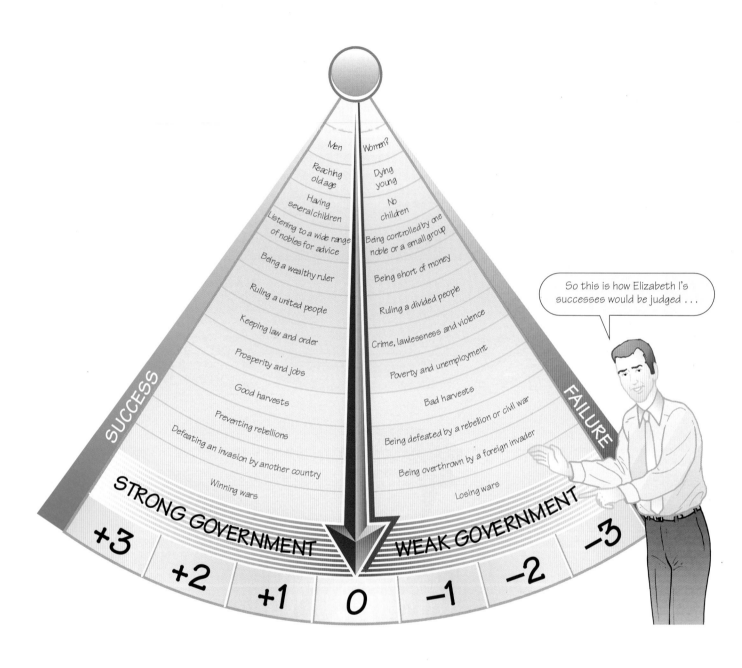

Men   Woman?

Reaching old age | Dying young

Having several children | No children

Listening to a wide range of nobles for advice | Being controlled by one noble or a small group

Being a wealthy ruler | Being short of money

Ruling a united people | Ruling a divided people

Keeping law and order | Crime, lawlessness and violence

Prosperity and jobs | Poverty and unemployment

Good harvests | Bad harvests

Preventing rebellions | Being defeated by a rebellion or civil war

Defeating an invasion by another country | Being overthrown by a foreign invader

Winning wars | Losing wars

SUCCESS   FAILURE

STRONG GOVERNMENT   WEAK GOVERNMENT

+3 +2 +1 0 −1 −2 −3

So this is how Elizabeth I's successes would be judged . . .

■ TASK

1. If you had been a new monarch in the sixteenth century, which piece of advice in Source 2 would you have found the most useful? Explain the reasons for your choice.

2. What might cause protests and rebellions against a monarch in the sixteenth century?

3. What could a sixteenth-century ruler do to prevent protests and rebellions?

4. Why would sixteenth-century rulers have to take notice of other countries?

5. How much would the success of a sixteenth-century ruler depend on good luck?

6. Add more ideas to the list of qualities needed to be a successful monarch which you began on page 16.

Had the earlier Tudor monarchs been successful rulers?

Elizabeth I was the fifth member of the Tudor family to rule England and Wales. Her grandfather, father, brother and elder sister had all been monarchs before her. Now you are going to investigate the three monarchs who ruled immediately before Elizabeth. How successful had they been as rulers of the country? When you are asked later on in the book to measure Elizabeth's success, it will be useful to know whether she did any better or worse than the monarchs who ruled before her.

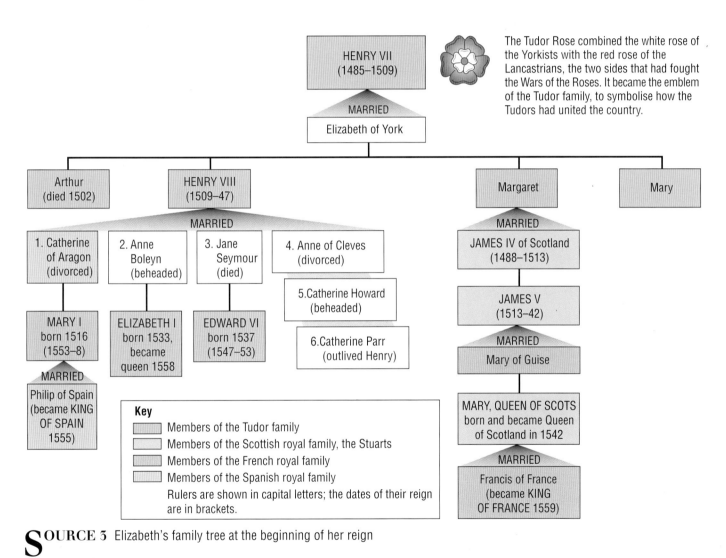

The Tudor Rose combined the white rose of the Yorkists with the red rose of the Lancastrians, the two sides that had fought the Wars of the Roses. It became the emblem of the Tudor family, to symbolise how the Tudors had united the country.

Key
- Members of the Tudor family
- Members of the Scottish royal family, the Stuarts
- Members of the French royal family
- Members of the Spanish royal family

Rulers are shown in capital letters; the dates of their reign are in brackets.

SOURCE 3 Elizabeth's family tree at the beginning of her reign

■ TASK

1. Who were Elizabeth's parents?
2. Did Elizabeth have any brothers or sisters?
3. Who was Elizabeth's grandfather?
4. When she became Queen in 1558, Elizabeth was unmarried.
   a) Who was the heir (next in line) to the throne?
   b) Can you suggest why many people in England were very worried about this?

■ ACTIVITY

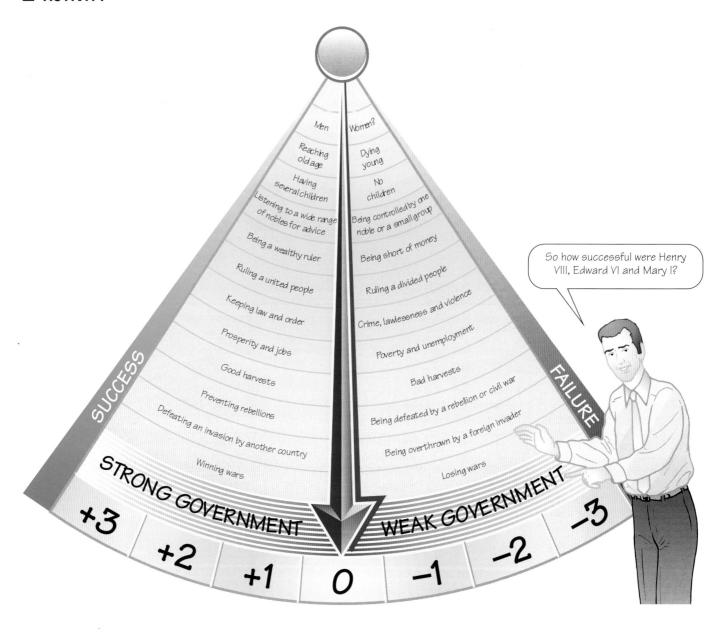

Your class should work in three groups. Each group should choose ONE of the Tudor monarchs who ruled before Elizabeth.

Study the information on these pages about your chosen monarch and decide how successful s/he was. Your teacher will give you a chart to help you. Then report your findings to the rest of the class. When all the groups have reported back, discuss the following questions.

■ Who do you think was the most successful ruler and why?

■ Who do you think was the least successful ruler and why?

■ Most people in the first half of the sixteenth century thought that women were weak and unsuccessful rulers. Does your study of these monarchs support or oppose this opinion?

■ This book is about Elizabeth I's reign and how successful she was. Is it of any use to know how successful the rulers before her had been?

Henry VIII (1509–47) Henry VIII married Catherine of Aragon, a Spanish princess, in 1509. During the early years of his reign Henry fought wars against France, Scotland and Spain. They achieved little and were expensive.

By 1529 Henry had a daughter, Mary, but he needed a son. He wanted to divorce Catherine and marry Anne Boleyn, a young noblewoman. The Pope refused to grant a divorce. Henry's adviser, Thomas Cromwell, suggested that England should leave the Roman Catholic Church. In 1533–34 Henry became Head of the Church of England. He married Anne Boleyn and in September 1533 their daughter, Princess Elizabeth, was born. In 1536 Anne was accused of being unfaithful to Henry, and executed. Henry married four more times. His only son, Prince Edward, was born in 1537.

Between 1536 and 1540 Henry shut all the monasteries and seized their wealth. In 1536 a major rebellion, the Pilgrimage of Grace, broke out in the north of England. Henry sent an army to defeat the rebels and over 200 were executed. Henry sold most of the monastery lands to pay for new defences in the south-east, and for wars against France and Scotland.

Protestant ideas spread to England during Henry's reign. Henry hated these new ideas and punished many Protestants. In 1540 he executed Thomas Cromwell for supporting them. Henry also punished Catholics who remained loyal to the Pope, including his former friend and adviser, Sir Thomas More, who was executed in 1535.

Many wealthy people became better off during Henry's reign but other people were hit by rising prices and unemployment. Poverty grew and the number of beggars increased.

When Henry died in 1547 he was short of money.

Edward VI (1547–53) Edward was only nine years old in 1547. Nobles appointed by his father ruled the country for him. They wanted to make England and Scotland more friendly by marrying Edward to Mary, Queen of Scots but Mary was sent to France. She married a French prince.

The Church of England was made more Protestant. Decorations were removed from churches and a new prayer book, written in English, was introduced. In 1549, Catholics in Devon and Cornwall rebelled. 2500 of them were killed.

Poverty grew. Harvests were bad and prices rose. Thousands of spinners and weavers lost their jobs. Many farm workers lost their jobs too, when landowners began keeping sheep instead of growing crops. This caused a rebellion in Norfolk in 1549. It was crushed and 3000 rebels were killed.

Edward died shortly before his sixteenth birthday. The government was short of money.

Mary I (1553–58) Mary was half-Spanish and a strong Roman Catholic. She was very popular at first, but then she announced plans to marry Philip of Spain, who was also a strong Catholic. Many people thought that this would lead to Spain controlling the country. In 1554 a rebellion broke out. Mary defeated it, executing 90 of the rebels. She also imprisoned Princess Elizabeth in the Tower of London because she was afraid that Elizabeth was plotting against her.

Mary married Philip and restored the Roman Catholic religion. She burnt to death over 300 Protestants who refused to change their beliefs. They were seen as MARTYRS. The Roman Catholic religion and Spanish influence became very unpopular. Discontent grew. There were two terrible harvests. Prices rose sharply and thousands died of starvation or disease.

Mary joined Spain in an unsuccessful war against France. In 1558 France captured Calais, a town on the French coast that England had ruled for hundreds of years. This was seen as a national disaster.

When Mary died in 1558 she was very unpopular. She had no child to succeed her and she left debts of £250,000.

What problems did Elizabeth I face in 1558?

YOU WILL BEGIN your study of Elizabeth I's reign by looking at what the country was like in 1558 when she became Queen. If you know what problems she faced when she became Queen, you will be able to work out, later on, how successful she was in dealing with them.

■ TASK

You are one of Elizabeth's advisers in November 1558. She has asked you to prepare an information pack about the country for her. Use the information on these two pages to prepare a report under these three headings:

■ What is going well in the country
■ What problems the country is facing
■ How the country's problems should be dealt with.

Government

Most people believed that monarchs were chosen by God to rule the country. Kings or queens governed with the help of a small group of advisers. Occasionally, they called meetings of Parliament to help them make laws or approve emergency taxes. They also appointed Justices of the Peace to help them impose law and order throughout the country.

The monarch was expected to pay all the normal costs of governing the country. The money came from customs duties, fines from the lawcourts and rents from land owned by the monarch. Monarchs were usually short of money but Mary had increased the Crown's income. The war with France, however, had been expensive and there were debts of £250,000.

Mary had strengthened the navy to protect the coast, but there was still not enough money to pay for a full-time army.

The economy

Most people worked in the countryside as labourers, growing crops on farms. Some landowners had started to keep sheep on their land instead of growing crops. Fewer workers were needed for this and many labourers were losing their jobs.

The country's most important industry was making woollen cloth. Many merchants had become wealthy by selling English cloth abroad. Then, in the early 1550s, this trade had collapsed. Thousands of spinners and weavers were thrown out of work.

Prices had been rising since the beginning of the sixteenth century. They rose very fast in the 1550s. Farmers faced higher rents and many people found that their wages were losing their value.

After several bad harvests in the 1550s, the harvest in 1558 was very good.

SOURCE 1 What England was like in 1558

What was the country like in 1558?

Cultural developments

The sixteenth century was a time of changing ideas. The RENAISSANCE had spread to England. People were becoming interested in the ideas and way of life of the Ancient Greeks and Romans. This led to the development of new styles of art, music and architecture. People began to question old ideas and became interested in learning and science. The invention of the printing press meant that books could now be mass-produced. This helped to spread new ideas. New schools and university colleges were opened. Wealthy people were better educated than ever before.

People were also becoming interested in other parts of the world. In the late fifteenth and early sixteenth centuries, Spanish and Portuguese sailors had made long voyages of exploration. They had reached India, discovered the 'NEW WORLD' of the Americas, and brought back great wealth to their countries.

Relations with other countries

The most powerful countries in Europe were France and Spain. Both were Roman Catholic countries. England was weak compared to them.

King Philip of Spain had been married to Queen Mary; now he hoped to marry Elizabeth. If England became Protestant again, however, he might organise Catholic countries to attack it.

France and England had been enemies for centuries. In 1558 they were at war. France controlled Scotland, although Protestant ideas were spreading there. Mary, Queen of Scots, was married to Francis, the heir to the French throne, and was living in France. In 1558 Mary declared that she, not Elizabeth, was the rightful Queen of England. Many Catholics in England supported her.

Society

Three million people lived in England and Wales. They lived in a HIERARCHICAL society which most people believed was ordered by God. They were expected to know their place in society, obey people above them, and help to control and look after those below them. In each level of society women were thought to be inferior to men and were expected to obey them. Poverty and unemployment were growing amongst the lower classes at the bottom of the social hierarchy.

God

The Queen

Nobles and lords
(great landowners)
About 50 families

The gentry
(lesser landowners)
About 10,000 families

Wealthy merchants
About 30,000 families

Yeomen (farmers who owned their own land)
and **Tenant farmers** (who rented land
from a landowner) About 100,000 families

**Craftspeople, labourers,
servants, the poor**
About 500,000 families

Religion

In 1558 England was a country divided by religion. It had been a Roman Catholic country for nearly a thousand years, until Henry VIII's reign. Since then the Church had changed three times in twenty years. Catholics and Protestants had very different ideas about what sort of Church the country should have.

Catholics believed that:	Protestants believed that:
the Pope was head of the Church throughout the world	the monarch should be in charge of the country's Church
church services and the Bible should be in Latin	church services and the Bible should be in English
churches should be highly decorated	there should be little decoration in churches

There was a third group of more extreme Protestants, called PURITANS. They wanted much plainer churches and simple services. Many of them had fled abroad during Mary Tudor's reign. Now they were returning.

Mary Tudor had made the country Roman Catholic again but most people in England were Protestants. They wanted changes to the Church. Many people thought that religious differences were leading the country towards civil war.

Reactions to the new Queen

When Elizabeth became Queen she was very popular. Crowds cheered her in the streets. She was young, single and of completely English blood. She seemed to offer the country a fresh start. Some ambitious nobles hoped to marry her.

At the same time, many people were worried about having another woman ruling the country. After all, they said, everyone knew that women were much weaker rulers than men!

■ DECISION POINT, 1558

SOURCE 2   Elizabeth and her problems in 1558

> I have to pay the costs of governing the country out of my own money. But my sister Mary has left me debts of £250,000.

> My cousin Mary, Queen of Scots, claims that she is the rightful Queen of England. She is married to the heir to the French throne. Many English Catholics support her.

> My people follow different religions but my country must have one Church. Most of my people want a moderate Protestant Church but some want a Puritan Church – and others want to stay with the Roman Catholic religion.

> King Philip of Spain was married to my sister Mary. Spain is the most powerful country in Europe. If England becomes Protestant again, Philip might persuade all the Catholic countries to attack England.

> Poverty is growing and the lower classes are becoming discontented. At least there has been a good harvest this year.

> My navy is much stronger than it was, but I cannot afford a full-time army. I only have part-time soldiers.

> I am young and very popular with my people. If I make changes I must take care not to lose their support, especially the support of my rich and powerful landowners.

> My people expect me to get married as soon as possible. If I marry an English nobleman he might try to control me. Then my other nobles will become jealous. If I marry a foreign prince he might try to control me, too. This will make other foreign rulers, as well as my own people, angry.

> All of my wealthiest and most powerful subjects are men. They think that women are too weak to rule a country.

The new Queen and her problems

The Queen has read your information pack. She now knows that she faces several serious problems.

Elizabeth cannot deal with all these problems at once. She has to decide:

■ which is the most urgent problem facing the country

■ how she is going to deal with it.

In order to do this, she needs advice. She is about to have her first meeting with her advisers.

Divide the class into groups. One group should take the role of the new Queen. The others are her advisers. Each group of the Queen's advisers should prepare a speech in which they explain:

a) which problem is the most urgent

b) why it is the most urgent

c) how Elizabeth should deal with the problem.

The group representing Elizabeth should also discuss these points. The Queen will not want her advisers to think that she has no ideas of her own!

After they have heard the advisers' speeches, the group representing Elizabeth should decide:

a) which problem she will deal with first

b) why she has made this decision

c) how she will deal with the problem.

Then, announce the Queen's decision to her advisers.

■ TASK

1. Which of Elizabeth I's problems in 1558 were:

a) political

b) social and economic

c) religious

d) international?

2. Were Elizabeth I's problems in 1558 completely separate or were some of the problems linked? Explain your answer fully.

3. 'Elizabeth I came to the throne at a very difficult time.'

Do you agree or disagree with this statement? Explain your answer fully.

Did Elizabeth have the experience to become a successful ruler?

YOU HAVE INVESTIGATED the kind of person a monarch needed to be in order to become a successful ruler in the sixteenth century. You have also found out about the problems that the country faced when Elizabeth became Queen. Now you are going to consider whether Elizabeth was the right person to begin ruling the country at such a difficult time. What were her chances of becoming a successful monarch? Would her troubled childhood have been good or bad preparation for ruling the country? Did she have the character and personality necessary to become a successful ruler?

It is not easy to find out what Elizabeth was like before 1558. When she was young it was very unlikely that she would ever become Queen. She was not as important as Edward and Mary. They were both before her in the succession to the throne. This is why we only have a few sources about her to study. They were produced by different people at different times.

SOURCE 2 A portrait of Princess Elizabeth, aged about twelve. It was painted by an unknown artist in about 1545. It is the only painting we have of Elizabeth as a child

SOURCE 1 An extract from a letter written by Roger Asham, Elizabeth's tutor, in 1550

66 *My illustrious mistress, the Lady Elizabeth, shines like a star. So much solidity of understanding, such courtesy and dignity, which I have never observed at so early an age. She hath the most ardent [passionate] love of the true religion and the best kind of literature. Her mind is free from female weakness and she is endued [blessed] with a masculine power for hard work. No memory is more retentive [better] than hers.* 99

SOURCE 4 A description of Princess Elizabeth in 1554. It was written by an AMBASSADOR from Venice, in Italy

66 *She is now about 21 years old; her figure and face are very handsome, and such an air of majesty pervades [spreads through] all her actions that no one can fail to suppose she is a queen.* 99

SOURCE 3 An extract from a letter written by Elizabeth to Queen Mary in March 1554, shortly before she was imprisoned in the Tower. She drew lines across the blank spaces on her letters to prevent anyone adding a forged confession

66 *I never practised, advised, nor consented to anything that might be prejudicial [damaging] to your person in any way.*
Your Highness's most faithful subject, that hath been from the beginning and will be to my end, Elizabeth. 99

SOURCE 5 A description written by another ambassador from Venice, in 1556

66 *She is now twenty-three years old. Although her face is pleasant rather than handsome, she is tall and well-formed, with a good skin, though dark in colour. She has fine eyes and above all a beautiful hand which she displays.*
Her intellect and understanding are wonderful. As a linguist she excels [is better than] the Queen, for besides Latin she also knows Greek, and speaks Italian more than the Queen does, taking so much pleasure in it that from vanity she will never speak any other language with Italians. 99

SOURCE 6 An extract from a letter from the Spanish ambassador to Philip II, King of Spain, in November 1558, shortly after Elizabeth became Queen

66 *She seems to be greatly more feared than her sister and gives her orders and has her way as absolutely as her father had.* 99

■ REVIEW TASK

Study Sources 1–6 on page 25. Also look back at the information about Elizabeth's early life on pages 4–9.

1. What tragedies and difficulties had Elizabeth faced before she became Queen? What do you think she might have learnt from these experiences?
2. Choose the words and phrases from the list opposite which you think best describe what Elizabeth was like. Then complete a chart like the one below.

healthy	unhealthy	
very beautiful	ugly	quite good-looking
serious	fun-loving	hard-working
lazy	religious	not religious
intelligent	foolish	modest
vain	careful	careless
secretive	majestic	able to speak several languages
strong and determined	weak	

What Elizabeth was like	Supporting evidence	Would it help her to become a successful queen?

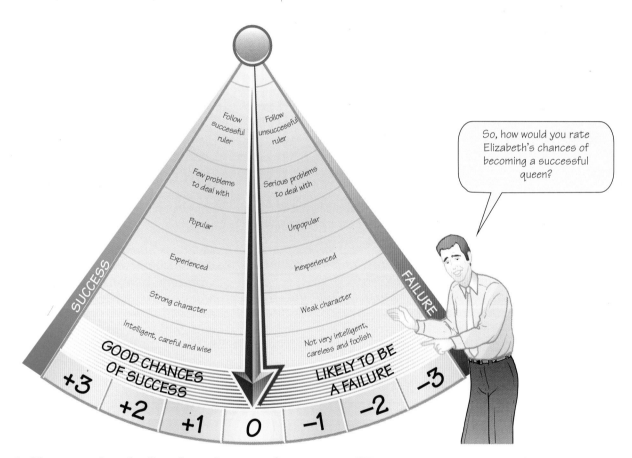

So, how would you rate Elizabeth's chances of becoming a successful queen?

3. Now complete the list of requirements for a sixteenth-century monarch which you began on page 16. For each item on your list, give Elizabeth I a mark from +3 to −3 and briefly explain your reasons.

Your teacher will give you a sheet to help you work out your answer.

Write an essay to answer this question: How good were Elizabeth I's chances of becoming a successful ruler when she became Queen in 1558?

Your teacher will give you a sheet to plan your answer. You will need to measure Elizabeth's chances of success against the criteria shown in the diagram.

chapter 2

DID ELIZABETH KEEP COMPLETE CONTROL OF GOVERNMENT?

SOURCE 1 From *The First Blast of the Trumpet against the Monstrous Regiment [government] of Women* by John Knox, a Scottish religious leader, 1558. His views were well known in England

66 *To promote a woman to bear rule, superiority, dominion [power] or empire above any nation; is contumely [insulting] to God, a thing most contrary to his revealed will and approved ordinance [order]; and finally it is the subversion [overturning] of good order, of all equity [fairness] and justice. For no man ever saw the lion make obedience and stoop before the lioness.* **99**

1. Did John Knox think that women could be good rulers?
2. What were his reasons?
3. Most people in 1558 thought that women were weak and unsuccessful rulers. Was there anything to support their view?
4. Was there any reason, apart from the fact that she was a woman, why some people thought Elizabeth should not rule England?

ELIZABETH I'S TASK of governing the country was not easy. England faced many problems. Elizabeth also had her own difficulties. She needed to appoint powerful nobles as her advisers but she had to show that she was in charge of them. This was particularly difficult for Elizabeth because she was a woman. Most people believed that women were too weak to govern the country.

In this chapter you will investigate how Elizabeth I governed the country. You will have to decide who really ruled Elizabethan England. Was Elizabeth a strong ruler who was really in charge of the government of her country? Or, as many people feared, was she a weak ruler who was controlled by her advisers?

How did Elizabeth govern her country? Was she really in charge – or was she controlled by her advisers?

How did Elizabeth try to win her people's support?

ELIZABETH NEEDED TO win the support of her people, especially her most powerful subjects, in order to govern the country successfully. She also needed to make foreign rulers respect her. Good publicity was one important way of winning support and respect. Politicians today can use newspapers, photographs, radio broadcasts, television programmes and the Internet. Elizabeth I could not use any of these methods. Was she able to create a good 'publicity machine'?

Elizabeth's coronation

Elizabeth's first opportunity to achieve good publicity was her coronation. After consulting her ASTROLOGERS, she decided that the coronation should take place in London on 15 January 1559. She was determined to make it as impressive as possible. There were colourful processions and a royal journey by barge along the River Thames. Huge crowds lined the streets. The coronation ceremony was held in Westminster Abbey. Most of Elizabeth's nobles and many important foreign visitors attended. There was a grand banquet for them afterwards. Celebrations in London lasted for the next ten days. All this cost at least £16,000, a huge sum of money.

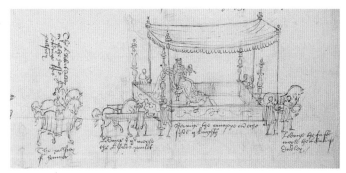

SOURCE 1 From a drawing of Elizabeth's coronation procession, 1559. It shows Elizabeth being carried on a platform covered in golden silk. Her nobles, officials and servants are following her

Sceptre

Orb

SOURCE 2 Elizabeth's coronation portrait, issued by the government in 1559. She is holding the orb and sceptre, the symbols of a monarch's power and authority

SOURCE 3 A modern account of the preparations for Elizabeth's coronation, from *Elizabeth I, A Study in Power and Intellect*, by Paul Johnson, 1974

  Timber was brought from the Windsor forest for seating. Other materials were shipped over from Antwerp [a town in what is now Belgium]. The Yeoman of the Guard got new scarlet coats, with silver and gold ornaments. All the Queen's household, down to the jesters [clowns], Will and Jane Somers, were measured for new clothes. The thirty-nine ladies who attended Elizabeth were each provided with sixteen yards of velvet and two yards of cloth of gold. The senior officers of state had crimson velvet and the PRIVY COUNCILLORS crimson satin. Elizabeth herself had four state dresses made; one, for her procession through the city, of twenty-three yards of gold and silver with ermine [white fur] trimmings, and silver and gold lace coverings. Her coronation robes, with their great cloak of ermine and embroidered silk, can still be seen in her official portrait, but she had two other state dresses, of crimson and violet velvet, and changed her outfit twice during the ceremony.

■ ACTIVITY

You are visiting London to see Elizabeth's coronation. Use Sources 1–3 to write a letter to your parents. Include in your letter:

■ a description of what you saw
■ what you think about the new Queen.

1. Why do you think Elizabeth consulted astrologers before deciding when to hold her coronation?
2. Elizabeth faced debts of £250,000 when she became Queen in 1558. Why, then, do you think she spent so much money on her coronation?
3. Who did Elizabeth want her coronation to impress? Do you think that she succeeded?

Progresses

Very few of Elizabeth's people were able to travel to London to see her, so Elizabeth decided to go on tours around the country. These were called progresses. They took place during the summer. She travelled with most of her advisers, officials, servants and guards. They stayed in nobles' houses and were given free accommodation, food and drink, entertainment and gifts. Elizabeth's progresses were held in the south-east and the Midlands. She never visited the north of England, Wales or the south-west.

SOURCE 4 A picture, painted in 1601, showing one of Elizabeth's progresses

SOURCE 5 An extract from the diary of Sir Julius Caesar. Elizabeth stayed at his house for one night in 1590

66 *The Queen visited my house in Mitcham and supped and lodged there, and dined the next day. I presented her with a gown of cloth of silver, richly embroidered; a black mantle [cloak] with pure gold; a hat of taffeta [a smooth, shiny fabric like silk], white with several flowers; a jewel of gold set with rubies and diamonds. Her Majesty left my house after dinner with exceeding good contentment. This entertainment cost £700.* **99**

4. a) What was a progress?
   b) Why did Elizabeth go on them?
5. Study Source 4. Elizabeth was 68 years old when this painting was made. How easy is it to tell this from the painting?
6. Study Source 5. Elizabeth's visit to Sir Julius Caesar's house cost him a huge amount of money. Do you think he would have thought that it was worth it?

29

Portraits

Most of Elizabeth's people were never able to see her in real life. For them, the only way of 'seeing' the Queen was by looking at pictures of her on coins, medals and portraits. Many nobles wanted to display paintings of the Queen in their country houses. Portraits of her were also sent abroad, often as gifts to foreign rulers.

Elizabeth I's portraits were not supposed to show what she actually looked like. As she grew older, her real appearance needed to be disguised more and more. She caught smallpox in 1562. It left large scars on her face. By the 1590s her teeth had turned black, she was wrinkled and had to wear a wig because she had lost her hair. Elizabeth did not like having her portrait painted and rarely sat for artists. But she realised how important portraits were. They were a powerful form of PROPAGANDA. Elizabeth used them to create an image which she wanted her people to believe.

Artists had to get the government's permission before they were allowed to paint pictures of the Queen. They had to use approved faces, jewels and fabrics in their paintings.

Eventually, Elizabeth's portraits made her look more like a goddess than a human being.

SOURCE 6 A medallion made in the 1580s. It was made of cheap metal so that poorer people could afford to buy it

Legitimacy and purity
Roman Catholics believed that Elizabeth was illegitimate and had no right to be Queen. Tudor roses, the orb and sceptre, the sword of justice and the crown were included in her portraits to show that she was the rightful Queen. To show her purity, Elizabeth's face and clothes were usually white. She was often shown wearing pearls, white roses and white fur. In one portrait Elizabeth is shown with an ermine on her arm. It was believed that the ermine would rather die than get its fur dirty.

Success and wisdom
Elizabeth wanted to show that she was ruling the country wisely and successfully. She was often shown as Astraea, a goddess who brought eternal springtime after troubled times. Sometimes she was shown with spring flowers, or a serpent (a symbol of wisdom), holding a rainbow or bringing in sunshine after a storm. The Armada Portrait (Source 8) was painted immediately after Spain had tried to invade the country. It deliberately shows Elizabeth controlling the victory.

What did Elizabeth want her portraits to show?

Strength and power
Elizabeth wanted her paintings to show that she was strong and powerful. Symbols of strength, such as pillars, were used. In one painting she is shown standing on a map of England. In another, her hand is on top of a globe (see Source 8).

Wealth
It was important to disguise the Queen's financial difficulties. She was always shown wearing magnificent dresses which were studded with expensive pearls and jewels.

Ageless
As Elizabeth grew older, it became increasingly important to hide the signs of her age because this was a sign of weakness. A smooth white 'face mask' was used to make the Queen look eternally youthful.

SOURCE 7 How Elizabeth used her portraits to create an image

■ TASK

1. Draw a larger version of the table below in your book. Then use the information on pages 30–33 to complete the second and third columns.

Problems Elizabeth faced	What Elizabeth wanted people to think	How her portraits showed these qualities
Women were thought to be weak rulers		
Catholics thought she was illegitimate		
She was short of money		
Women were thought to be unsuccessful rulers		
She was getting old and frail		

2. In what ways is Source 6 different from Sources 8–10? In what ways is it similar?
3. Choose one of the portraits of Queen Elizabeth I (Sources 8–10). Look closely at the way Elizabeth is presented and the symbols that have been included in the portrait. Then explain the purpose of the portrait you have chosen.
4. Historians have to be very careful when using propaganda, but it can contain very valuable evidence about the past. Elizabeth's portraits are an example of propaganda.
   a) Explain why they have to be used very carefully.
   b) Explain why they contain valuable evidence.

SOURCE 8   The 'Armada Portrait' of Elizabeth I, painted in 1588

SOURCE 9 The 'Ermine Portrait' of Elizabeth I, painted by Nicholas Hilliard in 1585

SOURCE 10 The 'Ditchley Portrait' of Elizabeth I, painted in 1592 by Marcus Gheeraerts. She is shown standing on the village green of Ditchley in Oxfordshire. It was painted for Sir Henry Lee, a courtier who lived in Ditchley

■ TASK

Write an essay to answer the question: 'Did Elizabeth I make good use of publicity during her reign to win the support of her people?'

Your answer should be planned like this:

■ a short introduction explaining why Elizabeth needed good publicity
■ three paragraphs explaining how Elizabeth publicised herself, including her coronation, progresses and portraits
■ a short conclusion, explaining your overall answer to the question.

33

Did Elizabeth control central government?

ELIZABETH'S CORONATION, PROGRESSES and portraits all helped to show her as a wise, strong and successful ruler. But they were not enough. Even good publicity could not disguise failures. In the end, Elizabeth's success would depend on how well she governed the country. She needed to win the support of her wealthy and powerful landowners, but she could choose only a few of them as her closest advisers. This was a difficult balancing act for any monarch, but especially for a young woman at that time.

The Court

Elizabeth lived at Whitehall Palace in London. Her advisers, government officials, ladies-in-waiting and servants lived with her. This large community of people was known as the Court.

The Queen was the most important member of the Court. Daily life revolved around her. Her meetings, prayers and meals, as well as important banquets and dances, were all turned into glamorous ceremonies. They were designed to impress anyone who saw them.

Most of the Court travelled with the Queen when she stayed at her other palaces or went on a progress. It was rather like a large family. There were loyal and friendly relationships as well as rivalries and arguments – and many rumours of love affairs.

SOURCE 1 Queen Elizabeth at Court on her way to morning prayers. This modern drawing is based on an account written by a German traveller who visited the Court in 1598

The Court was the centre of political power in Elizabethan England. Wealthy and ambitious people went there to be noticed by the Queen and win her favour. If she gave them an important job in the government it would give them power, influence, and a valuable income. Some people went to Court just to meet one of the Queen's ministers. They could appoint people to less important positions in the government and introduce them to the Queen. The power to appoint people to important jobs is called PATRONAGE. Elizabeth used her power of patronage like a magnet to attract the loyalty and support of her most important subjects.

SOURCE 2 Lord Herbert of Cherbury describes his first visit to Court in 1600

❝ It was the manner of those times for all men to kneel down before the great Queen Elizabeth. I was likewise upon my knees when she passed us by to the Chapel at Whitehall. As soon as she saw me, she stopped and demanded 'Who is this?' Everybody there present looked upon me, but no man knew me, until Sir James Croft told who I was, and that I had married Sir William Herbert of St Julian's daughter. ❞

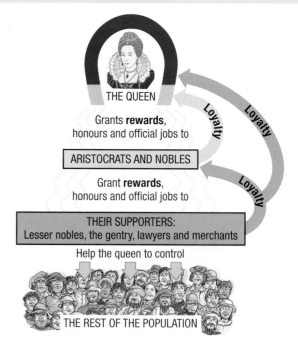

SOURCE 3 How the system of patronage worked

1. Explain:
a) how the system of patronage worked
b) how Elizabeth used it to keep her most important, powerful subjects loyal to her.

The Privy Council

Sixteenth-century monarchs appointed a council of advisers or ministers to help them govern the country. It was called the Privy Council. After the monarch, it was the most important part of the government. Members of the Privy Council were usually chosen from the nobles, gentry and the Church. Their main purpose was to give advice. They could not tell the monarch what to do. Monarchs could ignore their advice if they chose. They could also replace them.

Elizabeth's first and most important task in 1558 was to appoint her Privy Council.

■ DECISION POINT, 1558

It is November 1558. Elizabeth has just become Queen. She is trying to decide who to appoint to her Privy Council.

SOURCE 4 Elizabeth thinking about who to appoint to her Privy Council

■ ACTIVITY

In groups, discuss each of the issues Elizabeth is thinking about in Source 4. Consider the advantages and disadvantages of each possible course of action before deciding what type of people you think Elizabeth should appoint to the Privy Council. Your teacher will give you a sheet to help you. Then each group should present its decisions to the rest of the class.

Did Elizabeth choose her Privy Councillors well?

By January 1559 Elizabeth had appointed nineteen experienced men to her Privy Council. They held a range of different views. Ten had been members of Mary's Privy Council. None were strong Catholics. Elizabeth appointed William Cecil as her Secretary of State: the most important position on the Privy Council.

■ TASK

Your task is to decide how good Elizabeth was at choosing her advisers.

1. Study the information below. Rate each Councillor against these criteria:

   ■ high social status   ■ well-educated
   ■ hardworking   ■ loyal
   ■ religion   ■ other qualities.

2. How good were Elizabeth's choices? Explain your answer fully.

SIR WILLIAM CECIL, LORD BURGHLEY (1520–98) APPOINTED: 1558

Background: Lincolnshire gentry. Educated at grammar school. Studied law at Cambridge University.
Previous experience: Elected to Parliament 1547. Privy Councillor for Edward VI. 1550: Princess Elizabeth appointed him to look after her lands.
Personal qualities: Hard-working. Like Elizabeth, wanted to unite the country and avoid war. Didn't like making changes or rushed decisions. A moderate Protestant.
Service to Elizabeth: Elizabeth made him Secretary of State in 1558 and Lord Burghley in 1571. He worked hard – knew about all government business. Managed meetings of Parliament. 1572: made Lord Treasurer, in charge of the government's finances. Wasn't afraid to disagree with the Queen or other Privy Councillors. Elizabeth trusted him completely. He was a loyal adviser for 40 years.

ROBERT DUDLEY, EARL OF LEICESTER (1533–88) APPOINTED: 1562

Background: Youngest son of the Duke of Northumberland. Well educated. The same age as Elizabeth – they were childhood friends. 1553: his father executed for plotting against Mary Tudor.
Previous experience: Fought against France during Mary Tudor's reign. Went to Court in 1558. Elizabeth called him her 'sweet Robin'. Showered him with gifts. Rumours spread that they were in love.
Personal qualities: Young and good-looking in 1558. Very skilful horseman, good organiser, very ambitious. A Puritan.
Service to Elizabeth: Made Earl of Leicester in 1564. Disliked William Cecil – often disagreed with him. A loyal adviser to Elizabeth but they had several quarrels. 1585: Elizabeth made him commander of an army sent to the Netherlands. Leicester quarrelled with his generals. He soon returned to England.

SIR CHRISTOPHER HATTON (1540–91) APPOINTED: 1577

Background: Northamptonshire gentry. Went to Oxford University. Then studied law.
Previous experience: Elizabeth saw him at Court in 1561, was impressed by his dancing; gave him several government jobs and land. Elected to Parliament in 1571 and 1572.
Personal qualities: Moderate, kind and intelligent. A good dancer. A moderate Protestant. Hated Puritans. Sympathised with Catholics.
Service to Elizabeth: Made a knight in 1577. Organised the Queen's progresses. Elected to Parliament several times. Helped Elizabeth to pass laws and control MPs. 1587: made Lord Chancellor, in charge of judges and lawcourts.

SIR FRANCIS WALSINGHAM (1532–90) APPOINTED: 1573

Background: Gentry from Kent. Went to Cambridge University. Fled abroad during Mary Tudor's reign. Studied at Padua University, Italy. 1560: returned to England.
Previous experience: Elected to Parliament, 1562. 1568: began working for the government – his foreign languages and contacts abroad made him useful.
1571: helped discover a Catholic plot to murder Elizabeth.
Personal qualities: Spoke French and Italian. Knew many important people in Europe. Very efficient, good organiser, a strong Puritan.
Service to Elizabeth: Knighted 1577. Worked mainly on foreign affairs. Often travelled abroad. Put in charge of Elizabeth's secret service – controlled a network of spies and informers all over Europe. Often disagreed with William Cecil – wasn't afraid to tell the Queen. Often made her angry but she knew he was completely loyal to her. 1586: he found evidence that Mary, Queen of Scots, was involved in a plot to murder Elizabeth.

ROBERT DEVEREUX, EARL OF ESSEX (1567–1601) APPOINTED: 1593

Background: The son of the Earl of Essex and stepson of the Earl of Leicester. Went to Cambridge University.
Previous experience: Went to Court in 1584. Immediately attracted Elizabeth's favour. Was given several government jobs; fought in the Netherlands, France and Spain. Very knowledgeable about foreign affairs.
Personal qualities: Young, good-looking; very ambitious and short-tempered. Hated the Cecil family.
Service to Elizabeth: Commanded attacks on Spain and Ireland. Often quarrelled with Elizabeth. 1601: led a rebellion, executed for treason. (You will find out more about the Earl of Essex on pages 148–149.)

Did Elizabeth control her Privy Councillors?

The Privy Council met nearly every day, although Elizabeth did not always attend its meetings. Her Privy Councillors were powerful, ambitious men. Elizabeth could not allow them to control her. If she did, other nobles would become jealous and might even plan a rebellion to overthrow her.

Elizabeth was determined to show that she would take the most important decisions of the reign. But she was a cautious ruler. She did not like making big changes or being rushed into making decisions. This often frustrated her councillors, but they were completely loyal to her. There were only two exceptions: the Duke of Norfolk and the Earl of Essex. They were both executed for treason.

SOURCE 5 An extract from Elizabeth's speech to her Lords, three days after becoming Queen, November 1558

I consider a multitude [large number] doth make disorder and confusion than good council.

SOURCE 6 A disagreement between Elizabeth and the Earl of Essex in 1598, described by William Camden, 1615

He uncivilly turned his back upon her and gave her a scornful look. She, not enduring such behaviour, gave him a box [punch] upon the ear and bade him get away and get hanged.

SOURCE 7 Sir John Harington, Elizabeth's godson, writing in about 1606

Her best councillors were oft sore troubled to know her will; so secretively did she make her decisions. When business turned to better advantage, she did most cunningly commit the good issue to her own honour [take the credit]. But when anything fell contrary to her will and interest, the Council were desperate to defend their actions and not blemish the Queen's good judgement.

SOURCE 8 Sir Robert Naunton, a member of Elizabeth's Court, writing in the 1630s

She ruled much by factions [small groups] and parties, which she made, upheld and weakened as her own great judgement advised.

SOURCE 9 An extract from a report by the Spanish ambassador to the King of Spain

The Queen turned to Secretary Walsingham and said a few words to him; after which she threw a slipper at Walsingham and hit him in the face. She is constantly behaving in such a rude manner as this.

SOURCE 10 Elizabeth's comments to William Cecil when she appointed him to the Privy Council, November 1558

I have this judgement of you, that you will not be corrupted with any gift, you will be faithful to the state, and without respect of my private will, you will give me the best advice; if you know anything to be declared to me in secret, you will tell only me and I will keep it confidential.

SOURCE 11 An extract from another report by the Spanish ambassador

Her temper was so bad that no Councillor dared to mention business to her and when even Cecil did so, she told him that she had been strong enough to lift him out of the dirt, and she was able to cast him down again.

SOURCE 12 A comment Elizabeth made in 1603 to Robert Cecil, after he said that she must rest in bed. From a report by the Spanish ambassador

Little man, Little man! The word 'must' is not used to princes!

■ TASK

1. Study Sources 5–12. What examples can you find of Elizabeth using these methods in her dealings with her Privy Councillors:

   ■ having a small Privy Council
   ■ expecting her councillors to be completely loyal to her
   ■ making her decisions in private
   ■ taking the credit for successes but not the blame when things went wrong
   ■ encouraging rivalries amongst her Councillors
   ■ being rude to them?

2. Briefly explain why Elizabeth used each method.
3. Did these methods help Elizabeth to keep complete control over her Privy Councillors? Explain the reasons for your answer.

Did Elizabeth lose control of Parliament?

> OVER TO OUR special correspondent in Westminster . . .
>
> 'All the lords and bishops have arrived. They are wearing their finest robes. They find their seats and then everything goes quiet. There is a loud fanfare and the Queen enters the chamber with her attendants, the Lord Chancellor and the Secretary of State. Her Majesty is wearing a dress of the finest silk, trimmed with white fur and studded with jewels. She sits on the throne. The crown is placed on her head and she is given the orb and sceptre to hold. The Commons file into the chamber, in silence, their heads bowed. Then Her Majesty stands. She begins her speech. "My faithful, loving and obedient subjects, the Lords and Commons in this present Parliament assembled. The matters and causes whereupon we have summoned you here . . ."'

This is how a modern television journalist might have reported Elizabeth I opening one of her Parliaments. A similar ceremony is still held every year. It has hardly changed since the sixteenth century. The importance of Parliament, however, has changed a lot.

In the sixteenth century, Parliament was much less powerful than it is today. It could only meet if it was called by a monarch. This did not happen very often. By Elizabeth's reign, however, MPs were better educated than ever before. They knew that Henry VIII had used Parliament to help him break away from the Roman Catholic Church and pass other important laws. MPs were becoming more willing to complain about the Church or the way the country was being governed. Some historians have claimed that Elizabeth lost control of Parliament.

They say that this eventually led to the Civil War between Charles I and Parliament in the 1640s. We are going to investigate this claim.

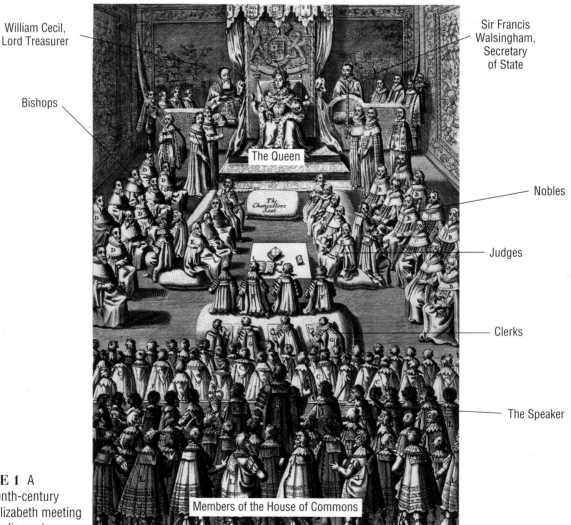

William Cecil, Lord Treasurer

Bishops

The Queen

Sir Francis Walsingham, Secretary of State

Nobles

Judges

Clerks

The Speaker

Members of the House of Commons

SOURCE 1 A seventeenth-century drawing of Elizabeth meeting one of her Parliaments

Why did Elizabeth call Parliament?

Elizabeth did not have to call Parliament at all. She could close it whenever she liked. She called Parliament only when it was needed. It met thirteen times during her 45-year reign: an average of just three weeks each year.

Elizabeth called Parliament for three main reasons:

■ to help pass ACTS OF PARLIAMENT – laws which were approved by both Houses of Parliament and the monarch
■ to approve taxes, which could only be collected if Parliament agreed to them
■ to provide her with support and advice – it was very useful for monarchs to know the opinions of MPs and win their support.

Elizabeth only expected her MPs to talk about certain issues. They were not supposed to discuss her personal affairs, religion or foreign policy. These were Elizabeth's private 'matters of state'.

She used a variety of methods to control Parliament, as you can see in Source 3 on page 40. She also made sure that several of her Privy Councillors sat in the House of Lords or were elected to the Commons. They helped to win support for government measures. Elizabeth appointed the Speaker of the House of Commons. He chose the topics MPs were allowed to discuss and which MPs were allowed to speak about them. If there were difficulties, Elizabeth could always use the royal veto (her power to reject a law), or close Parliament.

Why were meetings of Parliament important for MPs?

When Parliament met, MPs had a valuable opportunity to voice their opinion on how the country was being governed. They believed that they had three special privileges or rights:

■ freedom of speech – the right to discuss anything they wanted to, especially if they had complaints against the government
■ freedom from arrest – no MP could be arrested or imprisoned while Parliament was meeting
■ freedom to discuss their own ideas for new laws.

1. Did sixteenth-century Parliaments represent the whole population?
2. Can you tell from Source 1 who were the most important members of Parliament? Who were the least important?
3. Explain how
a) Elizabeth
b) MPs
gained from meetings of Parliament.
4. Was Parliament an important part of the system of government in the sixteenth century?
5. Do you think it was inevitable that Elizabeth would have difficulties with her Parliaments?

■ ACTIVITY

A new Parliament is about to meet. MPs from all over the country are arriving in Westminster. Choose one of Elizabeth's Parliaments from the table in Source 3, on the next page.

a) Imagine you are one of Elizabeth's most important Privy Councillors. She has asked you to write her opening speech to this Parliament. Your speech should explain:

■ the Queen's reasons for calling this Parliament
■ what she wants MPs to do
■ what she does not want her MPs to talk about.

b) Write a conversation between two MPs who have just heard your speech. They are discussing what they plan to do. One MP is very ambitious and does not want to cause any trouble. He hopes that one day Elizabeth will appoint him to the Privy Council. The other MP wants to bring his complaints to the Queen's attention.

S OURCE 2 The membership of Parliament during Elizabeth's reign

The House of Lords
■ *Nearly 100 lords, bishops and judges had the right to sit in the House of Lords.*

The House of Commons
■ *About 450 men. They were mostly members of the gentry who owned land but there were also some lawyers, merchants and government officials.*
■ *They were elected by landowners and wealthy men in the towns. People from the lower classes and women could not vote.*

■ *Several Privy Councillors sat in both Houses of Parliament.*

SOURCE 3 Elizabeth and her Parliaments, 1558–1603

Date	Government business	MPs' complaints	How Elizabeth dealt with them
1559	MPs declared their loyalty to the new Queen. They helped to pass laws to create a new Protestant Church.	Some MPs asked Elizabeth to marry as soon as possible.	Elizabeth gave them a vague reply. Then she closed Parliament.
1563	MPs approved taxes to pay for military help Elizabeth had sent to Scotland. They passed a law which said that all APPRENTICESHIPS must last for seven years.	Some MPs asked Elizabeth to get married soon.	Elizabeth gave another vague reply and then closed Parliament.
1566	MPs agreed to taxes to pay for an army Elizabeth had sent to France.	A few MPs threatened to refuse to approve taxes until Elizabeth made plans to marry. Paul Wentworth, a Puritan, said that MPs had the right of free speech to discuss the Queen's marriage.	Elizabeth angrily told MPs that it was not convenient to discuss her personal affairs. Then she closed Parliament.
1571	MPs agreed to taxes to pay for defeating a rebellion in the north of England. They passed laws against the Pope and traitors.	Walter Strickland, a Puritan, introduced a BILL to replace the Prayer Book and make other changes to the Church.	Elizabeth accused some MPs of interfering in her private matters of state. Then she closed Parliament.
1572	A Catholic plot to murder Elizabeth had been discovered. MPs discussed the Queen's safety.	MPs believed that Mary, Queen of Scots, had been involved in the plot. They demanded that she should be executed.	Elizabeth refused to execute Mary. Then she closed Parliament.
1576	MPs agreed to taxes.	Peter Wentworth, a Puritan, complained that MPs were not being allowed to discuss anything they wanted to.	Wentworth was imprisoned in the Tower of London for one month. Then Elizabeth closed Parliament.
1581	MPs approved taxes to pay for an army Elizabeth had sent to Ireland. They passed new laws to punish Catholics. Then Elizabeth closed Parliament.		
1584–1585	Another plot to murder the Queen had been discovered. MPs agreed to punish anyone who benefited from Elizabeth's death. They passed a law to punish Catholic priests and granted taxes.	Puritan MPs demanded that there should be changes in the Church, before they would agree to new taxes.	Elizabeth ordered her MPs to stop talking about religion, but asked her bishops to carry out checks on the clergy. Then she closed Parliament.
1586–1587	War had broken out with Spain and there had been another plot to murder the Queen. MPs granted taxes for the war.	MPs demanded that Mary, Queen of Scots, should be executed. Anthony Cope, a Puritan, tried to introduce a Bill to abolish bishops and replace the Prayer Book. Peter Wentworth supported his right to speak. Job Throckmorton, a Puritan, spoke for a war against France and asked Elizabeth to become Queen of the Netherlands.	Elizabeth gave a vague answer to MPs' demands to put Mary to death, but agreed to her execution a few months later. She imprisoned Cope, Wentworth, Throckmorton and three other MPs for interfering in her private affairs. Then she closed Parliament.
1589	MPs approved taxes to pay for the cost of defeating the Spanish Armada.	Some MPs complained about PURVEYANCES.	Elizabeth said that this was not MPs' business but she would look into their complaints. Then she closed Parliament.
1593	MPs granted taxes to pay for the war against Spain and passed a law to punish Catholics.	Peter Wentworth wanted Elizabeth to name her successor.	Elizabeth imprisoned Wentworth in the Tower of London. (He died there in 1597.) Then Parliament was closed.
1597–1598	MPs agreed to taxes. They passed laws to punish beggars and help the poor: the Elizabethan Poor Law.	Some MPs complained about MONOPOLIES.	Elizabeth said she would look into their complaints and closed Parliament.
1601	MPs approved taxes to pay for the war against Spain and the cost of sending an army to Ireland.	MPs complained about monopolies again. Some said that they should not grant taxes until monopolies were cancelled.	The Queen agreed to cancel some monopolies and look into the rest. She made a long 'Golden Speech' to flatter MPs and then closed Parliament.

SOURCE 4 An extract from *Elizabeth I*, by Christopher Haigh, 1988

66 *Elizabeth's councillors nominated MPs, planned business in advance and tried to manage proceedings. Parliament was a most useful means of applying pressure on the Queen to accept policies she disliked – such as over marriage and the succession in 1563 and 1566, over religious reform in 1571, over anti-Catholic laws in 1581 and over the execution of Mary, Queen of Scots, in 1586.* 99

■ TASK 1

Use Sources 3 and 4 to answer the questions below. For Part A you could use a spreadsheet program to present your findings as bar graphs or pie charts.

Part A: working out your findings
1. How many times did Elizabeth call Parliament:
a) to approve taxes?
b) to help her pass laws?
c) to provide advice and support?
2. Elizabeth's Parliaments dealt with the following issues: religion; marriage and the succession; foreign affairs; MPs' privileges; finance; Mary, Queen of Scots; the Queen's safety; social issues.
a) Taking each of these issues in turn, how many times did Elizabeth and her Parliaments disagree about them?
b) How many times did they agree about them?
3. How many times did MPs threaten Elizabeth's powers as Queen and in what ways?
4. How often did Elizabeth use these methods to deal with her MPs:
a) getting angry with them?

b) punishing them?
c) using persuasion to win their support?
d) using delaying tactics?
e) giving in to their demands?
f) closing Parliament to stop things getting out of control?

Part B: interpreting your findings
Use your findings to the questions in Part A to answer these questions.
1. Why did Elizabeth usually call Parliament?
2. Which issues did Elizabeth and her MPs
a) agree
b) disagree
about the most?
c) Do you think that Elizabeth agreed with her MPs more often than she disagreed with them?
3. Did MPs ever make serious attacks on Elizabeth's powers as Queen?
4. Which methods did Elizabeth use most often to deal with her MPs?
5. Which methods were the most successful in helping Elizabeth to control her MPs?

■ TASK 2

Write an essay to answer this question: how successfully did Elizabeth deal with her Parliaments?
You will need to write four detailed paragraphs to explain:

■ how Elizabeth and some of her MPs had different views about the purpose of Parliament
■ which issues Elizabeth and her MPs disagreed about and how important they were

■ which issues Elizabeth and her MPs agreed about and how important they were
■ the methods Elizabeth used to control her Parliaments and how successful they were.

Finally, write a brief conclusion to explain your overall answer to the question you were given at the start of this enquiry: did Elizabeth lose control of Parliament? Your teacher will give you a sheet to help you.

Case study: why did Elizabeth never marry?

WHEN ELIZABETH BECAME queen, most people expected that there would be a royal wedding soon. Unmarried monarchs usually got married quickly. They needed children to succeed them. Elizabeth was the last of Henry VIII's children. Without a child to succeed her the rule of the Tudor family would come to an end. In fact, this is exactly what happened. Elizabeth I, the 'Virgin Queen', is the only queen of England who never married. You are now going to investigate why Elizabeth never married. This case study can tell us a lot about whether Elizabeth was really in control of government. Was it her decision – or was she forced into staying single?

Did anyone want to marry Elizabeth?

The short answer to this question is yes! There was no shortage of men who wanted to marry Elizabeth. Many English nobles and European princes hoped to marry the new Queen of England. They sent gifts to win her favour.

Elizabeth's Privy Councillors regularly advised her to get married. Many Members of Parliament asked her to marry, too (see page 40). Elizabeth never gave them a definite answer.

I will be much more wealthy and powerful if I marry Elizabeth. Everyone knows that women are weak. I will be able to control her and become the real ruler of the country – I will be 'the power behind the throne'.

If I marry the Queen of England I can make myself and my country more powerful. I will be able to rule England. I will also gain an ally for my country. If my country is ever at war, I can make sure that England fights on our side.

An English noble   A foreign prince

SOURCE 1 Why many English nobles and foreign princes wanted to marry Elizabeth

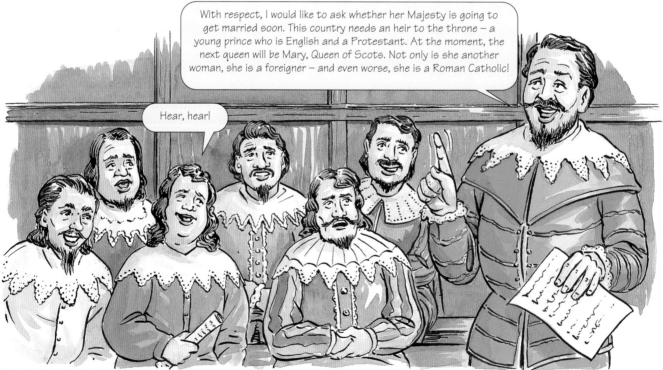

With respect, I would like to ask whether her Majesty is going to get married soon. This country needs an heir to the throne – a young prince who is English and a Protestant. At the moment, the next queen will be Mary, Queen of Scots. Not only is she another woman, she is a foreigner – and even worse, she is a Roman Catholic!

Hear, hear!

SOURCE 2 Most Members of Parliament wanted Elizabeth to get married

Why didn't Elizabeth marry Robert Dudley?

Throughout the first few years of Elizabeth's reign there were many rumours that she was about to marry. Several European princes, including Philip of Spain, proposed marriage to her. The strongest rumours of a royal wedding came in 1560. Many people believed that Elizabeth was about to marry an English nobleman – Lord Robert Dudley.

Robert Dudley (see page 36) was good-looking, intelligent and the same age as Elizabeth. By 1560 Elizabeth was spending a lot of time with him. Many people believed that she and Dudley were in love. Several other nobles at court became jealous.

SOURCE 3 Robert Dudley, painted by Nicholas Hilliard in about 1575. In this year, Elizabeth stayed at Dudley's home, Kenilworth Castle, for three weeks during one of her progresses

SOURCE 4 The Spanish ambassador, writing about Elizabeth's relationship with Robert Dudley

❝ She, Robert and I being alone in the gallery, they began joking. They went so far with their jokes that Robert told her that if she liked I could be the minister to perform the marriage ceremony. She was not unhappy to hear it, but said she was not sure whether I knew enough English. ❞

Dudley was an ambitious man. He wanted to marry Elizabeth. Many historians think that Elizabeth was in love with him. There was one big problem: he had a wife. He had married Amy Robsart when he was seventeen. Rumours spread that he wanted to murder her so that he could marry Elizabeth. Then, in September 1560, Amy was found dead at the bottom of the stairs in their Oxfordshire home. An enquiry decided that her death was an accident, but many people did not believe it. They thought that Dudley had really murdered her. Some people even thought that Elizabeth was involved.

■ DECISION POINT, SEPTEMBER 1560

Work in groups of two or three. You are Elizabeth I. You would like to marry Robert Dudley. News has just arrived that his wife has been found dead. You have heard the rumours that he has murdered her, but you don't believe them. You have to decide what to do. Will you:

a) marry Robert Dudley as soon as possible?
b) wait a few months until the rumours have stopped and then marry him?
c) ban him from Court and never see him again?
d) allow him to stay at Court but tell him that you can never marry him?
e) go to a marriage guidance counsellor?
f) something else?

Think about the advantages and disadvantages of each choice. Then make your decision. Announce it to the rest of the class and explain your reasons. Your teacher will tell you what Elizabeth really decided.

What did Elizabeth say about getting married?

Elizabeth never explained why she did not marry. She kept her thoughts private. Source 8 suggests what some of those thoughts might have been. When Parliament asked her to marry, she gave only vague replies. Later in the reign, when her MPs asked her to name her successor, she always refused.

> **SOURCE 5** Elizabeth's reply to Parliament's first request, in 1559, that she should marry

66 Whenever it shall please God to incline my heart to another kind of life, you may well assure yourselves that I will not do anything that my realm will have a good cause to be discontented with. I will never decide anything that shall be prejudicial [damaging] to the realm. And in the end, this shall be sufficient for me, that a marble stone shall declare that a Queen, having reigned such a time, lived and died a virgin. 99

> **SOURCE 6** Another of Elizabeth's replies to Parliament, 1566

66 I say again, I will marry as soon as I can conveniently. And I hope to have children, otherwise I would never marry. At this present time, it is not convenient. 99

> **SOURCE 7** Elizabeth's reaction to Robert Dudley, Earl of Leicester, when he tried to give orders to her servants

66 I will have here but one mistress and no master. 99

> **SOURCE 8** Some of the possible reasons why Elizabeth never married

My sister Mary's marriage to Philip of Spain was very unpopular. It caused a rebellion in 1554. My people hate having foreign rulers.

If I marry an English nobleman many other nobles will be disappointed. They might feel excluded from power and start a rebellion. All the time I am unmarried they will still hope to marry me and so they will be loyal.

Several foreign princes want to marry me, so their countries are being friendly. If I marry one of them England might lose the friendship of the other countries; they might be offended and become our enemies.

If I marry, my husband might try to control me and rule the country instead of me. My people already think that women are weak rulers. I am determined to be a strong ruler.

1. a) Why did most of Elizabeth's people **expect** her to marry?
   b) Why did most of them **want** her to get married?
2. What were the advantages and disadvantages to Elizabeth of:
   a) marrying an English noble?
   b) marrying a foreign prince?
   c) not getting married?
3. Why do you think Elizabeth did not marry Robert Dudley?

■ TASK

1. Do you think Elizabeth ever really meant to get married? Explain the reasons for your answer.
2. Why do you think Elizabeth never married? Explain your reasons fully and say what you think the most important reason was.
3. 'Elizabeth's decision not to marry shows that she was in control. It was her decision and no one else's.' Do you agree or disagree with this statement? Explain the reasons for your answer.

Did Elizabeth control local government?

ELIZABETH, HER COURT and the Privy Council were all based in London. Parliament met nearby in Westminster. When Elizabeth went on her progresses she never travelled too far away from the capital. But most of Elizabeth's three million people lived far away from London. Elizabeth never visited many parts of England and Wales. If she was going to govern the country successfully she had to control all her people. This was not easy. Elizabeth did not have a permanent army or a police force to help her. Transport and communications were slow. A journey on horseback along bumpy roads from London to York took nearly five days. How did Elizabeth try to make all her people obey her orders and laws?

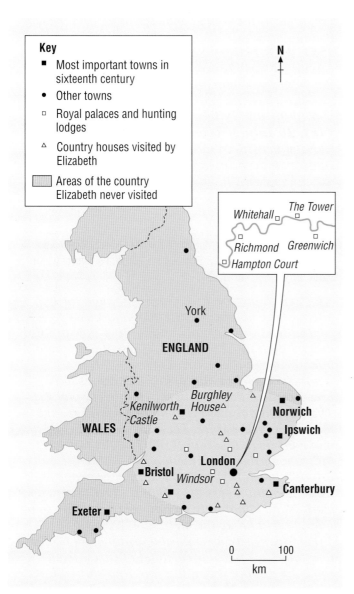

SOURCE 1 Parts of the country that Elizabeth visited during her reign

Controlling the countryside and towns

Elizabeth appointed officials around the country, to help her control local areas. There was a Lord Lieutenant in each county. He was usually a wealthy noble who kept the Queen and her ministers informed of what was happening in the county. In an emergency, the Queen would order him to call up part-time soldiers to form the county army. He had to make sure that the county's soldiers were well trained and that their weapons were kept in good condition. In the towns, wealthy citizens elected councils to look after the town's affairs and keep law and order.

Justices of the Peace

The local officials with whom most people came into contact were the Justices of the Peace (JPs). Elizabeth appointed about 40 of them in every county. They were usually gentry landowners who knew their area well. Their work was voluntary and they were not paid, but there were always plenty of landowners who wanted to become JPs. It was a great honour to be a JP. It meant that you were the most important person in the area. Although it rarely happened, the Queen could dismiss a JP if she was not satisfied with his work. Elizabeth relied greatly on her JPs. Without them, she would not have been able to rule the country effectively.

The Queen expected her Justices of the Peace to carry out a range of duties. Although it was only supposed to be part-time work, JPs were given more and more to do during Elizabeth's reign. They were often given instructions from the Privy Council to carry out, or new laws from Parliament to enforce. They had lesser officials such as constables and NIGHT-WATCHMEN to help them. So what did JPs actually do? The following sources will help you answer this question.

SOURCE 2 An extract from *De Republica Anglorum*, by Sir Thomas Smith, one of Elizabeth's Privy Councillors, 1565

66 *The Justices of the Peace be those who repress [punish] robbers, thieves and VAGABONDS, plots and conspiracies, riots and violences, and all other misdemeanours [bad behaviour] in the country. Each of them hath authority upon complaint made to him of any theft, robbery, manslaughter, murder, violence, riots, unlawful games, or any such disturbance of the peace and quiet of the realm, to commit the persons whom he supposeth offenders to the prison. A few lines signed with his hand is enough for that purpose. He and his fellows do meet four times in the year to enquire of all the misdemeanours.*

The Justices of the Peace do meet also at other times by command of the Queen upon suspicion of war, to take order for the safety of the county, sometimes to raise able men [as soldiers], and sometimes to take order for the excessive wages of servants and labourers, for unlawful games, for evil orders in ale-houses and taverns, for punishment of idle and vagabond persons. There never was in any country devised a more wise, gentle or certain way to rule the people, whereby they are kept always in good order. 99

SOURCE 4 Extracts from the journal of William Lambarde, a JP in Kent, 1581–83

66 *August 1581 Sir Thomas Cotton, Sir Christopher Alleyn, Thomas Willoughby, Robert Richers and I sat at Borough Green for the licensing of alehouses. We took bond of Roger Meare of Mereworth, innkeeper, for keeping good order in his alehouse, he being bound in £10.*
1581, 23 August Sir Christopher Alleyn, my father-in-law, and I joined in the examination of eight persons who disguised their clothing and language as the rogues called gypsies, and we sent them to the gaol.
1583, 23 February Sir Christopher Alleyn and I examined various people at Sevenoaks concerning the wilful poisoning of William Brightrede by Thomas Heyward and Parnel, his now wife, then wife of the said William.
1583, 20 July At Cobham Hall my Lord Christopher Alleyn and I wrote to all the constables in the area to notify to them the taxation needed to pay for the gaol and the house of correction. 99

SOURCE 5 An extract from a letter from Edward Hext, a Somerset JP, to Lord Burghley, Elizabeth's Secretary of State, 25 September 1596

66 *Right honourable and my very good lord, having long observed the crimes and thefts committed in this county and finding they multiply daily, I do think it my duty to present unto your honourable and grave consideration, this report. 173 wicked and desperate persons have been executed this year in the county of Somerset. They would not work and no one would receive them into their service. These are not all the thieves and robbers in this county, for I know that every fifth person that commiteth a felony [theft] is not brought to trial. Many wicked thieves escape and infect great numbers; they change their names and clothes and commonly go into other counties so as no man will know them.*

This year there assembled a group of 80 people and they stole a whole cartload of cheese from someone driving it to a fair and they shared it out amongst them. 99

SOURCE 3 A sixteenth-century drawing of a night-watchman

1. What pieces of equipment is the night-watchman shown carrying in Source 3? What do you think he needed them for?

2. What kinds of people did Elizabeth appoint to be her Justices of the Peace?
3. a) Why did Elizabeth I have to rely upon part-time, unpaid JPs to enforce her laws in local areas?
   b) Why, if they were not paid, did so many local gentry want to become JPs?
4. Use Sources 2–9 to make a list of the kinds of work Justices of the Peace did for the Queen. Present your list as a 'spider' diagram.

5. Thomas Smith (Source 2) praised the JPs and said that they always kept the people 'in good order'. From the evidence, do you think that JPs:
   a) were completely loyal to Elizabeth?
   b) did their best to make sure that local people obeyed her?
   c) were totally successful?

SOURCE 6 Instructions issued in 1544 by Henry VIII. JPs were still expected to carry them out during Elizabeth's reign

66 *Many persons have accumulated a great number and multitude of corns and grain, far above what is necessary for their household, without bringing it into any market to be sold, intending thereby for the prices of corn to rise. All Justices of the Peace shall with all convenient speed search the houses, barns and yards of such persons.* 99

SOURCE 7 An extract from an Act of Parliament, 1572

66 *When the number of poor people forced to live upon ALMS be known, the justices, mayors, sheriffs, bailiffs and other officers shall set down a weekly charge towards the relief [help] of the said poor people, and shall tax all the inhabitants to such weekly charge as all of them shall contribute towards the relief of the said poor people.* 99

SOURCE 8 Extracts from the records of local lawcourts in West Yorkshire, 1597–98

66 *From information given to this court by the constables, Adam Hutchonson and Thomas Hodgson of Barnsley, alekeepers, are men of bad behaviour and do maintain ill rule in their houses. It is therefore ordered that they shall not run any alehouses. It is ordered that no brewers in this area shall brew any ale or beer to be sold at a greater price than a penny per quart, unless they have a special licence from a Justice of the Peace.*

The highway leading from Leeds to Wikebrigg is in great decay to the great hindrance of all her Majesty's subjects who travel that way. Therefore the Justices here present do order every person occupying land in Leeds to send labourers to repair the highway before August 25. 99

SOURCE 9 An extract from a letter from the Privy Council to the JPs in Norfolk

66 *You received letters from us eight months ago to make careful enquiry of all the provisions needed for her Majesty's visit. We understand not of any performance by you of this, her Majesty's commandment. We require you, in her Majesty's name, that presently you do proceed to carry out our orders.* 99

■ **ACTIVITY**

Script a conversation between two Justices of the Peace. One of them has just been appointed by the Queen. He explains why he is so pleased to be a JP. The other man is a very experienced JP who comes from the next village. He explains to the new JP what sort of work he will have to do.

■ **ACTIVITY**

You are one of the Queen's Justices of the Peace. Use Sources 2–9 to write a diary entry, describing a typical week's work.

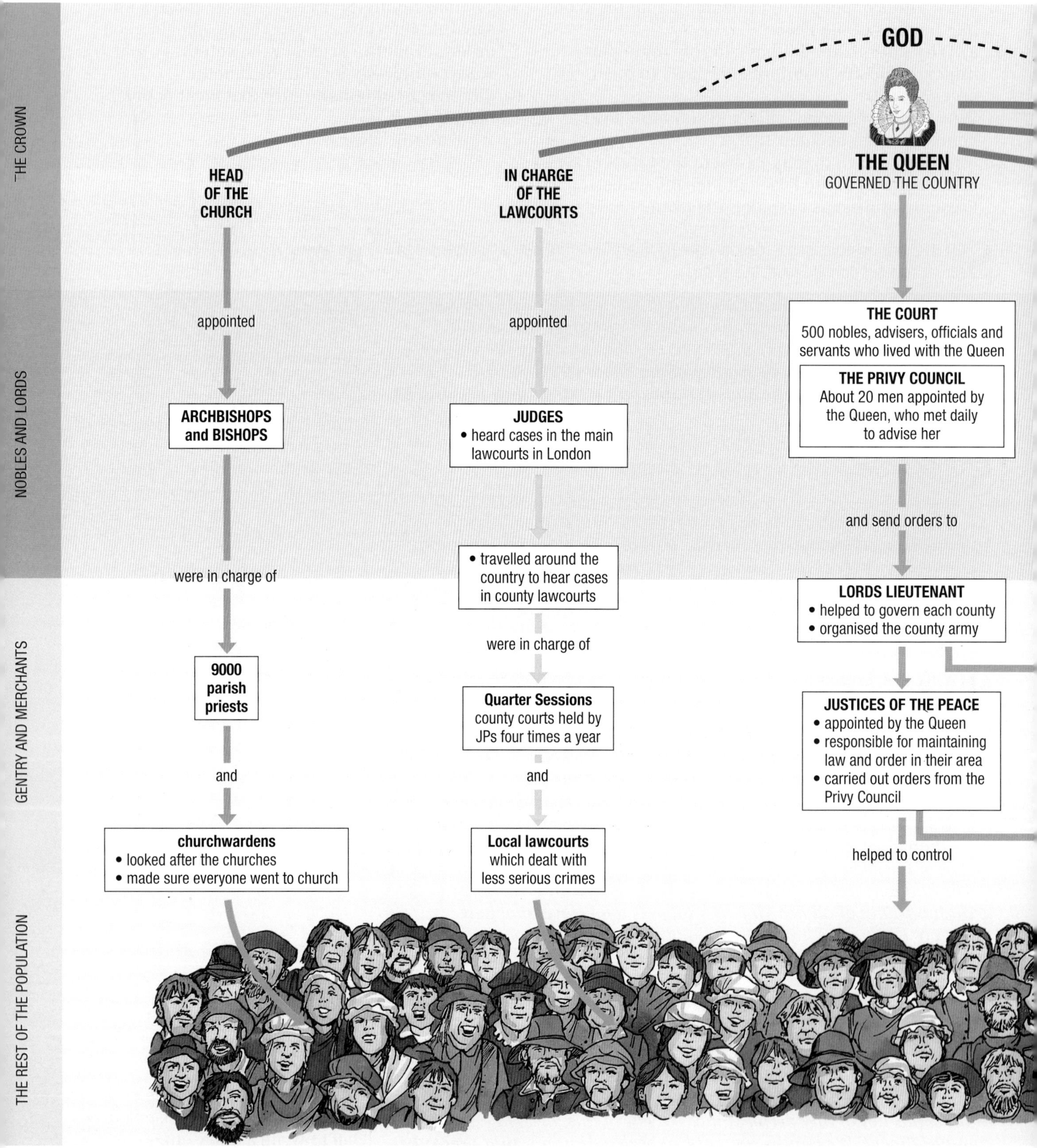

THE CROWN

NOBLES AND LORDS

GENTRY AND MERCHANTS

THE REST OF THE POPULATION

GOD

THE QUEEN
GOVERNED THE COUNTRY

HEAD OF THE CHURCH

appointed

ARCHBISHOPS and BISHOPS

were in charge of

9000 parish priests

and

churchwardens
• looked after the churches
• made sure everyone went to church

IN CHARGE OF THE LAWCOURTS

appointed

JUDGES
• heard cases in the main lawcourts in London

• travelled around the country to hear cases in county lawcourts

were in charge of

Quarter Sessions
county courts held by JPs four times a year

and

Local lawcourts
which dealt with less serious crimes

THE COURT
500 nobles, advisers, officials and servants who lived with the Queen

THE PRIVY COUNCIL
About 20 men appointed by the Queen, who met daily to advise her

and send orders to

LORDS LIEUTENANT
• helped to govern each county
• organised the county army

JUSTICES OF THE PEACE
• appointed by the Queen
• responsible for maintaining law and order in their area
• carried out orders from the Privy Council

helped to control

SOURCE 10 The system of government in Elizabethan England

HER WEALTH CAME FROM HER LANDS AND FROM CUSTOMS DUTIES

COMMANDED THE NAVY TO PROTECT THE COAST, AND PART–TIME SOLDIERS IN EVERY COUNTY

occasionally called

NATIONAL GOVERNMENT

PARLIAMENT
- advised the Queen
- agreed to pass new laws
- approved taxes in an emergency

THE HOUSE OF LORDS
- 90 members: lords, bishops, judges

The House of Commons
- 450 members: gentry, merchants, lawyers, government officials
- Elected by wealthy citizens

LOCAL GOVERNMENT

Town councils
- mayors and aldermen elected by wealthy citizens
- responsible for maintaining law and order in towns

were in charge of

were in charge of

Local officials
- constables collected taxes, arrested criminals
- overseers of the poor

The lower classes had no say in how the country was governed and they were expected to obey their social superiors

49

■ REVIEW TASK

Did Elizabeth I keep complete control of government?

At the beginning of this chapter you saw that many people feared Elizabeth was going to be a weak ruler. They thought that she would not be strong enough to control the country.

Use what you have found out in this chapter to write an essay to answer this question: was Elizabeth I a weak ruler who was completely unable to control the government of her country?

You will need to explain how successful you think Elizabeth was in dealing with these issues:

- getting publicity to win her people's support
- choosing and controlling her Privy Councillors
- dealing with Parliament
- deciding whether or not to get married
- controlling local areas.

Use them as sub-headings in your answer. Remember to support your ideas with examples. Then write your overall conclusion to the question.

Your teacher will give you a sheet to help you to assess Elizabeth's success rating, using the criteria in the swingometer diagram. You can use your assessment to help you plan your essay.

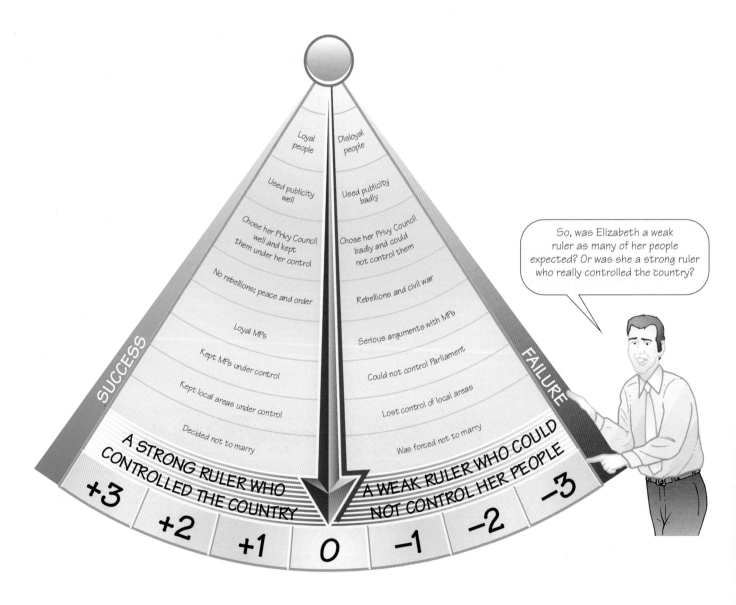

So, was Elizabeth a weak ruler as many of her people expected? Or was she a strong ruler who really controlled the country?

chapter 3

DID ELIZABETH PROTECT HER PEOPLE FROM POVERTY AND CRIME?

SIXTEENTH-CENTURY monarchs were expected to protect their people from poverty and crime. Everyone wanted to be better off and live in safety. These were high expectations. In this chapter, we will investigate how successful Elizabeth was in meeting them. Did all her people become better off during her reign? Or was there more and more poverty? Was she able to keep her people safe from crime and violence?

> What were people's lives like during Elizabeth's reign? How successful was she in protecting them from poverty and crime?

SOURCE 1 Two extremes – terrible poverty and incredible wealth

In the early 1570s a churchman from Essex travelled around the country to find out what the lives of people in England were like. His name was William Harrison. In 1577 he published a book called *The Description of England*. You can read his main findings in Source 2.

1. Do you think that William Harrison is a reliable source for historians?
2. Which of the two scenes in Source 1 do Harrison's findings seem to support?
3. Do his findings prove that this view of Elizabeth's reign is true?
4. What kinds of source could you use to check his findings?

> Old people tell me that, during their lifetimes, people have become much better off.
>
> CHANGES IN THE LAST 50 YEARS
>
> Now houses are built of stone and brick, not wood.
>
> They have fireplaces and chimneys.
>
> Windows have glass in them.
>
> Houses now have many rooms, on several floors.
>
> There are oak panels on the walls to keep rooms warm.
>
> Tapestries and painted cloths are hung on the walls.
>
> Everyone has much more furniture, such as cupboards – more than ever before.
>
> People now have cups, plates and spoons made of silver and pewter, not wood.
>
> They sleep on feather mattresses and pillows, not straw and logs.

SOURCE 2 William Harrison's findings

Did Elizabeth's people become better off?

PEOPLE'S HOMES CAN be useful sources for historians. They can show us how well off their owners were. They can also help us to work out what their lives were like. During Elizabeth's reign many people built themselves impressive new houses to live in. They were built in the latest style and often contained expensive furniture, paintings and tapestries. This was a way for people to display their wealth. So many new houses were built at this time that some historians have described this period as 'The Great Rebuilding'. Some of these houses still survive today. Now you are going to investigate one of them.

Case study: Hardwick Hall, Derbyshire

Hardwick Hall was built for Elizabeth, Countess of Shrewsbury, who became known as Bess of Hardwick. She was the wealthiest and most powerful woman in Elizabethan England – apart from the Queen. Bess was born in 1520. She was the daughter of a Derbyshire gentleman, who was not particularly wealthy or important. Bess married four times, and each of her marriages made her richer and more powerful. Her last husband was the Earl of Shrewsbury. When he died in 1590 Bess was a very wealthy widow. She began rebuilding her family home into a magnificent new house called Hardwick Hall. It took about seven years to finish. Bess lived there until she died in 1608.

SOURCE 1 A portrait of Bess of Hardwick painted in about 1580 when she was 60 years old. It was painted to hang with other portraits of her family in the Long Gallery at Hardwick Hall

■ TALKING POINT

What are the advantages of studying Elizabethan houses in order to find out about people's lives during her reign? Can you think of any disadvantages?

SOURCE 2

SOURCE 3

OURCE 4

OURCE 5

1. Match the following captions correctly with Sources 2–5:
   - ■ the kitchen
   - ■ the Long Gallery (used for indoor exercise, dancing and conversation)
   - ■ the exterior of Hardwick Hall
   - ■ the High Great Chamber (used for receiving important guests and holding banquets).

2. Why do you think Hardwick Hall was so large?

3. Study Source 2. How did the design of Hardwick Hall show who owned it?

4. Look again at Source 2. The rooms for servants, the family and important guests were all on different floors.

a) On which floors, do you think, were the rooms shown in Sources 3–5?

b) Does the design of Hardwick Hall tell you anything about Elizabethan society?

■ ACTIVITY

You are a guide at Hardwick Hall. Today you are taking a group of blind people around the house. You have to help them to 'see' the house, so you must describe it to them accurately and in detail. Explain how you will describe:

- ■ the outside of Hardwick Hall
- ■ the three rooms in Sources 3–5 (pay attention to the size of each room, the walls, the floor, the ceiling, the furniture and equipment, and what the room was used for).

■ TASK

1. Did Bess of Hardwick become better off during Elizabeth's reign?

2. Look again at William Harrison's findings on page 51. Which of the features he describes have you seen in your study of Hardwick Hall?

3. Is Hardwick Hall a useful source for your investigation into the lives of Elizabeth's people?

What about other people's lives?

So far you have only studied one Elizabethan house. Good history students should never base their ideas on just one piece of evidence! Now you are going to continue your investigation by examining some evidence about the homes of other people.

SOURCE 6 Burghley House, Lincolnshire. It was built by William Cecil, Lord Burghley, in three stages between 1552 and 1589. He also built himself two other large houses, one in London and one in Hertfordshire

SOURCE 7 Montacute House, Somerset. It was built by Edward Phelips, a member of a gentry family, in the 1590s

SOURCE 8 A yeoman farmer's house in Kent. It was built in the 1490s. The chimney and glass windows were added during Elizabeth's reign

SOURCE 9 Westwood Manor, Wiltshire. It was the home of Thomas Horton, a cloth merchant

SOURCE 10 Extracts from the INVENTORY of Christopher Scott, a merchant in Canterbury, Kent, 1568

" The Great Chamber over the shop: 3 feather beds, 2 bolsters [long pillows], 3 blankets, a cloth canopy, 5 green and red curtains. A cupboard with blue velvet cloth. 2 tables and a long bench. 23 cushions. A screen, chair and bench. A chest. A cloth hanging. A glass lantern. Value: £13 12s.

In the Attic: a feather bed, a bolster, a blanket, a cover, a bedstead with hangings. A set of pewter dishes. 24 saucers. 12 soup bowls. 4 dishes. 2 basins and a jug. A heating dish. A chair, a long bench and a cupboard. Value £6 11s 4d.

In the Chamber over the Great Chamber: 2 feather beds, 2 bolsters, a cover, a bedspread and 3 curtains. A bed, blanket, cover and bolster. 7 pillows and 3 cushions. A table, cupboard and carpet. A blue velvet canopy. A scarlet gown with velvet. A satin gown with velvet. A gown. A jacket with velvet sleeves. 19 pairs of sheets, 10 table cloths, 14 pillow cases, 4 dozen napkins. Value: £26 7s 4d.

Silver plate: 57 ounces. 2 silver bowls. Value: £73 19s 9d.

Cloth in the shop: £146 3s 4d. "

■ **TASK**

Do Sources 2–10 support William Harrison's findings on page 51? Your teacher will give you a sheet to help you.

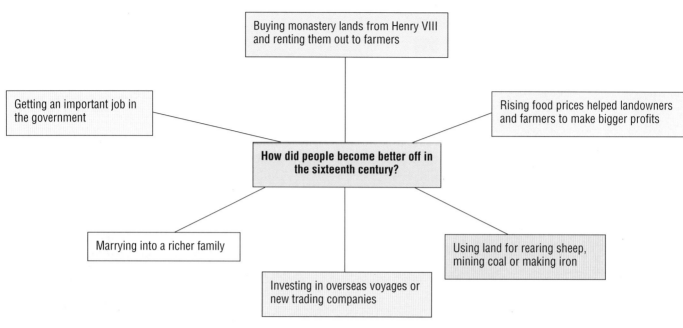

SOURCE 11 How people became better off in the sixteenth century

■ TASK

Look at the cartoons below. They show a student like you. He has been investigating how well off people were during Elizabeth's reign. What would you advise him to do next? Explain the reasons for your answer.

What about the lower classes?

We divide our people commonly into four sorts.
- Gentlemen: nobles, lords and gentry
- Citizens and burgesses in the towns: merchants, master craftsmen and lawyers
- Yeomen: farmers who own their land
- The fourth sort: farm labourers, servants, shopkeepers, and craftspeople such as tailors, shoemakers, carpenters and bricklayers

SOURCE 12 William Harrison's views

You have found out about wealthy people who did well during Elizabeth's reign. But that is not the whole picture. Most people belonged to William Harrison's 'fourth sort'. They did not own land or businesses. To provide their families with food, clothes and a home, they had to work. Unlike today, they could not go to a job centre or claim benefit if they could not find work. The government was not expected to give this sort of direct help.

So, did the lower classes become better off during Elizabeth's reign? It is not easy to answer this question. Their homes and possessions have not survived. We cannot read what they thought about their lives. Few of them could read or write. The only written accounts we have were produced by wealthy people. The following sources, however, contain some clues.

SOURCE 13 A rhyme, thought to date from the sixteenth century

66 *Hark, hark! The dogs do bark,*
The beggars are coming to town,
Some in rags and some in tags,
And one in a velvet gown. 99

5. a) Is Source 13 a reliable source?
b) If it does date from Elizabeth's reign, is it a useful source?

SOURCE 14 Philip Stubbs, a Puritan writing about beggars in 1583

66 *They lie in the streets in dirt and are permitted to die like dogs or beasts without any mercy or compassion.* 99

SOURCE 15 A drawing dating from Elizabeth's reign

6. Describe what is happening in Source 15.
7. Study Source 16.
a) Does it suggest that poor people were becoming better or worse off?
b) Harrison states that there were 10,000 beggars. Do you think that this is an accurate figure?

SOURCE 16 An extract from *The Description of England*, by William Harrison, 1577

66 *It is not yet threescore years since this trade of begging began. But how it has increased since then. They are now supposed, of one sex and another, to number 10,000 people as I have heard reported.* 99

■ TASK

Did Elizabeth's people become better off during her reign? Write an essay using Harrison's 'four sorts of people' as sub-headings in your answer.

Why did poverty get worse?

YOU HAVE SEEN that many rich people became much better off during Elizabeth's reign. But there is little doubt that the poor got poorer. They found it more and more difficult to make ends meet. Many lost their jobs. The numbers of beggars on the streets rose considerably. So why did poverty get worse during Elizabeth's reign? What were the most important causes of poverty? Were Elizabeth and her councillors to blame – or was it caused by forces outside their control which they did not really understand?

A rising population

The population of England and Wales had fallen in the later Middle Ages, especially after the Black Death of 1348–49. In the sixteenth century it began to rise again. By 1600 there were many more people in the country. This meant that more food, clothes, houses and jobs were needed. But there were not enough, so more people became poor.

1. a) By how much did the population rise in the sixteenth century?
b) In the early 1500s the population was rising slowly. When did it begin to rise faster?
c) When did the population rise fastest?
d) Did the population begin to rise before or after Elizabeth became Queen?

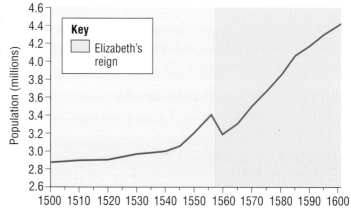

SOURCE 1 The population of England and Wales, 1501–1601

Inflation

The sixteenth century was a period of INFLATION throughout Europe. Most people's wages did not keep up with the rising prices. Poorer people, who were paid low wages to start with, were the worst off. Buying food cost more and more of their money, leaving them with little or nothing to spend on anything else.

The causes of inflation were not understood in the sixteenth century. Modern economists think that prices rise for three main reasons:

- shortage of goods
- a bigger demand for the same amount of goods
- people having more money to spend.

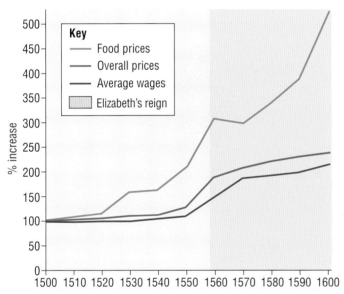

SOURCE 2 Prices and wages, 1500–1600

2. a) By how much did prices rise in the sixteenth century?
  b) Did food prices rise faster, slower or at the same rate as other prices?
  c) When did prices begin to rise sharply?
  d) Look at Sources 1 and 2. Does inflation seem to have anything to do with the rising population?
  e) In which years did prices rise fastest?
  f) Can you suggest any possible reasons why prices rose fastest at these times?

More silver in Europe

In the early sixteenth century Spain conquered large areas of Central and South America. There were many gold and silver mines in the 'New World'. From the 1540s onwards huge quantities of silver were shipped to Spain. Mines in central Europe were also producing more and more silver. Most of it was melted down to make coins or BULLION. Trade helped to spread it throughout Europe.

3 a) Do you think that more silver in Europe would have any effect on prices?
  b) Use Source 2 to check your answer.

Henry VIII's debasement of the coinage

English coins had always contained an amount of precious metal that was equal to the value of each coin. In the 1540s Henry VIII was short of money to pay for wars with France and Scotland. He decided to melt down the old coins and issue new ones. The new coins contained less gold and silver. Henry made a profit of nearly £1 million but he had 'debased' the coins. Merchants and traders could easily tell that the new coins were not as valuable as the old ones. So, when they sold their goods, they asked for more coins than they had asked for before. In 1560–61 Elizabeth called in the debased coins and issued new ones which contained a higher proportion of precious metal.

4. a) How did the debasement of the coinage affect prices?
  b) Does Source 2 support your answer?
  c) Did Elizabeth's issue of new coins solve the problem?

Bad harvests

Everyone in Elizabethan England depended on food from the country's farms. Farmers, however, were at the mercy of the weather. There were several bad harvests in the sixteenth century. As a result there were food shortages and the price of food rocketed. There was a real threat of starvation for the poorest people.

Quality of harvest

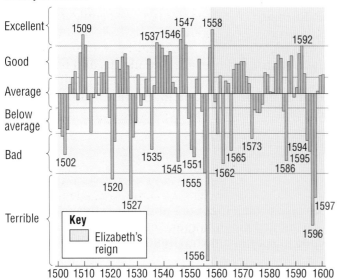

SOURCE 3 Harvests, 1500–1600

5. a) When were the worst harvests of the sixteenth century?

b) Look at Source 1 on page 58. Did these bad harvests have any effect on the population rise?

c) Look at Source 2 on page 59. Was there a connection between bad harvests and food prices?

SOURCE 4 Harvesting corn in the sixteenth century

SOURCE 5 Sheep farming

Changes in farming

Many landowners looked for more profitable ways of using their land. Some of them decided to keep sheep instead of growing crops. Many farm labourers lost their jobs and went to the towns in search of work. The landowners also enclosed their fields with hedges. The new fields often included the common land where villagers had grazed their animals.

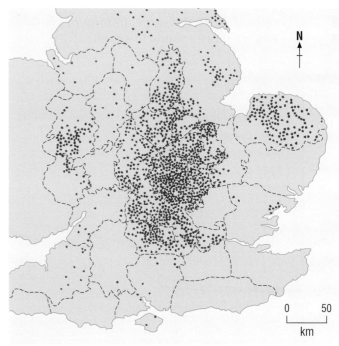

SOURCE 6 Areas affected by ENCLOSURES in the sixteenth century

6. a) Why did landlords have to enclose (put fences around) their fields if they wanted to keep sheep?

b) Use Sources 4 and 5 to explain why these changes led to more poverty.

c) Study Source 6. Did these changes affect the whole country?

Rack-renting

Many people in the sixteenth century blamed the increase in poverty on greedy 'RACK-RENTING' landlords. Landowners rented out most of their land to farmers. But, as prices rose, they found that their rents were losing their value. So they increased them. Poorer farmers who could not afford to pay the higher rents were evicted. Many of them went to the towns to find work.

7. Why do you think many landowners increased the rents they charged their farmers?

Changes in the cloth trade

The most important industry in sixteenth-century England was the cloth industry. Woollen cloth was the country's main EXPORT. Large quantities were sold in Europe. Many cloth merchants became very wealthy. There was plenty of work for spinners and weavers. Then, for reasons beyond the government's control, the cloth trade collapsed. Tens of thousands of people were thrown out of work.

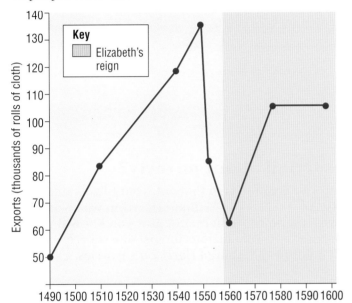

SOURCE 7 Cloth exports from London in the sixteenth century. London was the country's biggest port

8. a) Did the collapse in the cloth trade begin before or after Elizabeth became Queen?
    b) Did the cloth trade completely recover during Elizabeth's reign?

Wars

Tudor monarchs fought several expensive wars. This could have led to more poverty in three main ways:

■ high taxes (monarchs had to raise money to pay for the cost of fighting)
■ high government spending
■ soldiers and sailors being left without jobs when the fighting ended.

> **S**OURCE 8 The main periods of war under the Tudors
>
> *1520s: Henry VIII's wars against France and Spain*
> *1540s: Henry VIII's wars against France and Scotland*
> *1590s: Elizabeth I's war against Spain*

The dissolution of the monasteries

The monasteries helped many poor people in the Middle Ages by giving them food, clothing and money. Then, between 1536 and 1540, Henry VIII closed all the monasteries. The monks and nuns were given pensions and some of them found new jobs in the Church. But their servants lost their jobs and an important source of charity for poor people was taken away.

Monopolies

In the 1590s Elizabeth made money by selling monopolies. These gave individual nobles and merchants the sole right to manufacture or sell particular goods. Monopolies were very unpopular. Many people said they caused prices to rise.

9. Look at Source 2 on page 59 again. Is there any evidence to suggest that wars might have affected prices?
10. Do you think that monopolies caused inflation or just made it worse?

■ TASK 1

What were the most important causes of poverty in Elizabethan England? Look back at the cartoon of the students discussing the causes of events on page 58. Then draw a flow diagram to show:

■ the causes of poverty in the sixteenth century
■ how they were interconnected (draw arrows to show how one cause led to another)
■ which were the most important causes of poverty (draw large boxes around the most important causes and smaller boxes around the less important ones).

■ TASK 2

Write an essay to answer the question: was Elizabeth I responsible for the rise in poverty during her reign? You will need to consider the following issues:

■ which causes of poverty were not really understood in the sixteenth century?
■ which causes of poverty began before Elizabeth became Queen? (Elizabeth can't be blamed for them!)
■ which causes began or got much worse while she was Queen?
   was she to blame for them?
   did Elizabeth do anything to stop them? Could she have done more?

Were Elizabethans worried about poverty?

> With us the poor are commonly divided into three sorts.
>
> ■ Some are poor by impotency such as the fatherless child, the aged, blind and lame, and the person with an incurable disease.
> ■ The second are poor by misfortune, like the wounded soldier, the evicted householder and the sick person.
> ■ The third consists of idle beggars like rioters, vagabonds, rogues and strumpets [prostitutes]. They are poor through their own fault. They stray and wander about, hating all work. Some with sound and perfect limbs pretend to have all sorts of diseases. They are thieves who consume the charity of well-disposed people in a most detestable and wicked manner.

SOURCE 1 William Harrison's views

Were people worried about poverty?

The next stage of your investigation is to find out what Elizabethans thought about poverty. As you can see, William Harrison was worried. He thought poverty was a serious problem. But now you know that historians should not base their conclusions on just one source. We need to find out if other people shared Harrison's worries.

SOURCE 3 An extract from a letter written by Edward Hext, a Somerset JP, to Lord Burghley, Elizabeth's Secretary of State, 25 September 1596

66 *I do not see how it is possible for the country to bear the burdens of the thievings of the infinite numbers of the wicked, wandering idle people of the land. Though they labour not, they live idly in the alehouses day and night, eating and drinking excessively.* **99**

SOURCE 4 The opinion of Thomas Dekker, an Elizabethan writer, 1608

66 *Rogues are not driven to misery by mere want, but to be given money which by night is spent merrily.* **99**

SOURCE 5 An extract from *Utopia* by Sir Thomas More, 1516. (More was a lawyer and government minister during Henry VIII's reign)

66 *Poor wretched souls. Men, women, fatherless children, widows, woeful mothers with their young babes – away they trudge. All their household stuff, which is worth very little, they be forced to sell for hardly anything. And when they have wandered about till they have spent that, what can they do but steal, and then be hanged, or go about begging?* **99**

1. Were the people quoted in Sources 3–5 worried about poverty?
2. Were any of them sympathetic towards the poor?

■ **ACTIVITY**

SOURCE 2 a homeless young women in London today

There are many homeless people today. Some of them beg on the streets from passers-by. People have different views about beggars. Carry out a survey in your class or year group. How many students think:

■ beggars are lazy scroungers who should be punished?
■ individuals and charities should give them help?
■ the government should help them?
■ something else?

Vagabonds

William Harrison said that there were many people who were genuinely poor. His 'third sort of poor' caused the most worry. These were the vagabonds or wandering beggars. They were fit and strong but deliberately avoided work. They travelled in groups around the country, robbing and stealing as well as begging. Ordinary people were terrified by the vagabonds. Thomas Harman, a JP, was so worried that he wrote a book to warn people about them. He said that they cheated people into giving them money. He claimed that they even had their own slang language called 'canting', which no one else could understand.

3. Do you think that Thomas Harman's evidence about vagabonds is completely reliable? Explain the reasons for your answer.

SOURCE 6 An extract adapted from Thomas Harman's book, *A Warning against Vagabonds*, 1567

66 **Anglers** carry long wooden sticks. They beg during the day. In the evening they attach a hook to their stick and use it to steal clothes from people's washing lines.

Clapperdudgeons pretend to be badly wounded. They use arsenic to make their skin bleed. Then they soak dirty rags in the blood and tie them around their arms and legs.

A **doxy** carries a large pack on her back. She keeps all the things she has stolen in it. She knits as she begs and always wears a needle in her hat. She steals chickens by feeding them bread tied on a hook. The hook chokes and kills the chicken. Then she hides the chicken under her cloak.

Counterfeit cranks dress in old, dirty clothes and pretend to have epilepsy. They suck soap to make themselves foam at the mouth and pretend to have a fit when people come near them.

Abraham men pretend to be mad. They walk around half-naked, making strange wailing noises. 99

SOURCE 7 Some words from the canting language used by vagabonds

66 nab – a head   bouse – drink   nab-cheat – hat   bene – good
glaziers – eyes   pannum – bread   smelling cheat – nose
a grunting cheat – pig   prattling cheat – tongue
a cackling cheat – a chicken   togman – coat   grannum – corn
to filch – to rob   a ken – a house   Rome-vill – London 99

ACTIVITY 1

These five pictures are based on sixteenth-century drawings of vagabonds. Match each drawing to one of the different types of vagabond described by Thomas Harman in Source 6.

1.
2.
3.
4.
5.

ACTIVITY 2

Use the words in Source 7 to write a short conversation between two vagabonds in London. They are planning to steal something.

Why were Elizabethans so worried about poverty?

You have seen that many people thought that poverty was a serious problem. They were especially worried about the vagabonds. So, why were they so worried? Did they feel threatened by the rising numbers of poor people they saw around them? Were different kinds of people worried for the same reasons?

■ TASK

1. The people whom we call 'Elizabethans' were really different groups of people, all with their own concerns. Read the information on the opposite page. Then, fill in the speech bubbles on the sheet your teacher will give you, to show what each of the people below might have said about beggars – and why they felt so strongly about them.

A beggar

A poor woman

A Privy Councillor

A Justice of the Peace

A Puritan

2. Elizabethans all lived in the same country at the same period of time. Why then did they have such different reasons for being worried about poverty?

Scaremongering

Many people thought that there were huge numbers of vagabonds travelling around the country. Exaggerated writings by people like Thomas Harman helped to stir up a lot of unnecessary panic. Historians today think that there were nowhere near as many beggars as people at the time thought.

Disease

There were many outbreaks of plague and other infectious diseases in the sixteenth century. Many people died at an early age but no one understood why. Most people believed that wandering groups of vagabonds spread deadly diseases.

Crime

Beggars often turned to crime. Some of them robbed people in the streets and broke into their houses. There was no police force to catch criminals. The Justices of the Peace were responsible for enforcing law and order in local areas. They wanted to do a good job for the Queen. They thought that beggars were a serious threat to their authority.

Rebellions

Sixteenth-century governments were always worried by the danger of rebellions. They did not have a permanent army to deal with them. Rising numbers of poor people made the threat of rebellion even greater. Powerful people who opposed Elizabeth, such as discontented nobles or Mary, Queen of Scots, might try to win the support of the poor for a rebellion against the government.

Charity

Rich and powerful people were not only expected to control the lower classes. They also had a duty to help local people who had fallen on hard times. Many landowners took this seriously. They gave gifts of money and food to the poor. The monasteries helped them care for the poor until Henry VIII closed them down. By Elizabeth's reign, many landowners could not cope with the growing numbers of poor people. They simply could not afford to help them all.

Why were Elizabethans so worried about poverty?

Idleness

Most people believed that everyone should work hard to look after themselves and their families. They believed that beggars set a bad example. The Puritans felt very strongly about the importance of hard work. They believed that idleness was a sin because it displeased God. They thought that it was the Devil who made people idle, and so anyone who refused to work should be severely punished. Some of Elizabeth's Privy Councillors, Members of Parliament and JPs were Puritans.

What did the poor think?

It is not easy to know what the poor themselves thought about poverty. They would certainly have seen beggars being whipped in the streets. Some poor people probably felt sorry for them and might have blamed rich people for being too greedy and cruel. Others would have been frightened by the beggars. The beggars might steal the few possessions they had. Perhaps they thought that beggars were giving all poor people a bad name. But this is largely guesswork – and guesswork is not good history!

The social order

In the sixteenth century most people believed that everyone had a fixed place in society. Everyone was expected to obey their social superiors. As long as this happened, the wealth and power of the upper classes were protected. Large numbers of discontented beggars wandering around the countryside threatened the social order. They did not seem to know their place and were not obeying their superiors. If this continued, tens of thousands of poor people might rebel and overthrow the ruling classes. This had nearly happened two hundred years earlier in the Peasants' Revolt of 1381.

How successfully did Elizabeth deal with poverty?

YOU HAVE FOUND out that poverty got worse during Elizabeth's reign, and that many people were worried. The next part of your investigation is to find out how successfully Elizabeth dealt with the problem. First, we will examine how poverty had been dealt with before Elizabeth became Queen.

How did the earlier Tudors deal with poverty?

At the beginning of the sixteenth century the government's approach to poverty was shaped by two main beliefs.

- Plenty of work was available for everyone. If people were poor it was their own fault. People without jobs were all lazy. They should be punished in order to set an example to others.

- Poverty was not a national problem. It only affected a few parts of the country. It was best to let local people, such as Justices of the Peace and town councillors, decide what to do in their own areas. Governments had much more important business to deal with, such as defending the country.

Slowly both of these ideas began to change. The numbers of poor people kept increasing. Governments gradually realised that some people, such as orphan children, the sick and the old, were genuinely unable to work and deserved help. They were called the impotent (or helpless) poor. Governments also began to think that poverty, especially begging, threatened law and order. This led to the passing of four laws before Elizabeth's reign began.

1495: HENRY VII ordered that beggars should be put in the STOCKS for three days. Then they should be sent back to the last place where they had lived.

1531: HENRY VIII passed a law ordering that people who were genuinely unable to work should be given a licence to beg. Anyone begging without a licence should be 'tied to the end of a cart, naked, and be beaten with whips till his body be bloody. He shall then return to the place where he was born.'

1536: HENRY VIII asked people to give money in church every Sunday for the poor. This was voluntary. The money would be handed out to local poor people to stop them begging.

1547: THE BEGINNING OF EDWARD VI'S REIGN. A new law ordered that all beggars should be whipped and branded on the forehead with the letter V. Then they would become a slave for two years. If they tried to escape they would be made a slave for life. If they tried to escape again they would be executed. This law was repealed (cancelled) in 1550.

SOURCE 1 Laws before 1558 which dealt with poverty

■ TASK

1. Each of the following ideas was believed in 1500:
a) wandering beggars must be punished
b) all poor people were idle and too lazy to work
c) governments should not deal with poverty
d) governments should not force local people to deal with poverty if they did not want to
e) poverty was not a national problem.

Which of these ideas had changed by the time Elizabeth became Queen in 1558? Which had stayed the same? Give examples to support your answers.

2. 'The early Tudors were completely successful in dealing with poverty.' Do you agree or disagree with this statement? Explain the reasons for your answer.

How did Elizabeth deal with poverty?

Elizabeth's Privy Councillors and Parliaments discussed the problem of poverty many times. Worried JPs wrote letters about it to the Privy Council throughout the reign. But Elizabeth thought that there were some much more important problems, such as religion and foreign policy, which needed her personal attention. She left less important issues like poverty to William Cecil and her other ministers. Like the Queen, they thought that poverty was best dealt with at a local level by the JPs and town councillors.

Dealing with poverty in the towns

The most serious effects of poverty were felt in towns. Many unemployed people went to the towns hoping to find work. As the number of beggars on the streets grew, so did crime. Town councillors were very worried about the STURDY BEGGARS, but they quickly realised that there were many poor people who were genuinely unable to work. They felt forced to take action. Now, you will examine how three towns dealt with the poor.

London

London's population grew from less than 50,000 in 1500 to 200,000 in 1600. Thousands of poor people flocked to the capital.

SOURCE 2 An extract from the records of law courts in Middlesex

66 *1574: At Harrow Hill on 29 March John Allen, Elizabeth Turner, Humfrey Foxe, Henry Bower and Agnes Wort, being over 14 years old, and having no lawful means of livelihood, were vagrants, and had been vagrants in other parts of the country. Sentenced to be flogged severely and burnt on the right ear.*
1575: 9 June. Thomas Maynard, Oswald Thompson and John Barres, incorrigible vagrants without any lawful means of livelihood, were sentenced to be hung. 99

SOURCE 3 An extract from *A Survey of London*, by John Stow, 1603. Stow was a wealthy London merchant who researched the city's history

66 *There are several ancient hospitals in the city and its suburbs. St Bartholomew's in Smithfield is a hospital for sick poor people. St Thomas's in Southwark is a hospital for old people. Christ's Hospital in Newgate market is where poor fatherless children are brought up and nourished. They were given by Henry VIII to the city and are paid for by the generosity of the citizens. Bethlehem Hospital, commonly called Bedlam, was founded in 1297 for lunatic people. Bridewell is a HOUSE OF CORRECTION which was founded by King Edward VI to be a workhouse for the poor and idle persons of the city. A great number of vagrant persons are there set to work.* 99

SOURCE 4 An extract from the City of London records, 1547

66 *It is this day by the Lord Mayor, aldermen and commons in the Common Council, ordered that all the citizens and inhabitants of the city shall pay towards the maintaining of poor persons.* 99

Norwich and Ipswich

These two towns were important centres of cloth manufacturing. They were badly hit by the collapse of the cloth trade in the 1550s. Even so, large numbers of poor people from the surrounding countryside travelled to these towns. By 1570 there were over 2000 poor people in Norwich who needed help. The town councillors were forced to take action.

SOURCE 5 Extracts from Ipswich town records

66 *1551: Two in every parish shall inquire into the poor in their parish and inform the Bailiffs.*
1552: At the Tower Church citizens shall make offerings to the poor.
1557: No children of this town shall be permitted to beg. Adults who are allowed to beg shall have badges.
1569: The House of Blackfriars shall be henceforth a hospital for the poor people of this town called Christ's Hospital.
1591: The clothiers of this town shall set the poor to work. If any shall refuse the work they shall be punished. 99

SOURCE 6 Extracts from Norwich city records

66 1570: A count shall be made of all the poor people who live in the city. Their need for alms shall be reviewed weekly.
1571: There shall be a workplace [a Bridewell] for the men to grind malt and the women to spin. The prisoners shall work for their meat and drink for at least 21 days. They shall work for 15 hours a day in the summer and 14 hours in the winter. And those that refuse to do their works shall be punished by the whip.
??: No person shall beg in the streets or they shall be whipped six times. No person shall help or feed any such beggars at their door.
??: One officer shall go daily about the city, with a staff in his hand, and arrest any vagabonds.
??: There shall also be appointed select women to receive idle women or the poorest children, into their houses to work or learn letters. They shall be driven to work and learn until they shall of themselves be able to live from their own work with their families as others do. 99

SOURCE 7 Two extracts from the Norwich Census of the Poor, 1570

66 NAMES OF THE POOR TO BE REVIEWED WEEKLY:
Richard Rich, 35 years old, a farm labourer, who keepeth not with his wife and helpeth her little. Margaret, his wife, 40 years old, spins wool. Joan her daughter, of the age of 12 years, also spins. Simon her son, 12 years old, goes to school. And Alice, 8 years old, and Faith, of 3 years.
Peter Browne, a cobbler, 50 years old and hath little work. Agnes, his wife, of the age of 52 years, that worketh not having been sick since Christmas. She spins wool. There are three daughters, one of 18 years, one of 13 years and the other of 14 years. They all spin when they can get work, but now they are without work. 99

SOURCE 8 Extracts from Norwich parish records for 1598–99

66 Paid to those who are very sick £2 7s 3d
Paid for the keeping of two of Bradley's children £3
Paid for nursing a young infant left in the parish 1s 8d
Paid to the constables for sending away vagrants 4s 8d 99

■ TASK

1. Make a larger copy of the table below. Using Sources 2–8, list the methods which were used in these three towns to deal with poverty.

How the towns dealt with the poor

Town	The impotent poor	Sturdy beggars
London		
Norwich		
Ipswich		

2. From what you have studied so far, who do you think looked after the poor better: the towns or the government? Explain the reasons for your answer.

The role of the government

Elizabeth's Privy Councillors were often told by the JPs and Members of Parliament that poverty was not just a local problem. It was growing throughout the whole country. It became increasingly obvious that many people were genuinely unable to work and needed help. The Privy Council was impressed with the measures developed in towns like London, Norwich and Ipswich. Eventually, they realised that punishing beggars and voluntary measures to help the deserving poor were not enough. But it took moments of crisis to persuade them to take action.

The 1570s

The government was very worried about social unrest in the early 1570s. There had been a serious rebellion in the north in 1569. A plot to murder Elizabeth was discovered in 1571. None of the harvests between 1573 and 1577 were good. A new law to deal with the poor was passed when Parliament met in 1572. Another law was passed when Parliament met four years later.

SOURCE 9 The Act of 1572

- *Beggars were to be whipped and bored through the ear. If they were caught begging three times they were to be executed.*
- *JPs and town officials were to count the numbers of poor people in their area. Local people must pay a Poor Rate to pay for the cost of helping the poor. Overseers of the Poor were appointed to help the JPs carry out this work.*

SOURCE 10 The Act of 1576

- *JPs were to build two Houses of Correction in each county. Beggars would be put in them and forced to work.*
- *JPs must keep a stock of materials in every town, so that people who were genuinely unable to find a job could be given some work.*

SOURCE 11 The Elizabethan Poor Law, 1601

- *JPs had to appoint four Overseers of the Poor in each parish.*
- *The Overseers had to make sure that orphan children had apprenticeships. They had to provide a stock of materials so that the able-bodied poor could be given work.*
- *People who were too old or sick to work were to have ALMSHOUSES to live in.*
- *Begging was strictly forbidden. Anyone found begging was to be whipped until 'his back be bloody' and then returned to his place of birth. If this was not known he was to be put into a House of Correction.*
- *The JPs had to make sure that everyone who lived in the local area paid a Poor Rate to pay for these measures. Anyone who refused could be imprisoned. Charitable gifts by wealthy people were still to be encouraged.*

The late 1590s

The government became even more worried about poverty in the 1590s. England was at war with Spain and people had to pay high taxes. Even worse, there was a series of disastrous harvests. The price of food rocketed. Some people starved to death. There was a serious risk of rebellion.

All the measures to deal with poverty were reviewed when Parliament met in 1597 and 1601. A series of laws were passed to create a new, nationwide, compulsory system of poor relief. These laws became known as the Elizabethan Poor Law.

Was government action successful?

Elizabeth's Poor Laws did not end poverty. It continued to rise. More money was raised for the poor by private charity than by the Poor Rate. The Poor Laws, however, did help thousands of people. Although poverty led to unrest and occasional riots it did not cause a single rebellion during the reign. The social order remained intact. Elizabeth's Poor Law of 1601 remained in use for the next 200 years.

■ TASK

1. What was new about the Acts of 1572 and 1576?
2. Explain how the Poor Law of 1601
a) helped the impotent poor
b) punished sturdy beggars
c) was paid for.

3. Was there anything new about the Poor Law of 1601?
4. How much had the government's attitude towards poverty changed by the end of Elizabeth's reign?
5. Were Elizabeth's Poor Laws successful?

■ ACTIVITY

It is 1603. News has just reached a village that the Queen has died. A group of local people are outside the tavern. They are discussing Elizabeth's Poor Laws and whether they have made any difference to their lives. Script a conversation which might have taken place between these people:

- an unemployed farm labourer
- a weaver, who has often been unemployed, but now has work
- a 50-year-old couple, who are too ill to work
- a 12-year-old orphan girl
- a sturdy beggar
- a farmer who rents a small plot of land
- a local JP, a wealthy landowner.

How successfully did Elizabeth deal with crime?

ELIZABETH'S PEOPLE HOPED that she would protect them from crime. She made the laws, but did she enforce them? Did crime rise or fall?

Elizabethans complained that crime was getting worse. Some historians have tried to find out whether they were right. They studied the records of lawcourts. Here are their findings:

- only 20 per cent of criminals were ever caught
- the most common crime was theft
- most thieves came from the lower classes
- most thieves stole so that they could buy food
- crime increased during Elizabeth's reign; the biggest increase occurred between 1596 and 1598.

Did Elizabeth not deal with crime more effectively because she was not really interested in tackling the problem? Or did she do her best in the circumstances?

1. Were crime and poverty connected?
2. Why did crime rise between 1596 and 1598? (Source 3 on page 60 will help you.)

Did Elizabeth try to deal with crime?

Sixteenth-century rulers did all they could to persuade people to obey the law. Churchmen, for example, were ordered to tell people that it was their duty to obey the law.

Another method of persuasion was to make sure that criminals were caught. Elizabeth relied on her JPs and town councillors to catch criminals. Then her judges and lawcourts dealt with them. The Queen's main lawcourts were in London. She appointed the best lawyers as her judges. They dealt with the most serious crimes, arguments about land, and people who failed to pay rents or taxes to the Queen. The Court of Star Chamber was a special court which met in the Queen's palace. Her Privy Councillors were the judges. They dealt with nobles who were accused of treason and people who tried to spread dangerous ideas. Most crimes, however, were dealt with in local lawcourts.

1. Assize Courts

The jury has found you guilty of murder. I sentence you to death by hanging.

The Queen's judges held courts in every county twice a year. They heard cases that were too serious for the Justices of the Peace.

2. Quarter Sessions

We find you guilty of being an idle vagabond. We sentence you to be whipped through the streets.

The JPs held courts in the main county towns four times a year. The 'Quarter Sessions' dealt with serious local crimes.

3. Petty Sessions

We find you guilty of stealing four eggs from your neighbour. You will be placed in the pillory for eight hours tomorrow.

The JPs also held regular courts in their local areas, to deal with less serious offences.

SOURCE 1 The main local lawcourts in Elizabethan England

■ TASK

Copy and complete the table below.

Type of local court	Where it was held	Type of crime it dealt with	Who decided on the verdict	Who decided on the sentence
Assize Court				
Quarter Sessions				
Petty Sessions				

Punishments

Another way of persuading people to obey the law is to show them that criminals are punished. Like today, many crimes in the sixteenth century were never solved, but criminals who were caught were punished. Wealthy people who broke the law were usually made to pay a fine. This made them less powerful and increased the wealth of the Crown. But ordinary people could not pay large fines. Other methods were used to punish them – and to show everyone else that they were being punished.

SOURCE 2 The punishment for treason (plotting against the king or queen), described by Sir Thomas Smith in 1565

❝ A traitor is first to be hanged, taken down alive, his bowels taken out and burned before his face, then he is beheaded, and his body cut up into quarters and then put on display in various places. ❞

SOURCE 4 Beggars being punished, from Holinshed's Chronicle, 1577

SOURCE 5 Sir Thomas Smith describing crimes for which there was capital punishment (i.e. death), 1565

❝ For any felony [serious theft], manslaughter, robbery, murder, rape, and such capital crimes as touch not treason, we have by the law of England no other punishment, but to hang till they be dead. Beheading, torturing, dismembering [the cutting off of limbs], breaking upon the wheel, impaling, and such cruel torments as be used in other nations we have not.

If a wife shall kill her husband she shall be burned alive. If the servant kills his master, he shall be drawn to the place of execution on a hurdle. Poisoners, if the person dies, by a new law made in Henry VIII's time, shall be boiled to death. ❞

SOURCE 3 Traitors' heads on public display on London Bridge, from an early seventeenth-century drawing of London

SOURCE 6 A sixteenth-century drawing showing a witch being punished. If she floated, she was believed to be using magical powers – so she must be a witch and was executed. If she drowned, she was innocent

SOURCE 7 An extract from the records of the Assize judges in Surrey

66 *HOLLYDAY, William of Croydon, labourer, accused of highway robbery. On 31 March 1576 he assaulted Robert Ware in the highway at Lambeth and stole from him 15s in money, a black cloak worth 7s and a dagger worth 3s 4d. Guilty. To hang.* 99

SOURCE 8 A sixteenth-century drawing of a pillory. Making criminals stand in a pillory for several hours was a common punishment for less serious crimes

SOURCE 9 A heretic being burnt at the stake during Mary Tudor's reign, from John Foxe's *Book of Martyrs*, 1563. Heretics were followers of what was thought to be a false religion; in this case they were Protestants

Could the government have done better?

You have found out that Elizabeth tried to persuade people to obey her laws. She had lawcourts which severely punished criminals. So why did crime continue to rise? Why were so few criminals caught?

Governments today try to deal with crime. They have a well-equipped police force to catch criminals. Soldiers can be used in an emergency. There are many prisons for offenders. This costs taxpayers billions of pounds. Things were very different in the sixteenth century. Elizabeth relied on her JPs to catch criminals. They were unpaid and their work was voluntary. There was no police force, no full-time army and few prisons. These would have cost huge sums of money, which Elizabeth could not afford. She struggled to pay for just the normal costs of governing the country. Even this was becoming more expensive because prices were rising. Taxes were unpopular and could only be asked for in an emergency. Elizabeth had to cope with crime using the few resources she had.

■ TASK 1

1. Make a copy of the following table. Complete it by using evidence from Sources 2–9, to show the kinds of punishment that were used for people who broke the law in the sixteenth century.

Crime	Punishment

2. Why do you think most punishments were carried out in public?
3. 'Elizabethans were cruel people.' Do you agree or disagree with this statement? Explain the reasons for your answer.

■ TASK 2

Did Elizabeth do her best to protect her people from crime? To answer this question write an introduction to explain how crime got worse – and why. Then write three paragraphs explaining:

■ who caught and dealt with criminals
■ how criminals were punished
■ the difficulties Elizabeth faced in trying to enforce law and order.

Finish your answer by briefly explaining whether you think Elizabeth tried her best to deal with crime, or whether you think she could have done better.

■ REVIEW TASK

Did Elizabeth protect her people from poverty and crime?

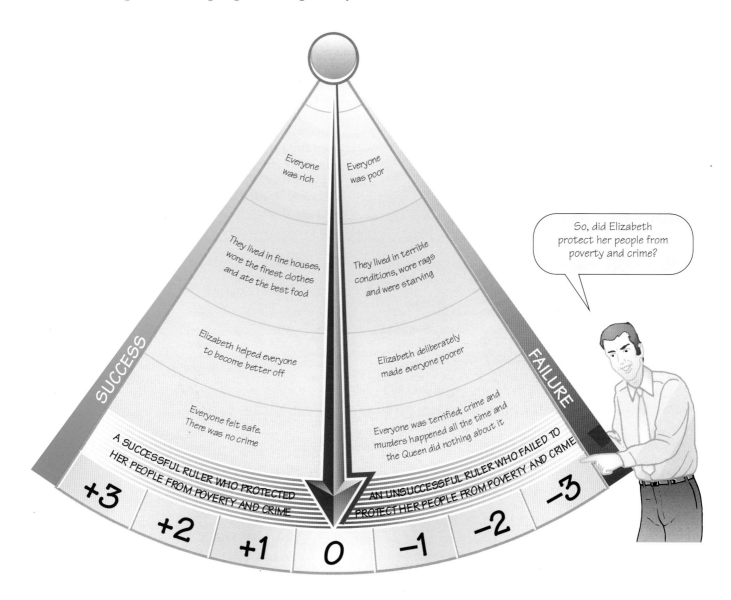

This chapter began with two cartoons. One showed wealthy and happy people. The other showed poverty and crime. Now is the time to decide whether Elizabethan England was like either of those cartoons.

Answer this question: did Elizabeth I protect her people from poverty and crime?

Begin your answer by writing a sentence to explain what life in Elizabethan England was like.

Was it really like either of the cartoons on page 51? Then explain, in separate paragraphs:

■ how well rich people lived
■ how well poor people lived
■ whether Elizabeth was to blame for poverty
■ how successfully poverty was dealt with
■ how successfully crime was dealt with
■ whether Elizabeth did the best she could.

Finally, write your overall conclusion.

chapter 4

HOW WELL DID ELIZABETH DEAL WITH THE COUNTRY'S RELIGIOUS PROBLEMS?

A FEW WEEKS ago you found out about the problems Elizabeth faced in 1558. You were asked to decide which was her most serious problem. Did you think it was religion? If you did, Elizabeth would have agreed with you. Religion seemed likely to cause a civil war in England. It was the first problem Elizabeth tackled.

In this chapter you are going to investigate why religion was a serious problem for Elizabeth and how successful she was in dealing with it. Unlike poverty and crime, she did not leave her Privy Councillors to decide what to do – she dealt with religious problems personally. Was she able to solve them? Or did they get worse?

Why was religion important?

Most people went to a church service every Sunday. Their baptisms, marriages and funerals were held in the local church. The Church also helped the poor, ran schools for children and organised dances and feasts.

The Church gave people hope, as well as help. Disease was a constant danger and relatively few people could expect to live into old age. Many women died in childbirth. Many babies died. Many people were poor and the threat of starvation was never far away. The Christian religion taught them to live good lives. Then they would go to heaven when they died.

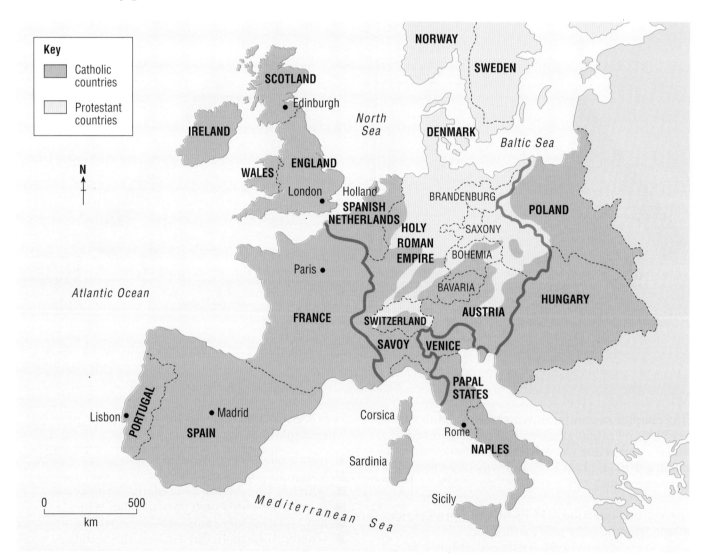

SOURCE 1 A map showing how Europe was divided by religion in 1558 when Elizabeth became Queen

Why was religion a problem?

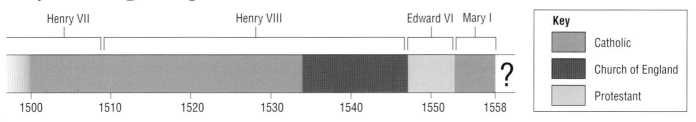

SOURCE 2 A timeline showing the religious changes that took place under the Tudors, before Elizabeth's reign

When Elizabeth came to the throne in 1558 her people were seriously divided by religion. Her sister, Mary, had made Roman Catholicism the official religion, but most people were Protestants. There were also growing numbers of Puritans.

Each group believed that only the religion they followed should be allowed. To make matters even worse, Europe was divided by religion, too. The most powerful countries, France and Spain, were both Roman Catholic.

SOURCE 3 The religious problems Elizabeth faced

What did Elizabethans believe?

All of Elizabeth's people followed the Christian religion. But they had different views about how:

■ God should be worshipped
■ the Church should be organised.

There were three religious groups. Their beliefs are shown in the table below. You will often need to refer back to it as you work through this chapter.

Main features of the Church	Roman Catholics	Moderate Protestants (also known as Anglicans after 1559)	Puritans (also called 'the hotter type of Protestant')
Head of the Church	The Pope in Rome.	The king or queen.	Nobody.
How the Church was governed	Cardinals, archbishops and bishops to help the Pope.	Archbishops and bishops to help the monarch.	Churchgoers elected committees to make the rules.
Parish clergy	Only priests appointed by a bishop could hold church services. Not allowed to marry. Wore richly decorated robes called vestments.	Only clergy appointed by a bishop could hold church services. Allowed to marry. Wore vestments, but not too richly decorated.	Ordinary people as well as church ministers were allowed to preach. Allowed to marry. Wore plain black gowns.
The Bible	In Latin. Only priests were allowed to read it.	In English, for everyone to read.	In English, for everyone to read.
Services	The Mass, in Latin. During Mass, a miracle took place. The bread and wine given to people by the priest was turned into the actual body and blood of Jesus.	Holy Communion, in English. Clergy gave people bread and wine as a way of remembering that Jesus died for them.	Communion in English. The minister gave people bread and wine as a way of remembering that Jesus died for them.
Music	Singing hymns, church organs.	Singing hymns, church organs.	No music.
Decoration	Richly decorated altar cloths, wall paintings and statues of the saints.	Altar cloth, no wall paintings.	Very plain chapels: whitewashed walls, plain windows, no statues, plain tables and benches.
Attitude to other religions	Believers in other religions were HERETICS. They should be burnt to death.	Other religions must not be allowed. Believers in other religions should be punished.	Other religions must not be allowed. Believers in other religions must be punished.
Strengths in 1558	England was a Roman Catholic country. So were Spain, France and Scotland. Elizabeth's heir, Mary, Queen of Scots, was Roman Catholic.	Most people were moderate Protestants. They hated the Roman Catholic religion.	Puritan ideas were becoming popular in London and the south-east. Some MPs were Puritans.
Weaknesses in 1558	Mary Tudor's reign had made Roman Catholics very unpopular. They were a minority, and most lived in the north and west of England.	Mary Tudor had made England into a Roman Catholic country again. The most powerful countries in Europe were Roman Catholic.	There were few Puritans in England and Europe.

SOURCE 4 Religious beliefs in Elizabethan England

■ ACTIVITY

1. Which drawing shows:
a) a Roman Catholic priest?
b) a moderate Protestant priest?
c) a Puritan minister?

A.

B.

C.

2. Which drawing shows the inside of:
a) a Roman Catholic church?
b) a moderate Protestant church?
c) a Puritan chapel?

A.

B.

C.

■ TASK

Study Source 4. Your teacher will give you a sheet to help you answer questions 1–4.

1. What did Roman Catholics and moderate Protestants agree about? What did they disagree about?

2. What did Roman Catholics and Puritans agree about? What did they disagree about?

3. What did moderate Protestants and Puritans agree about? What did they disagree about?

4. Was religion an easy problem for Elizabeth to solve? Explain the reasons for your answer.

5. Is it more important for historians to understand what people in the past *did* or what they *believed*? Explain your answer.

What kind of Church did Elizabeth choose in 1559?

YOU HAVE SEEN why religion was such a serious and urgent problem for Elizabeth. Now you are going to investigate how she dealt with it. You will be trying to find answers to these questions:

■ what kind of Church did Elizabeth choose?
■ how did she make her decision?
■ how did her people react?

First of all, however, you need to know more about Elizabeth herself. What were her religious beliefs? They were important. In the sixteenth century, the religion of the country and the religion of its ruler had to be the same.

What did Elizabeth believe?

Religion was very important to Elizabeth. She prayed in her private chapel every morning. She had been brought up as a Protestant and refused to become a Roman Catholic during Mary Tudor's reign. Elizabeth disliked the authority of the Pope. But she liked ornaments and decoration in churches. She thought that priests should wear vestments and did not like them to get married.

Although Elizabeth had her own religious views, she thought that her most important task was to unite her country. She wanted her people to obey her and not cause any trouble. She did not want to punish anyone just for their religious beliefs. She knew that it would be impossible to satisfy all of her people. She wanted a Church that most of them could accept – even if this took time.

I do not like change. Making changes means taking risks. There can be dangerous consequences.

Yes, Your Majesty. But sometimes not making changes can have even more dangerous consequences.

SOURCE 1 Elizabeth discussing religion with William Cecil

■ DECISION POINT, 1558

It is December 1558. Elizabeth has been Queen for one month. Religion is her most urgent and serious problem. You are one of her advisers. There will be an important meeting of the Privy Council tomorrow. You will be expected to advise the Queen about the sort of Church that there should be. Should it be a Roman Catholic, a moderate Protestant or a Puritan Church? Having all three religions is NOT allowed! Use a larger copy of the table below to plan your speech.

Type of Church	Advantages	Disadvantages
Roman Catholic		
Moderate Protestant		
Puritan		

My advice:

What did Elizabeth decide?

Elizabeth discussed the situation with her councillors. They made plans for a new Church. Then she decided to call Parliament. It met in February 1559. There were MPs from all the religious groups, but most of them were moderate Protestants. Elizabeth wanted her MPs to approve her plans quickly but some MPs did not like them. Two bishops who complained were imprisoned. However, Elizabeth did agree to make some changes to her plans. After four months her MPs agreed to create a new Church of England. They passed two Acts of Parliament. These are known as the Elizabethan Church Settlement.

■ TALKING POINT

Elizabeth could have ordered her people to obey her plans for a new Church. Why do you think she called Parliament instead?

SOURCE 2 The Elizabethan Church Settlement of 1559

The Act of Supremacy

- *England became a Protestant country again.*
- *Elizabeth became head of the Church of England, instead of the Pope. Her title was 'Supreme Governor'.*
- *Bishops would help her govern the new Church.*
- *All judges, government officials, JPs, MPs and clergy had to take an oath accepting Elizabeth's title. If they refused, they could be imprisoned. If they refused three times, they could be executed.*

The Act of Uniformity

- *A new Protestant Prayer Book had to be used in every church.*
- *Church services had to be in English. Bread and wine were to be taken, but the reasons why were left vague.*
- *The Bible was in English.*
- *Ornaments and decoration were allowed in churches.*
- *The clergy had to wear vestments and were allowed to marry.*
- *All clergy had to take an oath agreeing to use the new Prayer Book.*
- *RECUSANTS (anyone who refused to go to church) had to pay a fine of 1 shilling (5p) a week. This was a large sum for the poor, but a small amount for rich people.*

How did the new Church work in practice?

Elizabeth did not want the new Church to be too strict. She hoped that most people would gradually accept it. Her new Archbishop of Canterbury, Matthew Parker, was a moderate Protestant who did not really want to punish people who had different religious views. He was popular with most people. Most churchmen took the oath of loyalty to the new Church; only 250 out of 9000 priests (less than 3 per cent) refused and lost their jobs. The fines for recusancy were not strictly enforced. In many places they were not collected at all.

By 1568 most people had accepted the new Church. There were no serious protests or rebellions. Elizabeth's new Church and her lenient approach seemed to have worked.

■ TASK

How successful was Elizabeth's Church at first?

1. Make a larger copy of the table below. Then complete it to show which features of the new Church the different religious groups would have liked, and which they would have disliked.

Elizabeth's Church Settlement of 1559

Group	What they liked about the Church	What they disliked
Catholics		
Moderate Protestants		
Puritans		

2. Explain whether you agree or disagree with each of these views about Elizabeth's Church Settlement.
a) 'It was a middle way between Catholic and Protestant beliefs.'
b) 'It was exactly the kind of Church that Elizabeth wanted.'
c) 'It was a strict Church in theory, but not in practice.'
d) 'By trying to please everyone it failed to please anyone.'

Were Mary, Queen of Scots, and the Catholics dangerous threats to Elizabeth?

SOURCE 1 A portrait of Mary, Queen of Scots, painted in the 1550s

IT WAS A Sunday afternoon in May 1568. A small fishing boat landed on the coast of north-west England. Several people stepped out. Among them was a tall, 26-year-old woman. She looked tired. She was wearing borrowed clothes and her head had been shaved so that she would not be recognised. The group was taken to Carlisle Castle. The young woman demanded to see Queen Elizabeth.

Elizabeth was shocked when she heard the news. The first crisis of her reign had begun ...

In this enquiry you are going to investigate:

■ why this unwelcome visitor caused problems for Elizabeth
■ how successful Elizabeth was in dealing with this woman and her supporters.

First, however, you need to know who the woman was and why Elizabeth was so worried about her arrival in England. She was Mary Stuart, the Queen of Scotland. She had been overthrown and imprisoned by her nobles in the previous year. In 1568 she escaped.

Why was Mary a threat to Elizabeth?

Mary, Queen of Scots, was Elizabeth's cousin and her heir. The heir to the throne always caused problems for monarchs. They could attract the support of discontented nobles who felt excluded from power. Elizabeth had learnt how dangerous this could be during Mary Tudor's reign, when she herself had been the heir. But Mary, Queen of Scots, was not just Elizabeth's heir. Mary also claimed that she was the rightful Queen of England. Many English Catholics supported her. She also had support in Europe, especially in France.

English Catholics had not caused Elizabeth any problems before Mary's arrival. But now the situation had changed. Mary could easily become the focus for plots and rebellions against Elizabeth.

1. Why was Mary a **double** threat to Elizabeth?
2. Why did Mary and many Catholics believe that Elizabeth was not the rightful Queen? (Look back at the family tree on page 19.)
3. Why could Mary cause Elizabeth problems even if she did nothing?

■ DECISION POINT, 1568

What should Elizabeth do with Mary, Queen of Scots?

It is May 1568. You are Elizabeth I. You have just heard that Mary has arrived in England. She is asking you to help her regain her throne. If you will not do this, she wants to be allowed to travel to France. The Scots want you to send Mary back to Scotland. They want to put her on trial. You believe that rulers are appointed by God and you do not like helping rebels.

What will you do? Your teacher will give you a larger copy of this table to help you make your decision. Then announce your decision – and explain your reasons – to the Privy Council.

Your options	Advantages	Disadvantages
Help Mary to regain her throne		
Allow her to go to France		
Send her back to Scotland		
Keep her in England		
Execute her		

Your decision:

MARIA
D   G
SCOTIÆ
PIÏSSIMA REGINA
FRANCIÆ DOTARIA
ANNO
ÆTATIS REGNIQz
36
ANGLICÆ CAPTIVIT
IO
S   H
1578

SOURCE 2 A portrait of Mary, Queen of Scots, painted in 1578. The caption in the corner describes her as 36 years old, the Queen of Scotland, widow of the King of France, and a prisoner in England

■ TASK

Study Source 2. Look closely at the way the artist has painted Mary; for example, look at her expression, her clothes and the objects in the painting. What was the artist trying to say about Mary?

Why did Elizabeth face demands for Mary's execution in 1572?

Elizabeth decided that Mary should stay in England as a closely guarded guest. There was soon serious trouble. When Parliament met in 1572 MPs had a simple solution. They wanted Elizabeth to execute Mary. On these two pages we will investigate:

■ what problems Elizabeth faced between 1568 and 1572
■ how much Mary was to blame for these problems
■ how Elizabeth dealt with her MPs' demands.

1569: the Northern Rebellion

In 1569 a serious rebellion broke out in the north of England. The Earls of Northumberland and Westmorland, who were Catholics, gathered 6000 soldiers. They wanted to rescue Mary, overthrow Elizabeth, put Mary on the throne and make the country Roman Catholic again. Mary did not agree to the rebellion because she did not think it would succeed. Elizabeth sent an army to crush the rebellion. Eight hundred rebels were executed and the two leaders fled.

1569: the Duke of Norfolk

Thomas Howard, the Duke of Norfolk, was a wealthy, powerful and ambitious noble. He wanted to marry Mary, Queen of Scots. Mary would only agree if Elizabeth approved of the plan. Elizabeth was furious when she heard about it. She expected nobles to get her permission if they wanted to marry. She banned the marriage. Norfolk promised to obey her decision.

1570: the Papal Bull of Excommunication

In 1570 there was worrying news. The Pope EXCOMMUNICATED Elizabeth from the Church. He called her a 'servant of wickedness' and said that she was not the rightful Queen. He ordered Catholics not to obey her.

In 1571 Parliament passed an Act against BULLS from Rome. It said that anyone who said that Elizabeth was a heretic or was not the rightful Queen was a traitor.

1571: the Ridolfi Plot

In 1571 William Cecil discovered a Catholic plot to overthrow Elizabeth. It was organised by Ridolfi, an Italian banker. Mary, the Duke of Norfolk, Philip of Spain and the Pope were all involved. The plan was for a Spanish army to help English Catholics overthrow Elizabeth and make Mary Queen. Then she would marry the Duke of Norfolk and make England a Roman Catholic country again.

The plot failed. Ridolfi and the Spanish ambassador were arrested and expelled from the country.

■ TASK

These four events caused Elizabeth serious problems. Taking each event in turn, explain:
a) what problems Elizabeth faced
b) how much Mary, Queen of Scots, was to blame for them
c) how Elizabeth dealt with the situation.

■ DECISION POINT, 1572

Should Elizabeth execute Mary, Queen of Scots?

It is May 1572 and Parliament is meeting. MPs are demanding that Mary, Queen of Scots, should be executed. One MP has called her 'the monstrous and huge dragon, the Queen of Scots'.

You are Elizabeth I. Should you follow your MPs' advice? Make a list of the advantages and the disadvantages of executing Mary, Queen of Scots. Then make your decision. Prepare a speech to tell your MPs what you have decided.

SOURCE 3 An extract from Parliament's charges against Mary, Queen of Scots, May 1572

❝ *She has wickedly challenged the crown of England.*
She has sought to withdraw the Duke of Norfolk from his natural obedience, against the Queen's express prohibition.
She has stirred the Earls of Northumberland and Westmorland to rebel.
She has practised [tried] to procure [get] new rebellion to be raised within this realm.
We, your true and obedient subjects, do most humbly beseech your Majesty to punish and correct all the treasons and wicked attempts of the said Mary. ❞

SOURCE 4 Elizabeth's difficulties in 1572

My MPs and most of my Privy Councillors want me to execute Mary.

There was no trouble before Mary arrived. If I execute her it might stop.

There is no real proof that Mary has been involved in the plots and rebellions against me.

She is my cousin. Can I put a member of my family to death?

If I execute her, English Catholics will be angry. They might organise a massive rebellion to overthrow me.

The Pope, Spain and France might decide to invade my country.

Mary is a monarch who was appointed by God. Can I go against God's will?

Executing a monarch would set a dangerous example. My enemies might do the same to me in the future.

Why was Mary, Queen of Scots, executed in 1587?

It is 8 February 1587. A crowd has gathered around a platform in the great hall of Fotheringhay Castle in Northamptonshire. The atmosphere is tense. A door opens and everyone looks towards it. Mary, Queen of Scots, is led into the room. She is wearing a black dress and has a white veil over her hair. She has a crucifix (a small cross) in her hand. There are tears in her eyes. She sits on a stool and prays in Latin. Then two women help her to remove her dress. She is wearing a crimson petticoat underneath it. Mary is blindfolded, kneels on a cushion and lays her head on the block. Then the axe falls. The executioner holds up her head and shouts 'God save the Queen!' A small dog crawls out from under Mary's petticoat. It is dragged away.

Elizabeth is furious when she is told that the Queen of Scots is dead . . .

SOURCE 5 A drawing produced at the time by an unknown sixteenth-century artist, showing the execution of Mary, Queen of Scots

Elizabeth refused to execute Mary in 1572. Fifteen years later, however, Mary was executed. In the following pages you will investigate why. Was Mary guilty of treason or was she an innocent victim of circumstances? Did Elizabeth eventually agree to execute a fellow monarch, something she had refused to do for so long, or was she forced into it? Why was Elizabeth angry when she heard about her cousin's execution?

The St Bartholomew's Day Massacre, August 1572

Within weeks of Elizabeth's decision not to execute Mary horrifying news arrived from France. Thousands of Protestants had been massacred in Paris on St Bartholomew's Day. Mary's French relations were involved in the killings.

Catholic priests arrive in England

In the mid-1570s newly trained Catholic priests began arriving in England. Over the next ten years about 300 of them came here. They wanted to spread the Catholic religion and hold religious services for English Catholics. In 1580 the Pope sent specially trained priests called JESUITS to help them.

SOURCE 6 Written by one of the Pope's senior advisers in 1580

66 Since that guilty woman of England is cause of so much injury to the Catholic faith, there is no doubt that whoever sends her out of the world not only does not sin but gains merit. 99

Elizabeth and her ministers were frightened. They thought that these Catholic priests were organising more plots. Orders were issued to arrest them. When Parliament met in 1581, a new law was passed against Catholics. Recusants had to pay a bigger fine of £20 a month. Anyone who tried to persuade other people to become Catholic was now guilty of treason.

■ TALKING POINTS

1. Six of the people in Source 5 have a number next to them. What is the role of each person?
2. Source 5 shows that a crowd was present at the execution. Why do you think Mary was not executed in private?
3. Are there any questions you would like to ask about the artist who drew Source 5? Why?
4. Do you think that Source 5 is:
   a) a reliable source?
   b) a useful source?

The Throckmorton Plot, 1583

Another Catholic plot was discovered in 1583. Francis Throckmorton, a young Catholic, had helped to organise it. He was arrested and tortured. He said that the plan was for a French army to invade England and make Mary Queen. The Pope and King Philip of Spain had agreed to pay for it. He confessed that Mary knew about the plan.

Throckmorton was executed. The Spanish ambassador was expelled from England. Sir Francis Walsingham (see page 36) decided to find proof that Mary was involved in the plots. She was moved to Tutbury Castle in Staffordshire. She was not allowed to have visitors and all her letters were checked.

The murder of William of Orange, 1584

In 1584 more worrying news arrived. William of Orange, the leader of the Dutch Protestants, had been shot dead by a Catholic.

Elizabeth's Privy Councillors were worried that she could be the next Protestant leader to be murdered. When Parliament met in 1584 they encouraged MPs to pass the Bond of Association. It said that if Elizabeth was murdered, Parliament would make sure that the murderers were punished – as well as anyone who benefited from Elizabeth's death.

The outbreak of war with Spain, 1585

In 1585 war broke out between England and Spain. Philip II began building a huge fleet of ships to invade England. He was told that English Catholics would rebel against Elizabeth when the Spanish landed. Parliament ordered all Catholic priests to leave the country within 40 days. After that, they would be executed if they were caught.

5. The St Bartholomew's Day Massacre and the murder of William of Orange did not happen in England. Why, then, was the government so worried about them?
6. Who was the Bond of Association aimed at?
7. Why did the outbreak of war with Spain make the government even more worried about:
a) Mary, Queen of Scots?
b) English Catholics?

Babington's Plot, 1586

In 1586 Walsingham uncovered another Catholic plot. Anthony Babington planned to rescue Mary and murder Elizabeth. Secret letters from the plotters to Mary, and her replies, were hidden in beer barrels. Walsingham found the letters and read them. In one letter, Mary agreed to the plan. It was the evidence Walsingham needed.

Babington was arrested in August 1586 and confessed. In September he and six other plotters were executed. Walsingham and other Privy Councillors demanded that Mary should also be executed. When Parliament met in October, Elizabeth's MPs agreed.

■ TASK

Between 1572 and 1586 several events caused problems for Elizabeth. Take each event in turn and explain:
a) what problems it caused for Elizabeth
b) how much Mary, Queen of Scots, was to blame for what happened
c) how Elizabeth dealt with the situation.

■ DECISION POINT, 1586

Should Elizabeth execute Mary, Queen of Scots?

It is 1586. You are Elizabeth I. Your Privy Councillors and MPs are demanding that Mary, Queen of Scots, should be executed. Most of your people agree with them. Only you can make the decision. In 1572 you refused their demands. What will you do this time? You will have to consider:

■ the advantages of executing Mary
■ the disadvantages of executing Mary
■ whether the situation has changed at all since 1572.

Make a larger copy of the table below. Complete the table and answer the questions to help you make your decision. Then announce your decision to the Privy Council.

Advantages of executing Mary in 1586	Disadvantages of executing Mary in 1586

a) Has the situation changed since 1572?
b) Your decision:
c) Your most important reason:

Did Elizabeth agree to Mary's execution?
Elizabeth did not agree to execute Mary in 1586. She decided to put her on trial for treason. Mary was moved to Fotheringhay Castle in Northamptonshire. The trial took place there in October 1586.

■ ACTIVITY

Mary's trial, October 1586
Work in groups of six and divide into three pairs.

- The first pair should present the case against Mary. Prepare a speech to persuade the judges that Mary is guilty of treason.
- The second pair should take the role of Mary. Prepare a speech to defend yourself against the charge.
- The third pair are Mary's judges. You will have to decide whether she is guilty or innocent and how she should be punished. If you find her guilty of treason, execution is the only punishment you can give. Make sure that you know about everything that has happened since Mary arrived in England in 1568.

The first two pairs should make their speeches to the judges. Then the judges should decide on their verdict and sentence. Finally, all the judges should announce their decisions, and their reasons, to the whole class.

Mary was found guilty of treason and sentenced to death. Before Mary could be executed, however, Elizabeth had to sign a death warrant and send it to Fotheringhay. Her Privy Councillors begged her to sign. So did Parliament.

Another two months passed. Finally, on 1 February 1587, Elizabeth signed Mary's death warrant. Then she refused to let it go. Her Privy Councillors persuaded her secretary, William Davison, to take it to Fotheringhay. Mary was executed on 8 February. Before she died, she passed on her claim to Elizabeth's throne to King Philip of Spain.

Elizabeth was furious when she heard the news of Mary's execution. She said that she had never wanted the death warrant to be used. She wrote a letter to the young King James VI of Scotland, apologising for his mother's death. She refused to speak to William Cecil for a month. Davison was imprisoned in the Tower of London for eighteen months and banned from Court, but his salary was paid for the rest of his life.

8. Do you think that Elizabeth ever really made up her mind to execute Mary?
9. Most historians think that Elizabeth only pretended to be furious about Mary's execution. If they are right, why did Elizabeth behave in this way?

Did Mary's execution have serious consequences?

Mary had caused Elizabeth serious problems ever since she came to England in 1568. But Elizabeth thought that executing Mary would create even bigger problems. This helps to explain why she refused to execute her for so long, and why her behaviour after the discovery of Babington's Plot seems so strange. Was Elizabeth's cautious and indecisive policy successful? The only way that we can really answer this question is to find out what happened after Mary's execution.

France
The news of Mary's execution led to strong protests in France. Some French Catholics demanded revenge for her death. However, the French king, Henry III, was worried about the growing power of Spain and the threat of civil war in France. He wanted to keep on friendly terms with Elizabeth. He did nothing.

Spain
England and Spain were already at war by 1587. King Philip II was angry at the news of Mary's execution, but he had never really wanted Mary to be Queen of England. She would have been more friendly with France than with Spain. Her execution made no difference to his plans. He was already planning to send the ARMADA to invade England. It sailed in 1588.

Scotland
King James VI was Mary's son. He protested about his mother's execution, but said that he blamed the Privy Council, rather than Elizabeth. He took no further action.

English Catholics
Catholics in England caused no trouble. They did not rebel when the Armada sailed to attack England in the following year. There were no more Catholic plots for the rest of Elizabeth's reign.

■ TASK 1

'Elizabeth's dealings with Mary, Queen of Scots, show that she was a weak ruler who could not make a decision in a crisis.' Do you agree or disagree with this statement? Explain your answer fully.

Cover the following issues in your answer:

- was Elizabeth pressured into executing Mary?
- was it Elizabeth's decision, in the end, that Mary should be executed?
- were there good reasons why Elizabeth found it difficult to decide what to do with Mary?
- do the consequences of Mary's execution suggest that Elizabeth handled the situation well or badly?

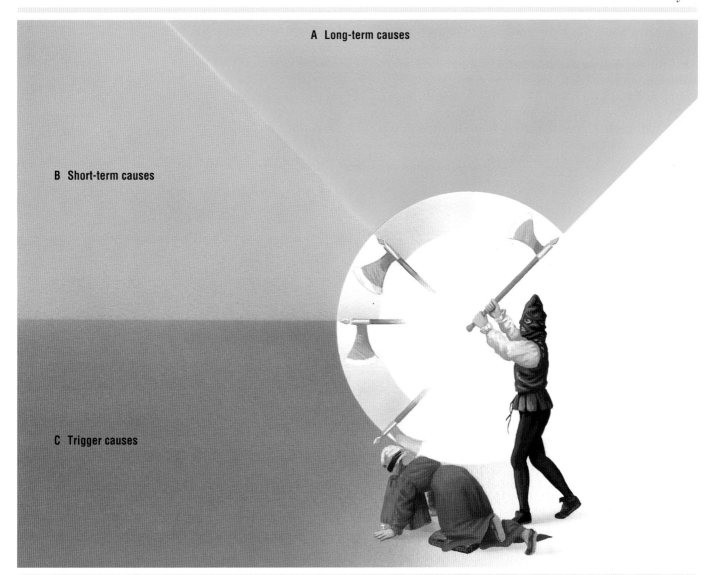

A Long-term causes

B Short-term causes

C Trigger causes

■ TASK 2

Write an essay to answer this question: why was Mary, Queen of Scots, executed in 1587?

Use the following headings in your answer to the question:

- long-term causes of Mary's execution (reasons why Mary was a threat to Elizabeth before and shortly after her arrival in England)

- short-term causes (reasons why Mary's execution became more likely during the later 1570s and 1580s)
- trigger causes (the 'last-minute' reasons why Mary was executed in February 1587).

Then write a short conclusion to explain briefly:

- the most important reason for Mary's execution
- if you think she deserved to be executed.

'Bloody Queen Elizabeth'?

MARY TUDOR HAS often been called 'Bloody Mary'. Three hundred Protestants were burnt to death as heretics during her short reign (1553–58). Some people have said that Elizabeth did not treat Roman Catholics any better. They say that she should be remembered as 'Bloody Queen Elizabeth'. You are going to investigate this claim.

Elizabeth treated Catholics leniently at first. Her attitude changed after Mary, Queen of Scots, came to England in 1568. Fines for not going to church were enforced. Stricter laws were introduced (see Source 2). Sir Francis Walsingham organised a network of spies and informers to keep a close eye on all suspected Catholics. In 1575 Catholic priests began arriving in England. The houses of known Catholics were searched. Catholic priests were hunted down by government agents. Nearly 200 Catholics were executed during Elizabeth's reign.

SOURCE 2 Laws passed by Parliament against Catholics during Elizabeth's reign

1559: Clergy, judges, government officials, MPs and JPs had to take an oath agreeing that Elizabeth was Head of the Church. If they refused they could be imprisoned. Recusants were to be fined 1 shilling (5p) per week.
1571: Anyone who questioned Elizabeth's right to be Queen or said she was a heretic was a traitor.
1581: Any priest holding a Catholic service, and anyone attending it, would pay a large fine and be imprisoned for a year. Fines for recusancy were increased to £20 a month. Anyone who tried to persuade people to disobey Elizabeth or become Catholic was guilty of treason.
1585: Catholic priests were ordered to leave the country within 40 days. Otherwise they would be executed.
1593: Catholics were banned from travelling more than five miles from their homes.

SOURCE 3 A 'priest's hole', a secret place where a Catholic priest could be hidden. This one is in a house in Nottinghamshire

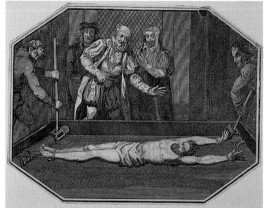

SOURCE 4 A Catholic priest being tortured on the rack in the Tower of London

> I do not punish people for their religious beliefs, but the Catholics have become more and more dangerous during my reign. A few have been executed but they were found guilty of treason.

> Your cruelty has got worse and worse. Catholics are punished, executed, and become martyrs. You have innocent blood on your hands.

SOURCE 1 Two views of how Catholics were treated during Elizabeth's reign

1. Do Sources 2, 3 and 4 **prove** that Elizabeth was cruel to all Catholics?

SOURCE 5 A modern account of the experiences of Edmund Campion, a Catholic priest

Edmund Campion trained as a Catholic priest in Europe. He returned to England in 1580 to spread the Catholic religion. Travelling in secret across the country, he held church services in several Catholic families' houses. He was arrested a year later and taken to the Tower. Elizabeth offered him his freedom if he became a Protestant. He refused. Even under torture, he said that he had only come to England to preach and had strict orders not to get involved in plots. He was found guilty of treason and executed in December 1581.

2. Edmund Campion (Source 5) has been called both a 'traitor' and a 'martyr'. Can you suggest why?

SOURCE 6 The numbers of Catholics executed during Elizabeth's reign

1558–76: none
1577: 1 priest
1578: 1 priest
1579–85: 35, including 27 priests
1587: 6 priests
1588: 31, including 21 priests
1590–1603: 88, including 53 priests

3. Source 6 shows that most of the executions of Catholics took place after 1585.
a) Can you suggest why?
b) How do these figures compare with Mary Tudor's treatment of Protestants?

SOURCE 7 A summary of some recent historians' views about the Catholics during Elizabeth's reign

- *The Roman Catholic religion almost died out during Elizabeth's reign. By 1603 there were only about 40,000 Roman Catholics in England – about 1 per cent of the population, a tiny minority of Elizabeth's people.*
- *The Catholic priests who came to England failed to convert many people.*
- *The vast majority of Catholics were loyal to Elizabeth. They just wanted to be left in peace to worship God as they pleased. Only a tiny minority of Catholics became involved in plots against Elizabeth.*
- *English Catholics did not cause any serious trouble at the most dangerous moments of Elizabeth's reign: neither in 1587 when Mary, Queen of Scots, was executed, nor in 1588 when the Spanish Armada sailed to attack England.*

4. Study Source 7. Is it more important for historians today to find out:
a) how dangerous Catholics really were?
b) why the government thought that they were dangerous? Explain the reasons for your answer.

SOURCE 8 Sir Christopher Hatton's view of Catholics, from a speech to Parliament in 1589

66 *Vile wretches, bloody priests and false traitors, here in our bosoms and beyond the seas. We have chopped off some of the enemy's branches but they will grow again.* 99

■ **ACTIVITY**

It is 1595. You have just been appointed to the Privy Council. The French and Spanish ambassadors have complained about how Catholics are being treated in England. Your first job is to meet them and explain:

- why the government thinks that Catholics are a serious threat
- why each of the government's laws (see Source 2) was necessary at the time.

Write your speech. Refer to the activities of English Catholics, Mary, Queen of Scots, Catholic priests, the Pope, and European countries.

■ **TASK**

Write an essay to answer this question: was Elizabeth a 'Bloody Queen'? Support your answer with examples from your investigation of Mary, Queen of Scots (pages 80–87) and the evidence you have studied in this enquiry. You can get a planning sheet from your teacher to help you.

Would you have survived as a Catholic priest in Elizabethan England?

■ ACTIVITY

Keep a journal to record your experiences as you play this game. Your teacher will give you a sheet to help you.

Instructions
You can play the game individually or in pairs.

 You will need a coin. Toss the coin when you this symbol.

? When you see this symbol you will have to make a decision. Each box represents one month. How long will you survive? How many Catholics will you be able to help? Good luck! Now go to 1.

START

1 It is January 1580. You are a newly qualified Catholic priest. You hate Elizabeth's Church. For years you have been training in the Netherlands and Rome. Now the Pope has told you to return to England. Your mission is to hold secret services for English Catholics and to spread the Catholic religion. The Pope hopes that you will help to make England a Roman Catholic country again.

You must travel in secret. If government agents find you, you will be arrested, tortured and probably executed. You are risking your life! NOW GO TO 2.

2 **?**

You have reached the coast of France. You decide to travel to England disguised as a merchant. Two sea captains who are sailing to England offer to take you. **Do you:**

a) sail to Dover, the nearest English port? GO TO 3.
b) sail to Lancashire? Most English Catholics live in the north of England. GO TO 4.

3

You land at Dover. Government agents stop you when you come ashore. You tell them that you are a merchant.

Heads: They believe you. GO TO 5.
Tails: They search your bags and find your book of Latin prayers. GO TO 17

4

You reach the coast of Lancashire. There are no government agents there. You meet your contacts and they take you to a large house owned by a wealthy Catholic. GO TO 8.

5 **?**

Your contact meets you and takes you to a safe house in London. He tells you that there are government spies everywhere. You meet other Catholic priests and decide to travel to the north of England. Your contact advises you to write a letter saying that you have come to England for strictly business reasons. He will send it to the Privy Council if you are ever arrested. **Do you:**

a) write a letter? GO TO 6.
b) refuse to write a letter? GO TO 7.

6

Heads: Your letter is kept in a safe place. GO TO 7.
Tails: Several copies of your letter are made. One of them reaches the government. Now they know you are in England. They order your arrest. GO TO 12.

7

You travel in disguise to the north of England. You have directions to a Catholic house. On your journey you meet government agents. You say that you are a trader.

Heads: They believe you. GO TO 8.
Tails: They search your bags and find a book of Latin prayers. GO TO 17.

---

8 **?**

You are welcomed by the owner of the house. He tells you that government agents called yesterday. You agree to hold a secret Catholic service for his family and servants. He asks if he can invite Catholic friends who live nearby. **Do you:**

a) disagree and say it is time to help another Catholic family? GO TO 12.
b) agree? GO TO 9.

9

You hold several services for the family, their servants and friends.

Heads: There are no problems. GO TO 10.
Tails: One of the servants is a government informer. GO TO 13.

10 **?**

You hold more services. After a few days the owner of the house tells you that some local Catholics are plotting to overthrow Elizabeth and put Mary, Queen of Scots, on the throne. He can take you to them if you want to help. What will you do?

a) Tell him that you cannot get involved in politics. It is time to go and help another Catholic family? GO TO 12.
b) Say that you want to help them. If the plot succeeds England will be a Roman Catholic country again soon. GO TO 11.

11

You meet the plotters, but the plot fails. They are all arrested and executed.

Heads: The plotters do not tell the government that you were involved. GO TO 12.
Tails: You are arrested too. GO TO 17.

1. Compare your experiences with other students in your class. Were they similar or different? They were probably different. Discuss the reasons why the missions of some Catholic priests lasted longer than others.

2. Do you think the failure of the Catholic missions to Elizabethan England was mainly due to:
a) priests' mistakes?
b) bad luck?
c) government action?

12

You travel in disguise to a Catholic house in the north. Government agents know you are in the area. During your journey they stop you. You say you are visiting relatives.

Heads: They believe you. GO TO 8.
Tails: They have a description of you from the government. They recognise you. GO TO 17.

---

13 **?**

The 'servant' tells the local JP. He calls up local soldiers and surrounds the house. The owner of the house says that he has a secret place where you can hide. **Do you:**

a) try to escape? GO TO 15.
b) go to the secret hiding place? GO TO 14.

14

You are taken to an upstairs room. The owner removes a wall panel to reveal a tiny hiding place. He gives you some bread and water. You get in and the panel is put back.

Heads: After several hours you are discovered. GO TO 17.
Tails: The government agents don't find you. GO TO 12.

15

You run across the garden and climb over a wall. Government agents chase after you.

Two heads: You escape. GO TO 12.
Two tails: You escape. GO TO 16.
A head and a tail: You are captured. GO TO 17.

16

You decide that it is too dangerous to stay in England. You reach the coast and find a sea captain who will take you to Europe. You set sail.

Heads: You escape abroad but government agents now have an accurate description of you. You can never return to England. END OF GAME.
Tails: Government agents intercept your boat. GO TO 17.

17

You are arrested and taken to the Tower of London. You are put in a dark prison cell.

Heads: GO TO 18.
Tails: GO TO 19.

---

18 **?**

After a few days you are taken to see the Queen. She offers to set you free if you reject the Roman Catholic religion and agree to join the Church of England. **Do you:**

a) Accept her offer? GO TO 23.
b) Refuse her offer? GO TO 19.

---

19 **?**

You are taken to a prison cell in the Tower of London. You are tortured for several days. Sir Francis Walsingham demands that you give him the names of all your Catholic contacts in England. He also accuses you of being in a plot to murder Elizabeth. He demands the names of the other plotters. **Do you:**

a) refuse to answer his questions? GO TO 20.
b) say that you are innocent? GO TO 20.
c) confess and give him the information he wants? GO TO 22.

20

You are tortured for several more days. The pain is agonising. Still you refuse to confess.

Heads: You are taken to face trial. GO TO 21.
Tails: You die in prison. END OF GAME.

---

21 **?**

You are put on trial for treason. You are accused of rejecting Elizabeth's right to be Queen and being involved in a plot to overthrow her. **Do you:**

a) refuse to answer any questions? GO TO 24.
b) confess? GO TO 24.
c) say that the Pope is your religious leader but you recognise Elizabeth as Queen and have not been involved in any plots against her? GO TO 24.

22

You are put on trial and found guilty of treason. Many other Catholics are arrested and taken to the Tower of London. GO TO 24.

23

You are pardoned by the Queen and set free. You return to your family. But for the rest of your life you think that you have betrayed the true religion. END OF GAME.

24

You are hanged as a traitor. Your body is cut into four pieces. They are sent to be put on display in different parts of the country. This is what happens to traitors! END OF GAME.

Were the Puritans a threat to Elizabeth?

THE ROMAN CATHOLICS were not the only religious group that worried Elizabeth. The Puritans also caused her problems. In this enquiry we will investigate:

■ what difficulties the Puritans caused for Elizabeth
■ why she was worried about them
■ how successful she was in dealing with them.

Who were the Puritans?

The Puritans were Protestants who wanted to 'purify' the Church of all traces of the old Catholic religion. One sixteenth-century writer called them 'the hotter type of Protestant'. Puritan ideas spread quickly during Edward VI's reign. Many Puritans fled abroad during Mary Tudor's reign, but they began returning to England in 1558.

1. Study Source 1, then look back at pages 76–79. Make two lists:
a) what Puritans liked about Elizabeth's new Church of England
b) what Puritans disliked about it.
2. Were the Puritans a single, united group?

SOURCE 1 The Puritans' beliefs

How Elizabeth dealt with the Puritans' attempts to change the Church

In 1559 most Puritans accepted Elizabeth's new Church. However, they soon began organising campaigns to persuade her to make more changes.

Elizabeth could not ignore the Puritans. Their ideas were spreading, especially in London and the south-east. The Earl of Leicester and Sir Francis Walsingham were Puritans; so were many of her MPs and Justices of the Peace. There were also many Puritans in the Church and in the universities.

S OURCE 2 How Elizabeth dealt with Puritan attempts to change the Church

Date	Puritan attempts to change the Church	How Elizabeth dealt with them
1566	Puritan MPs demanded that priests should wear plain black gowns.	Matthew Parker, Archbishop of Canterbury, issued new rules for the Church. All priests had to wear vestments. In London, 30 priests refused and were expelled from the Church.
1571	Walter Strickland, a Puritan MP, wanted to introduce a new Prayer Book and ban vestments. A big campaign was organised in London to support him.	Elizabeth closed Parliament before his ideas could be discussed.
1575–83	The Puritans organised prayer meetings, called 'Prophesyings', to spread their ideas. Edmund Grindal, the new Archbishop of Canterbury, was a Puritan and liked these meetings.	Elizabeth ordered Grindal to ban the meetings. He refused. Elizabeth suspended him. When he died in 1583, she appointed John Whitgift as his successor. He banned the meetings and expelled 200 Puritan priests for disobeying the rules of the Church.
1583	William Stubbs, a Puritan, wrote a pamphlet criticising Elizabeth for holding marriage talks with a Catholic prince from France.	Stubbs had his right hand cut off.
1586	Sir Anthony Cope, a Puritan MP, introduced a bill to abolish bishops and establish a new Prayer Book.	Cope and four of his supporters were imprisoned in the Tower of London.
1588–89	Some Puritans issued a series of anonymous pamphlets called the Marprelate Tracts. They contained strong complaints about the Church and the bishops.	Many people were offended by these pamphlets. The Puritans lost a lot of support. The authors were never identified.

The Puritans after 1590

The Puritan campaigns stopped in the late 1580s. There was no more trouble for the rest of Elizabeth's reign. Most of Elizabeth's people supported the Church of England. John Field, the most important Puritan leader, died in 1588. The Puritans' biggest supporters at Court died at about the same time: the Earl of Leicester in 1588 and Sir Francis Walsingham in 1590.

Elizabeth defeated the Puritans but she did not destroy them. Puritan ideas continued to spread. Historians think that they were an important cause of the Civil War between Charles I and Parliament in the 1640s.

Why was Elizabeth so worried about the Puritans?

The Puritans did not become involved in any plots to overthrow Elizabeth. They did not try to help a foreign country attack England. So why was Elizabeth so worried about them?

I don't like making changes, especially when they are unnecessary. Making changes always means taking risks.

I like some of the old Catholic ways – there is nothing wrong with some decoration in churches and priests wearing vestments.

The Puritans are a minority. Most of my people like the Church of England. I must keep their support.

I am in charge of the Church. Religion is one of my private matters of state. The Puritans have no right to ask for changes. They are attacking my authority.

If I make the changes the Puritans want, the Roman Catholics will be very angry.

Some Puritans want to get rid of bishops. This would destroy my power to rule the Church.

Church-goers electing committees to control the Church, indeed! What will the Puritans ask for next?

SOURCE 3 Elizabeth's views about the Puritans

3. The Puritans were always a minority of Elizabeth's people. Why, then, couldn't she simply ignore them?
4. Why, in her dealings with the Puritans, did Elizabeth also have to think about the Roman Catholics?
5. What did Elizabeth mean by the question in Source 3 'What will the Puritans ask for next?'

■ ACTIVITY

It is 1600. You are an adviser to the Archbishop of Canterbury. He is planning to discuss the Puritans with his bishops. He has asked you to draw up a secret report about the Puritans for the meeting. It should cover the following issues:

■ what the Puritans have tried to change in the Church since 1558
■ how successfully Elizabeth and her archbishops have dealt with them so far – have any mistakes been made?
■ how serious the Puritan threat to the Church is now (in 1600)
■ whether any further action against the Puritans is needed.

■ TASK

Why did the Puritans fail to change the Church during Elizabeth's reign? To answer this question:

■ make a list of reasons why the Puritans failed
■ choose some examples to support each reason
■ explain your reasons and examples in three or four paragraphs
■ briefly explain which you think was the most important reason for their failure in your last paragraph.

■ REVIEW TASK 1

Write an essay to answer this question: was it the Puritans or the Roman Catholics who were the greatest threat to Elizabethan England?

Organise your answer like this:

■ a short introduction – explain why both groups caused problems for Elizabeth

■ a detailed paragraph showing how and why the Puritans were a threat; support your points with examples

■ a detailed paragraph showing how and why the Roman Catholics were a threat; support your points with examples

■ a conclusion – explain who you think was the greatest threat and why.

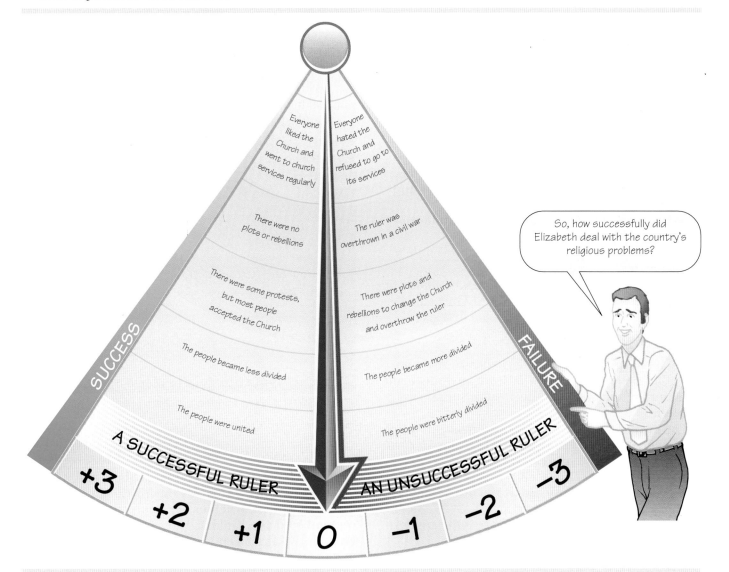

Everyone liked the Church and went to church services regularly

Everyone hated the Church and refused to go to its services

There were no plots or rebellions

The ruler was overthrown in a civil war

There were some protests, but most people accepted the Church

There were plots and rebellions to change the Church and overthrow the ruler

SUCCESS

FAILURE

The people became less divided

The people became more divided

The people were united

The people were bitterly divided

A SUCCESSFUL RULER

AN UNSUCCESSFUL RULER

+3   +2   +1   0   −1   −2   −3

So, how successfully did Elizabeth deal with the country's religious problems?

■ REVIEW TASK 2

Write an essay to answer this question: how successfully did Elizabeth I deal with the country's religious problems during her reign?

Consider the following issues in your answer:

■ how popular was Elizabeth's Church of England with her people?

■ how much trouble was caused by its opponents?

■ how effectively did Elizabeth deal with the Puritans?

■ how effectively did she deal with the Roman Catholics?

■ were the country's religious problems more serious or less serious at the end of Elizabeth's reign than they were in 1558?

chapter 5

WAS ELIZABETH'S REIGN A CULTURAL 'GOLDEN AGE'?

THERE IS A buzz of excitement in the air. The audience are flicking through their programmes and chatting quietly. Some people are still being shown to their seats. An announcement is made: 'Please would anyone with a mobile phone make sure that it is switched off.' The moment they have all been waiting for has nearly arrived. The lights are dimmed. There is silence.

Behind the scenes everything is ready. The actors and actresses have put their make-up on and have changed into their costumes. Some of them are reciting their lines. Others are pacing up and down nervously. The technicians are making final checks to the lighting and sound systems. Stage-hands have moved the scenery into place. The smoke machine is turned on.

The curtains open. The scene is a remote Scottish moor. Suddenly, there are crashes of thunder and flashes of lightning. Three witches appear.

'When shall we three meet again, in thunder, lightning or in rain?' asks the first witch.

'When the hurlyburly's done, when the battle's lost and won,' the second replies.

Finally, all three chant 'Fair is foul, and foul is fair. Hover through the fog and filthy air.' They vanish into the mist. The curtain closes. The first scene is over ...

What has this visit to a modern theatre got to do with Elizabethan England? Has it got anything to do with our investigation into Elizabeth's success as a ruler?

The theatre burst into life during Elizabeth's reign. The scene you have just read about is from *Macbeth* by William Shakespeare. He wrote at least 37 plays, most of them during Elizabeth's reign. They are the most famous plays ever written. You are probably studying one of them for your English GCSE. Most experts today think that Shakespeare is the greatest playwright who ever lived.

Elizabeth's reign is often called the 'Golden Age of English Drama'. This is all the more remarkable because in 1558 there were few signs of the great dramatic achievements to come. There was not a single theatre in the country when Elizabeth became Queen. Plays and acting were generally frowned upon. Many people thought that actors were no better than beggars.

SOURCE 1 A scene from a modern production of *Macbeth*

In this chapter we will investigate how and why the theatre developed so quickly during Elizabeth's reign. Then we will ask whether her reign deserves to be remembered as a 'Golden Age' of culture, a time of great musicians, scientists, artists, designers, writers and poets. Or is this view a myth (a false view of the past) that was deliberately spread by Elizabeth's propaganda machine at the time and by nostalgic writers ever since? And, if Elizabeth's reign really was a 'Golden Age' of culture, does this show that Elizabeth I was a successful ruler? Did she have any real control over these developments or would they have happened anyway?

What were Elizabethan theatres like?

THE ROMANS BUILT the first theatres in Britain. After they left Britain in about AD 400, these theatres soon became overgrown and ruined. For the next thousand years no theatres were built in this country. Plays, however, continued to be a popular form of entertainment. Groups of actors travelled around the country, together with acrobats, jugglers and minstrels. They performed stories from the Bible and miracle-plays on temporary platforms in market places and INN-YARDS.

Why were theatres built during Elizabeth's reign?

The authorities thought that wandering groups of people were a threat to law and order. Travelling actors were no exception. In 1572 Parliament ordered actors to be punished as vagabonds. Some nobles, however, protected groups of actors. In 1574, for example, the Earl of Leicester allowed one group to call itself 'Leicester's Company'. Performing in inn-yards and market squares, these actors attracted large audiences.

In 1576 a large building was opened at Shoreditch, just outside London. Its owner, James Burbage, wanted to use it just for performing plays. It was the first theatre in this country since Roman times. He called it 'The Theatre' and it was a great success. Other people soon copied his idea. More theatres were built nearby, including 'The Curtain' (1577), 'The Rose' (1587) and 'The Swan' (1596). The most famous theatre of them all was opened in 1599. It was called 'The Globe'. The first performance of many of Shakespeare's plays took place there.

1. Why do you think the authorities disapproved of actors?
2. Why were theatres better places for performing plays than market squares and inn-yards?

Elizabethan theatres

No Elizabethan theatres survive today. The Globe Theatre, for example, was accidentally burned down in 1613. A cannon that was being used for special effects set fire to the theatre's thatched roof. Although the Globe was rebuilt, it was closed down in 1644 and demolished during the English Civil War. To find out what Elizabethan theatres were like, we must piece together the clues from the few sources which have survived from Elizabeth's reign . . .

SOURCE 1 The interior of the Swan Theatre, drawn in 1596 by Johannes de Witt, a Dutch visitor to England. This is the only drawing of a theatre that survives from Elizabeth's reign

■ ACTIVITY

Reconstruct the Globe Theatre
A wealthy American film-maker is in London. He wants to build a full-scale reconstruction of the Globe Theatre on its original site. He is prepared to spend millions! You have been chosen to prepare a detailed design for the new Globe. Study Sources 1–5. Then draw up your plan. The film-maker wants you to include the following information:

■ where the new theatre should be built
■ the shape of the building
■ its size (height and width)
■ the type of roof
■ the position and size of the stage
■ the facilities for the actors
■ the facilities for the audience
■ a list of building materials required.

SOURCE 2 An extract from the contract to build the Fortune Theatre in London, 1600

❝ *This agreement made between Philip Henslowe and Edward Alleyn on the one part, and Peter Street, citizen and carpenter of London.*

The framework of the theatre is to be square and to be 80 foot square [7.5 m²] outside and 55 foot square [5 m²] inside, with a good, strong foundation of brick, lime and sand one foot [0.3m] high above the ground. There will be three floors, each of which shall contain four rooms for gentlemen, and other divisions for two-penny rooms, with seats to be placed in these rooms and throughout these galleries, as are made in the recently built Globe playhouse.

With a covered stage and a tiring house [dressing room]. The stage shall be 43 foot long [13 m] and in width extend to the middle of the yard of the theatre. ❞

SOURCE 3 An extract from the writings of Johannes de Witt, 1596

❝ *There are in London four theatres of noteworthy beauty, which have various names. In them a different play is presented to the people every day. The two finest of these, the Rose and the Swan, are situated south of the River Thames. The two others are outside the city to the north. There is also a fifth, of different structure, devoted to beast-baiting where many large bears, bulls and dogs are kept in dens and cages and are then made to fight each other, giving men a most delightful spectacle. Of all the theatres, the largest is the Swan; it has space for three thousand persons and is built of flint stones supported by wooden columns which are painted to look like marble. It looks like a Roman building.* ❞

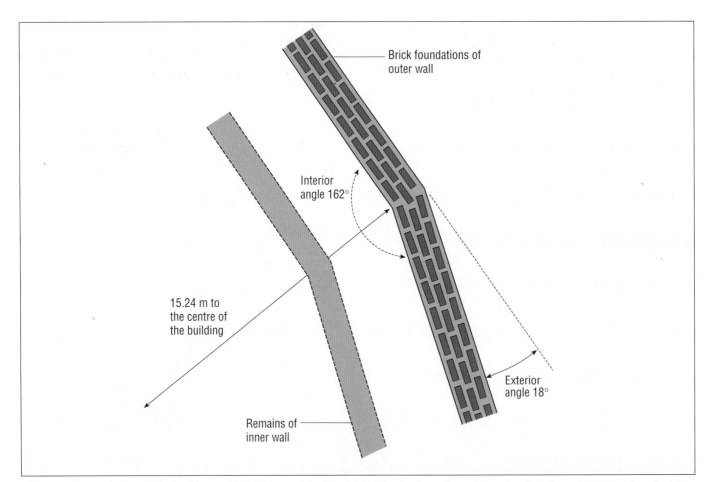

Brick foundations of outer wall

Interior angle 162°

15.24 m to the centre of the building

Remains of inner wall

Exterior angle 18°

SOURCE 4 Archaeological evidence, 1989. The remains of the Globe Theatre lie underneath modern buildings. In 1989 archaeologists had the chance to excavate a small part of them. Their work lasted for three months. They found a corner of the Globe's wall. From its angle, the archaeologists were able to work out, for the first time, the width and shape of the original Globe Theatre

SOURCE 5 From a drawing of London, 1647. The Globe Theatre and the 'Beere bayting' pit have been wrongly labelled. They should be the other way round

3. Which of these sources (2–5) contain evidence about the Globe Theatre?

4. Why do historians who want to find out about the Globe Theatre have to use evidence about other theatres as well?

5. Study Source 4.

a) How wide was the Globe Theatre?

b) What shape was the Globe Theatre?

c) Why had this information not been known before?

d) What could the archaeologists NOT tell about the Globe from their findings? Why?

e) Do their findings agree with Source 5? Explain the likely reasons.

6. 'All Elizabethan theatres were identical.' Do you agree or disagree with this statement? Explain your reasons.

Inn-yards Plays were often performed in inn-yards before theatres were built. The audience sat in covered galleries to watch the plays.

Bear-baiting pits Bear-baiting was another popular entertainment. The pits were circular buildings in which bears were tied to a post and attacked by dogs. The new theatres could easily be converted into bear-baiting pits if they were not successful.

Roman theatres Many wealthy people in the sixteenth century travelled to Italy to see the remains of Roman buildings, including theatres.

Mathematics John Dee was an influential Elizabethan mathematician who travelled in Europe. He believed that the design of buildings should obey the principles of proportion and symmetry.

Factors that influenced the design of Elizabethan theatres

SOURCE 6 Factors that influenced the design of Elizabethan theatres

The roof Most of the theatre was open to the sky. Plays were performed in the afternoon. There was no artificial lighting.

The galleries There were three galleries of covered seats around the yard. They could seat about 2000 people. They were for wealthy people, who paid extra to sit there.

The stage The stage was raised and it projected into the yard. There were no curtains across the front and very little scenery was used. Only the back part of the stage was roofed; the ceiling was usually painted with pictures of the heavens.

The yard (or pit) Poor people, or 'groundlings', stood in the yard to watch the plays. They were close to the actors and could be very noisy. The yard was open to the sky. People got wet if it rained.

SOURCE 7 The interior of a typical Elizabethan theatre. Elizabethan theatres were not all the same but they shared many common features. This is a modern reconstruction drawn especially for this book in 1999

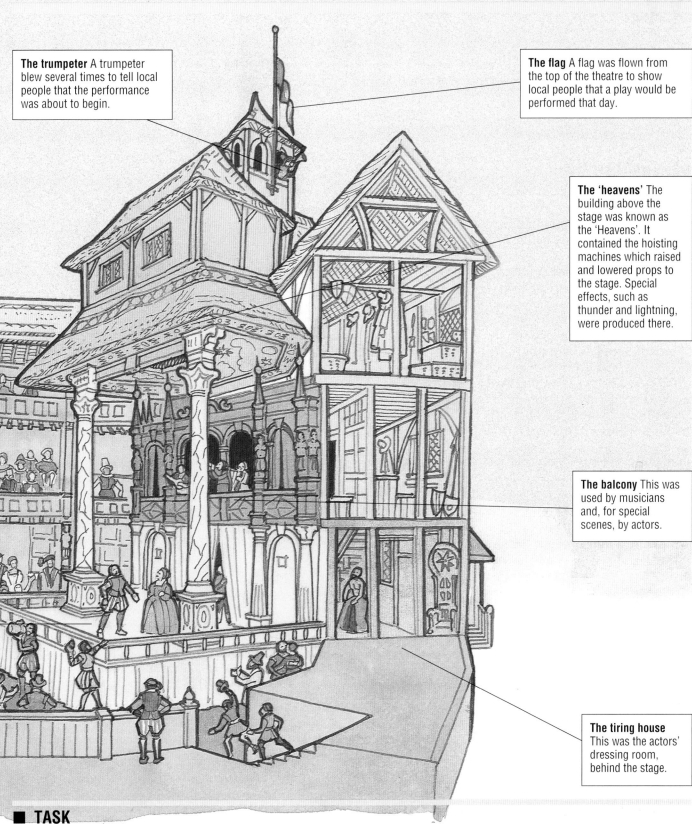

The trumpeter A trumpeter blew several times to tell local people that the performance was about to begin.

The flag A flag was flown from the top of the theatre to show local people that a play would be performed that day.

The 'heavens' The building above the stage was known as the 'Heavens'. It contained the hoisting machines which raised and lowered props to the stage. Special effects, such as thunder and lightning, were produced there.

The balcony This was used by musicians and, for special scenes, by actors.

The tiring house This was the actors' dressing room, behind the stage.

■ TASK

1. What evidence can you find in Sources 1–5 to support the main features shown in Source 7?
2. In what ways were Elizabethan theatres similar to theatres today?
3. In what ways were they different?
4. What problems did these differences cause for Elizabethan playwrights and actors?

Why was there opposition to the theatre?

ALTHOUGH IT MIGHT seem strange to us today, some Elizabethans objected to the theatre. In this enquiry we will investigate who they were – and why they opposed the theatre.

The authorities

Elizabethan London was a busy, noisy and overcrowded city. The Lord Mayor of London and his councillors were responsible for law and order in the capital. London's population rose from about 50,000 in 1500 to 200,000 in 1603. Many poor people flocked to London in search of work or charity. The authorities found it more and more difficult to control the city.

The new theatres were built just outside the city, either north of the city walls or on the south bank of the River Thames. This was outside the area that the city authorities controlled. They became very worried about the large crowds the theatres attracted. Only the Privy Council could give them the powers they needed to deal with the theatres; but some Privy Councillors liked plays and acting.

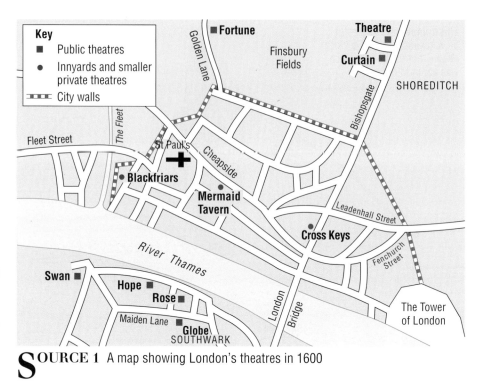

SOURCE 1 A map showing London's theatres in 1600

SOURCE 2 A declaration by the Council of the City of London, December 1574

66 *Great disorders and inconveniences have affected this city by the great multitudes [crowds] of people, especially youths, who go to plays and shows – especially quarrels and fights; drunkenness in inns which have open stages and galleries adjoining them; withdrawing of the Queen's subjects from church services on Sundays and holidays when plays are performed; the waste of money by poor persons; various robberies by picking and cutting of purses.* 99

SOURCE 3 An extract from a law passed in 1572

66 *All common players not belonging to any honourable person of great degree who wander about and have not a licence shall be taken, adjudged and deemed rogues, vagabonds and sturdy beggars.* 99

SOURCE 4 An extract from a letter from the Lord Mayor of London to the Privy Council, 1582

66 *All the afternoon the players took in people who were therefore absent from church. Further, the* PLAGUE *has increased and the season is hot and perilous. The continuing of performances would be most dangerous. I therefore request the Council to restrain such plays.* 99

SOURCE 5 An order from the Privy Council to the City of London authorities, date unknown but probably in the 1580s

66 *Your Lordships do permit the three companies of players to publicly present their plays in their several houses – the Globe in Maiden Lane on the Bankside, the Fortune in Golding Lane and the Curtain in Holywell in the county of Middlesex. Except that if there happen weekly to die of the plague above the number of thirty within the City of London. At which time, we think fit that they shall cease and forbear publicly to play until the sickness be reduced to the said number.* 99

SOURCE 6 A letter from the Lord Mayor and London councillors to the Privy Council, July 1597

66 *Theatres are places for vagrants, masterless men, thieves, horse-stealers, whoremongers, cheats, swindlers, traitors and other idle and dangerous persons to meet together to the great displeasure of Almighty God and the hurt and annoyance of her Majesty's people. We cannot prevent this for the theatres are outside the area of our control.*

They maintain idleness in such persons as have no work, and draw apprentices and servants from their work, and all sorts of people from attending sermons and other religious services, causing great damage to the trade and religion of this realm.

In times of sickness many who have sores amuse themselves by hearing a play, whereby others are infected. 99

The Puritans

Puritan beliefs spread during Elizabeth's reign, especially in London. The Puritans strongly disapproved of theatres. They associated theatres with the Ancient Romans. The Romans had crucified Jesus and persecuted Christians, sometimes by allowing lions to attack and kill them in their theatres. Most Puritans believed that theatres must be the work of the Devil.

SOURCE 7 An extract from a sermon by a Puritan preacher, 1580

66 *Whoever shall visit the chapel of Satan, I mean the theatre, shall find many young ruffians who are past all shame.* 99

SOURCE 8 An extract from a sermon by John Stockwood, a Puritan, preached outside St Paul's Cathedral in 1578

66 *Will not a filthy play, with the blast of a trumpet, sooner call a thousand there than a hour's tolling of church bells bring to a sermon a hundred people.* 99

■ **ACTIVITY**

You are the owner of an Elizabethan theatre. Write a letter to the Privy Council to defend your theatre against the complaints in this enquiry.

SOURCE 9 An extract from a sermon preached by Thomas White outside St Paul's Cathedral, 1578

66 *Look upon the common plays in London, and see the multitude that flocketh to them. Look at the expensive theatre houses, a monument to London's extravagance and foolishness. I understand that they are now forbidden because of the plague. I like this well, for a disease is only patched up if the cause is not cured. The cause of plagues is sin and the cause of sin is plays – therefore the cause of plagues are plays.* 99

SOURCE 10 An extract from *The Anatomy of Abuses*, by Philip Stubbes, 1583

66 *Do they not maintain vulgarity, foolishness and remind people of false religions? Do they not encourage prostitution and uncleanness? They are plain devourers of maidenly virginity and chastity. For proof of this, look at the flocking to theatres daily and hourly, night and day, to see plays where [there are] such suggestive gestures, bawdy [rude] speeches, laughing, kissing, winking and glancing of eyes.* 99

■ **TASK**

1. Study Sources 2–6. Then complete the table.

Why the London authorities opposed theatres

Reasons	Supporting evidence

2. Study Sources 7–10. Then complete the table.

Why the Puritans opposed theatres

Reasons	Supporting evidence

3. Were the reasons why the London authorities and the Puritans disliked the theatre similar or different? Explain your answer.
4. Do you think that any of London's Lord Mayors and councillors were Puritans? Explain the reasons for your answer.

Why was the Elizabethan theatre so successful?

AS YOU HAVE seen, some Elizabethans protested strongly against theatres. This makes it all the more surprising that the Elizabethan theatre was so successful. Theatres became very popular. Thousands of people went to them every week. By 1600 there were seven theatres in London and 40 companies of actors. Plays were also regularly performed in inns and private houses.

This enquiry will help you to explain why, despite the opposition, the Elizabethan theatre became so successful.

Elizabeth's support for the theatre

Elizabeth I never went to a theatre, but she enjoyed plays. She often invited companies of actors to perform for her at Court. She was an important patron of the theatre. Elizabeth even allowed one group of actors to call themselves 'The Queen's Men'.

SOURCE 1 An Italian duke describes the first performance of Shakespeare's *Twelfth Night* in 1600

66 *As soon as Her Majesty was set in her place, many knights and ladies began a great dance. When this ended, there was a comedy with pieces of music and dances.* 99

SOURCE 2 An extract from government records, 1572

66 *To the Lord Chamberlain's players at Whitehall, 25 February 1572, for a play presented by them before Her Majesty on St Stephen's Day, £6 13s 4d. And more in reward by Her Majesty making in all £10.* 99

SOURCE 3 An extract from *The English Gentleman*, by Richard Braithwaite, 1641

66 *Our late Queen Elizabeth of blessed memory, how well she approved of plays, calling them 'harmless spenders of time'. She gave countenance to their endeavours and encouraged them . . .* 99

The nobles

Many nobles invited actors to perform for them in their country houses, even when theatres were closed in London. Some nobles helped to protect groups of actors from being punished. Lord Hunsdon, Elizabeth's Lord Chamberlain, gave money to a group of actors. He allowed them to call themselves

'The Lord Chamberlain's Men'. William Shakespeare was a member of this company. Other nobles, like the Earl of Leicester, were patrons of companies of actors. Some nobles even thought that the theatre stopped the lower classes from causing trouble because it took their thoughts away from the problems in their lives, such as poverty and unemployment.

SOURCE 4 Sir John Harington, the Queen's godson, writing in 1606

66 *I think in stage plays may be much good, in well penned comedies and especially tragedies.* 99

1. What evidence is there that Elizabeth I:
a) saw plays?
b) enjoyed plays?
c) helped actors?
2. a) How did nobles help the theatre?
b) Why did they help the theatre?
3. Why was support from the Queen and the nobles important for actors and playwrights?

Why did people go to the theatre?

The main reason why most people went to the theatre must have been to watch the plays. Entrance fees were cheap and everyone could afford them. Theatre audiences contained people from all classes of society.

SOURCE 5 An extract from *Travels in England, 1599* by Thomas Platter, a Swiss traveller

66 *Whoever cares to stand below pays only one English penny, but if he wishes to sit he enters by another door, and pays another penny, while if he desires to sit in the most comfortable seats which are cushioned, where he not only sees everything well, but can also be seen, then he pays yet another English penny at another door.* 99

There were other attractions at the theatre, besides the plays. Refreshments were on sale. People could buy fruit and nuts to eat, and drinks such as wine or beer. In Source 5 Thomas Platter mentions that some wealthy people went to be seen. Going to the theatre was an opportunity to dress in your finest clothes and be noticed by other wealthy people. This could help you make business contacts or attract the attention of a young lady. The large crowds at theatres also attracted another kind of person as you have seen – criminals.

Elizabethan actors

Acting in an Elizabethan theatre was not easy. Actors had to perform a different play every day, often taking more than one part. They acted in front of noisy audiences, without modern scenery or lighting. Women were not allowed to act, so female characters had to be played by men or boys. As well as acting, they also had to sing and dance, play musical instruments and fight with swords.

Most actors were probably not especially talented, but the best actors became very famous.

- **Richard Burbage**, son of the owner of the first theatre, was the best tragic actor. He took the leading roles in many of Shakespeare's most well-known plays. Some parts, such as Othello, King Lear and Hamlet, were probably written with him in mind. Burbage later became an owner of the Globe Theatre and ran his own company of actors.
- **Edward Alleyn** was another tragic actor. He was famous for his strong voice and energy. He made enough money to buy land in Dulwich and open a college there.
- **Will Kempe** was a great comic actor who was famous for his dancing and his funny clothes.
- **Thomas Pope** was another well-known comedian. He was fat enough to play Sir John Falstaff and Sir Toby Belch, two of Shakespeare's most famous comic characters.

The plays

Elizabethan playwrights wrote some of the best plays ever written. Huge audiences, containing poor craftspeople and apprentices as well as wealthy nobles and merchants, flocked to watch them. First, we will find out about the playwrights. Then we will examine why their work was so popular.

Who wrote the plays?

Christopher Marlowe was the first famous Elizabethan playwright. He was born in Canterbury in 1564. He went to Cambridge University and then became a government spy. He wrote two well-known plays, *Tamberlaine the Great* (1586), about a cruel Asian warrior who conquered a large empire in the fourteenth century, and *Doctor Faustus* (1588). Marlowe was mysteriously killed in a fight in a London tavern in 1593.

The most well-known Elizabethan playwright is, of course, William Shakespeare. Surprisingly little is known about his life. We know that he was born in 1564 in Stratford-upon-Avon. By 1592 he had joined a company of actors in London and was beginning to write plays and poetry. By the time he died, in 1616, he had written at least 37 plays, at a rate of two a year. His first play, *Henry VI*, was probably written in 1590–91. His most famous plays include *Romeo and Juliet* (1595), *The Merchant of Venice* (1597), *Hamlet* (1600), *Othello* (1604), *Macbeth* (1606), *Anthony and Cleopatra* (1606) and *The Tempest* (1611).

Most people think that he was the greatest playwright of all time. Today, 400 years later, his plays are still performed all over the world.

SOURCE 6 A description of Richard Burbage, written by Richard Flecknoe in 1664

66 *He was a delightful actor, so wholly transforming himself into his part, as he never assumed himself again until the play was over. There was as much difference between him and one of our common actors, as between a singer who only mouths the words and an excellent singer, who knows all his graces, and can artfully vary and modulate [control] his voice and know how much breath to give to every syllable.* 99

SOURCE 7 The earliest known portrait of William Shakespeare. It was drawn by a Dutch artist in 1623, seven years after Shakespeare's death. It might have been copied from an earlier picture

1. From *Romeo and Juliet*, written by William Shakespeare in 1594–95. It is set in Verona, Italy. Romeo has fallen in love with Juliet. But their families have been enemies for many years. Romeo goes to her house one night to try to speak with her . . .

2. From *Richard III*, written by Shakespeare in 1592–93. It is set in fifteenth-century England. Richard, Duke of Gloucester, is determined to be King of England. He plans to murder his brother and nephews, who all have stronger claims to the throne . . .

3. From *Doctor Faustus*, written by Christopher Marlowe in about 1588. It is set in Germany. Doctor Faustus is a scholar. He signs a pact with the Devil. It gives him all the magical knowledge in the world for 24 years, but there is a terrible price to pay . . .

4. From *The Tempest*, written by Shakespeare in 1611. The King of Naples has been shipwrecked. His son, Ferdinand, wakes up alone on the shore of a strange island. He hears music and singing . . .

5. From *Julius Caesar*, written by Shakespeare in 1599–1600. It is set in Rome in the first century BC. Julius Caesar is the ruler of the Roman Empire and a successful general. Several politicians, including one of Caesar's friends, Brutus, think that he is becoming too powerful. They decide to murder him . . .

6. From *King Lear*, written by Shakespeare in 1605. It is set in early medieval Britain. Lear is the ageing King of Britain. Regan, his daughter, and her husband, the Duke of Cornwall, have quarrelled with him. They hear that the Earl of Gloucester has helped the King. They go to his castle, determined to punish him . . .

SOURCE 8 Six famous scenes from plays written by Elizabethan playwrights

Why were their plays so successful?

The plays of Marlowe and Shakespeare contained fascinating characters, gripping storylines and great poetry. A variety of clever dramatic techniques were used to overcome the practical difficulties presented by sixteenth-century theatres and to keep the audience's attention. Above all, their plays were in tune with people's interests at the time. They captured the 'spirit of the age'.

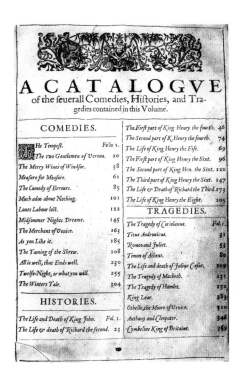

SOURCE 9 A list of Shakespeare's plays, from the first collected edition of his works, published in 1623

SOURCE 10 How playwrights dealt with the problems of Elizabethan theatres

Problem	Solutions	Example
No curtain to draw back or lights to lower to show when the play begins.	A dramatic start to seize everyone's attention.	*Macbeth* starts with thunder and lightning. Then three witches appear.
Curtains could not be drawn to show the end of scenes. Plays had to be continuous.	A distraction or a sub-plot alongside the main storyline.	Two bloodstained murderers in *Macbeth* are interrupted by a visitor. A drunken porter answers the door. This gives the actors time to change into clean clothes.
No artificial lighting to show the difference between night and day.	The words of the play tell the audience what time it is.	*Hamlet* begins at night. One character says 'Tis now struck twelve. Get thee to bed.'
There was little scenery.	The words of the play describe the scene.	*Henry V* begins on a battlefield in France. The narrator tells the audience to imagine 'the vasty fields of France . . . within this wooden O.'
	Special effects were used.	A trapdoor was used to make people appear or disappear.
		The sound of thunder was made by rolling a cannon-ball along a wooden floor.
		Pigs' bladders filled with blood were used to make stabbings or sword wounds look realistic.
Women were not allowed to act, so men had to play female roles.	Other actors described the beauty of female characters.	When Juliet appears at a window, Romeo compares her to the sun, calls her a 'bright angel' and a 'winged messenger of heaven'.
	Sometimes, female characters pretended to be men.	In *The Merchant of Venice*, Portia and Nerissa play a trick on their husbands by dressing up as men.
Audiences contained people from all classes of society.	Plays were as varied as possible. They included tragic and comic scenes, sub-plots, music and dancing.	

■ TASK 1

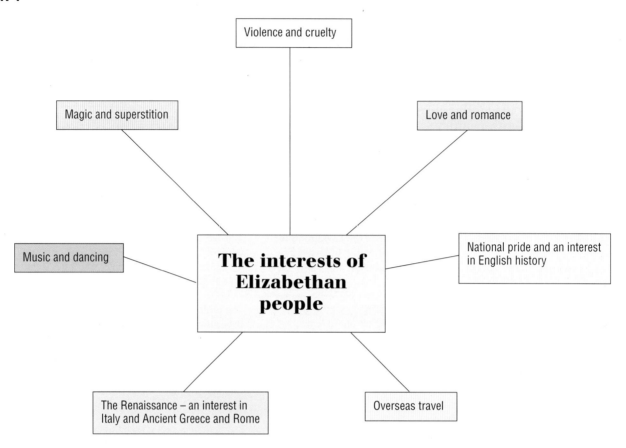

SOURCE 11 The interests of Elizabethan people that were reflected in the plays

Find examples to show how Elizabethan plays reflected each of the interests shown in Source 11. Use the information in this chapter (especially Source 8) and your own knowledge of any of Shakespeare's plays you have studied.

■ TASK 2

Write an essay to answer this question: why was the theatre so successful in Elizabeth's reign?

You will need to write four or five paragraphs. Each paragraph should contain one or two reasons. Explain how each reason helped the theatre to become so successful. Give some examples to support your explanation. You could refer to:

■ the Queen and the nobles
■ entrance charges

■ attractions for the audience
■ the acting
■ the plays.

In your conclusion explain which you think was the most important reason and why.

Your teacher will give you a sheet to help you plan your answer.

Was Elizabeth's reign a 'Golden Age' of culture?

AS YOU SAW at the beginning of this chapter, some people have said that there were other great cultural achievements during Elizabeth's reign besides the theatre. They have called her reign a 'Golden Age' of culture. In this enquiry we will investigate whether or not this is a valid view.

MUSIC and DANCE

Music and dancing were very popular. Brilliant musicians such as Orlando Gibbons and William Byrd wrote glorious music which is still played today. It was a great period for English music.

ART

The greatest artists were in Europe. The government hired foreign artists to paint most of the Queen's portraits. Nicholas Hilliard was the best English artist. He became famous for his superb miniature portraits.

MATHEMATICS

Some people were becoming interested in mathematics. John Dee found ways of drawing maps more accurately and was interested in the ideas of proportion and symmetry. John Napier discovered logarithms, although his work was not published until 1614.

LITERATURE and DRAMA

This was an astonishing period. Some of the greatest poetry, literature and drama in our history comes from Elizabeth's reign. The theatre burst into life with the great plays of Christopher Marlowe and William Shakespeare. Also, Edmund Spenser wrote a superb poem, called *The Faerie Queene*, to celebrate Elizabeth's reign.

HISTORY

People were becoming much more interested in history. William Camden wrote a history of Elizabeth's reign. Richard Hakluyt wrote a book about the voyages of English sailors. The work of these writers was important for two reasons. They studied sources, instead of just copying earlier writers; and they tried to explain why events happened rather than just listing them.

ARCHITECTURE

This was the time of 'The Great Rebuilding'. More people than ever before built themselves new houses, with upstairs rooms, glass windows, fireplaces and chimneys. The greatest English architect was Robert Smythson. He designed Hardwick Hall and many other country houses using the most recent designs from Europe.

SCIENCE

Important scientific discoveries about the planets and the human body were being made in Europe. In England, interest in science was only just beginning. Francis Bacon said that experiments were the only way to test new theories. William Harvey was educated during Elizabeth's reign. Later, in the 1620s, he discovered how the blood circulates around the body.

SOURCE 1   Some experts' views about the cultural achievements of Elizabeth's reign

■ ACTIVITY

Give each of the topics in Source 1 a score, from −3 (a dull, uninteresting period) to +3 (a time of brilliant achievement). Discuss the reasons for your scores.

Now we must ask two more questions.

■ Why were there so many cultural achievements during Elizabeth's reign?
■ If so many new things were happening did old, superstitious ideas suddenly die out?

Source 2 will help you to answer these questions.

SOURCE 2 Beliefs and social changes in Elizabethan England

Witchcraft

Most people believed that witches could use evil magic against them. Witches were accused of causing bad harvests, injuries or even death. More witches than Catholics were executed during Elizabeth's reign.

Illness and disease

No one understood the causes of disease. Many people died unexpectedly at an early age, especially babies. There were frequent outbreaks of plague. Old herbal remedies, prayers and charms were used to cure and prevent illness.

The printing press

All books were written by hand during the Middle Ages. The printing press was invented in the fifteenth century. It became much cheaper to produce books, and new ideas spread more easily. By Elizabeth's reign there were printing presses all over the country. More people were buying books than ever before.

The Renaissance

In Europe, many people were interested in the culture of the Ancient Greeks and Romans. They began to learn and question old ideas. These interests spread to England in the sixteenth century.

Protestantism

Protestants hated the old traditions of the Catholic Church, such as pilgrimages and the belief in miracles. They thought these ideas were just superstition. They wanted as many people as possible to read the Bible for themselves.

Education

For boys from well-off families, there were better opportunities for education than ever before. During Elizabeth's reign many new grammar schools and university colleges were opened.

Illiteracy

Most people were too poor to send their children to school. By 1600, only 30 per cent of men and fewer than 10 per cent of women could read or write.

Alchemy

During the Middle Ages, many scholars tried to discover a way of turning base (or worthless) metals into gold. These alchemists, as they were known, continued their efforts throughout the sixteenth century.

Elizabeth's role

Elizabeth was a patron of the arts. She loved music and dancing. She sang, and played the lute, the lyre and the virginals (a keyboard instrument). Elizabeth employed the best artists and invited the best actors and musicians to perform for her at Court.

Wealth

Many people became wealthy through agriculture and trade. This gave them more money to spend on entertainment, and on education for their sons.

Astrology

Most people believed that the stars and planets influenced their lives. Astrologers studied the heavens to predict the future. Their horoscopes and almanacs were very popular. Elizabeth asked John Dee, the most famous astrologer, to choose a day when the stars and planets were in favourable positions for her coronation day.

■ TASK

Study Source 2.

1. What examples can you find of old, superstitious ideas still surviving during Elizabeth's reign?

2. What reasons can you find to help explain why they survived?

3. Why, despite the survival of these old beliefs, were there so many cultural achievements in Elizabethan England?

■ REVIEW TASK

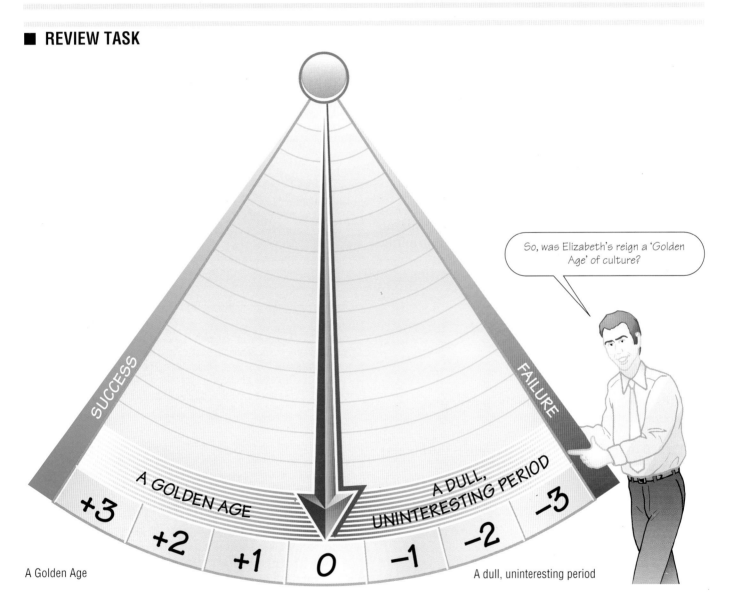

So, was Elizabeth's reign a 'Golden Age' of culture?

SUCCESS
FAILURE

A GOLDEN AGE
A DULL, UNINTERESTING PERIOD

+3   +2   +1   0   –1   –2   –3

A Golden Age   A dull, uninteresting period

1. Was there a 'Golden Age' of culture during Elizabeth's reign? Use what you have found out in this chapter to explain your answer.

2. How much credit does Elizabeth deserve for the cultural achievements that took place during her reign?

a) None (she tried to stop them)
b) Very little (she had nothing to do with them)
c) Some (she encouraged them)
d) A lot (she caused them).

Explain which verdict you agree with and give your reasons.

6 DID ELIZABETHAN ENGLAND BECOME A GREAT POWER?

SIXTEENTH-CENTURY monarchs were expected to protect their people from foreign attack. This meant keeping the country's defences strong. Any ruler who could not win a war or defeat an invasion would not survive for long. In 1558, when Elizabeth became Queen, England was a weak country. The biggest danger was that several European countries might join together to attack.

In this chapter we will investigate how successful Elizabeth was in protecting her people. How well did she deal with threats from other countries? Did she make England a 'Great Power' in the world?

■ ACTIVITY

It is 1558. Elizabeth has just appointed you to her Privy Council because you know a great deal about foreign affairs. Your first job is to prepare a briefing for her about the situation in Europe. She particularly wants to know about the following countries:

- France
- Spain
- the Netherlands
- Scotland
- Ireland.

She also wants to know about the power and influence of the Pope in Rome.

a) Which of these countries or people is the biggest threat to England and why?
b) With which country or person should England be most friendly and why?

Scotland
Scotland is a Catholic country but Protestant ideas are spreading fast. Its rulers, the Stuart family, have always been very friendly with France. Mary, Queen of Scots, is married to a French prince and claims that she is the rightful queen of England. Scotland and England have been enemies for centuries. They have fought many wars.

Ireland
English kings have always claimed to rule Ireland. In fact, England controls only a small area around Dublin. Most Irish people are Roman Catholics. An enemy could easily use Ireland as a base for attacking England.

The Netherlands
The Netherlands are ruled by Spain, but Protestant ideas are spreading. This is an important country for English trade. Many English merchants sell their goods here.

France
England and Spain are at war with France. It is a powerful country and it is friendly with Scotland. England and France have been enemies for centuries. They have fought many wars. France is a Roman Catholic country but Protestant ideas are spreading in some areas.

Spain
Spain is the wealthiest and most powerful European country. As well as ruling other lands in Europe, it controls a large empire in Central and South America. It is a strong Roman Catholic country and an enemy of France.

England and Spain have been friendly for most of the sixteenth century. Mary Tudor, Elizabeth's sister, was married to King Philip II of Spain. Now he hopes to marry Elizabeth.

The Pope
The Pope is head of the Roman Catholic Church. He lives in Rome. Catholics all over Europe are expected to obey him.

SOURCE 1 Europe in 1558

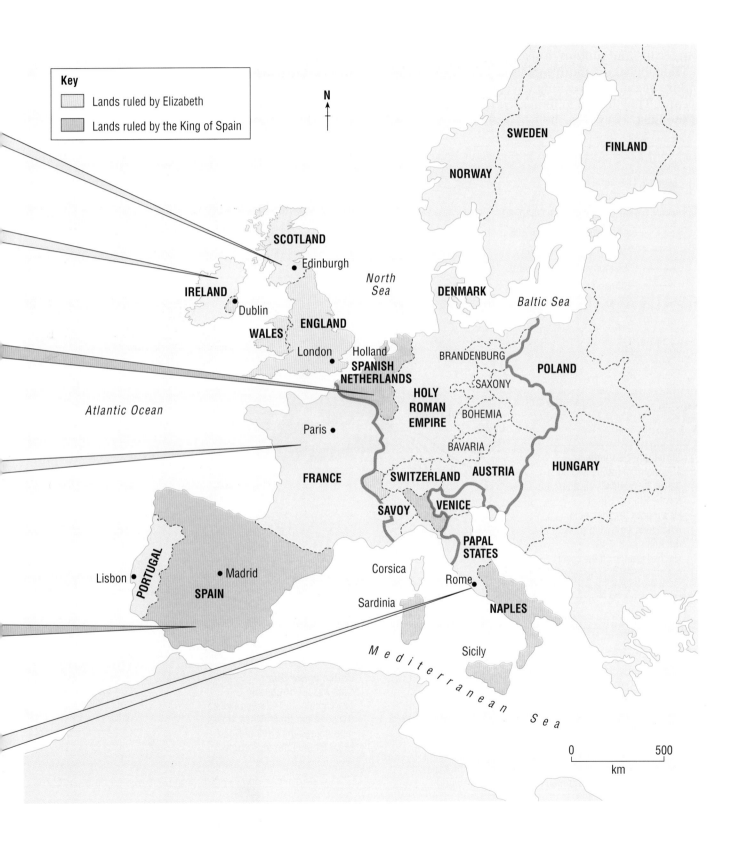

Key

Lands ruled by Elizabeth

Lands ruled by the King of Spain

N

SWEDEN

FINLAND

NORWAY

SCOTLAND

● Edinburgh

North Sea

DENMARK

Baltic Sea

IRELAND

● Dublin

ENGLAND

WALES

London ●   Holland

SPANISH NETHERLANDS

BRANDENBURG

POLAND

SAXONY

Atlantic Ocean

HOLY ROMAN EMPIRE

BOHEMIA

Paris ●

BAVARIA

FRANCE

SWITZERLAND   AUSTRIA   HUNGARY

SAVOY   VENICE

PAPAL STATES

Corsica

Rome ●

PORTUGAL

Lisbon ●   ● Madrid

Sardinia   NAPLES

SPAIN

M e d i t e r r a n e a n   S e a

Sicily

0   500

km

Why did Elizabethans go on overseas voyages?

DURING THE MIDDLE Ages Europeans knew little about the rest of the world. Valuable silks and spices were brought overland to Europe from India and China, but sailors did not dare sail into dangerous and unknown seas.

Then, between about 1430 and 1530, European sailors began making long voyages across the oceans. They hoped to find a sea route to the riches of the East. They were helped in their voyages by:

- the invention of new navigational instruments, such as the compass
- the development of fast, light ships called caravels and carracks. They had triangular 'lateen' sails which could be easily turned to catch the strong sideways winds of the open seas
- the invention of guns
- money and encouragement from kings and wealthy merchants.

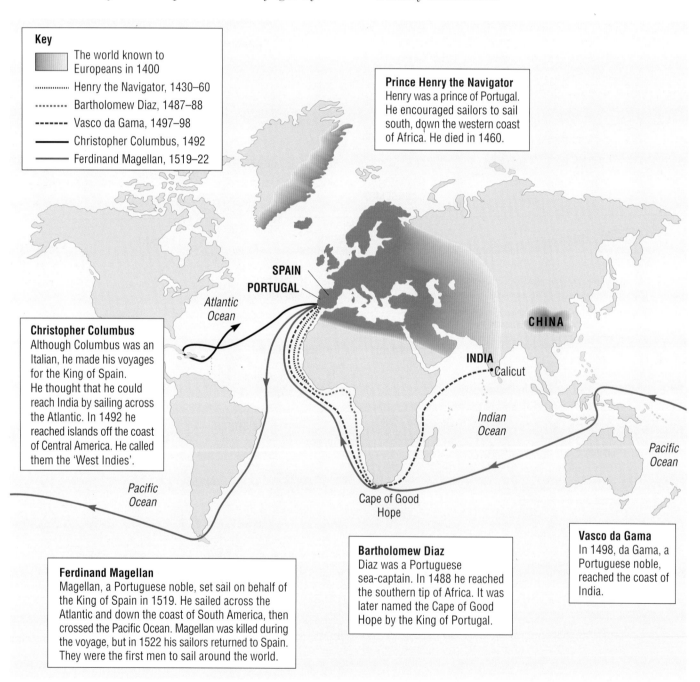

Key

- The world known to Europeans in 1400
- .... Henry the Navigator, 1430–60
- -------- Bartholomew Diaz, 1487–88
- ------ Vasco da Gama, 1497–98
- —— Christopher Columbus, 1492
- —— Ferdinand Magellan, 1519–22

Prince Henry the Navigator
Henry was a prince of Portugal. He encouraged sailors to sail south, down the western coast of Africa. He died in 1460.

Christopher Columbus
Although Columbus was an Italian, he made his voyages for the King of Spain. He thought that he could reach India by sailing across the Atlantic. In 1492 he reached islands off the coast of Central America. He called them the 'West Indies'.

Ferdinand Magellan
Magellan, a Portuguese noble, set sail on behalf of the King of Spain in 1519. He sailed across the Atlantic and down the coast of South America, then crossed the Pacific Ocean. Magellan was killed during the voyage, but in 1522 his sailors returned to Spain. They were the first men to sail around the world.

Bartholomew Diaz
Diaz was a Portuguese sea-captain. In 1488 he reached the southern tip of Africa. It was later named the Cape of Good Hope by the King of Portugal.

Vasco da Gama
In 1498, da Gama, a Portuguese noble, reached the coast of India.

SOURCE 1 European voyages of exploration, 1430–1530

1. Why did European sailors want to reach India?
2. Why did Columbus think that he could reach India by sailing across the Atlantic Ocean?
3. Which voyage was the most important?
4. Historians used to call this period 'The Age of Discovery'. Is 'discovery' a good word to describe the arrival of European sailors in parts of the world they had never seen before?

Spain and Portugal led the way in making these voyages. By 1550 Spain controlled a large EMPIRE in Central and South America. Every year ships full of silver and gold sailed for Spain from the 'New World'. Portugal also gained great wealth by establishing trading bases in India and around the coast of Africa.

During Elizabeth's reign many English seamen made overseas voyages. In this enquiry you will investigate why they went on such dangerous voyages – and how successful they were.

Why were Elizabethan sailors encouraged to go on overseas voyages?

Before 1550 few English people were interested in making long voyages of exploration. Most of the country's trade was with Europe. Then, in the 1550s, the cloth trade with Europe collapsed. Merchants needed to find new markets in which to sell their goods. More people became interested in voyages overseas.

This interest gathered pace during Elizabeth's reign. One man, Richard Hakluyt, wrote a book to encourage English sailors to make long voyages. He called it *The Principal Navigations, Voyages and Discoveries of the English Nation.*

5. Why did interest in making voyages grow in England after 1550?

■ TASK

1. What did Hakluyt think England would gain from overseas voyages?
2. What did he think people who lived in other parts of the world would gain from them?
3. Hakluyt did not actually go on any overseas voyages. Is Source 2, therefore, of no use to the historian?

SOURCE 2 Extract from Hakluyt's *Principal Navigations,* 1589

❝ *By these voyages our navy shall be enlarged. The Kings of Spain and Portugal, since the first discovery of the Indies, have greatly enriched themselves and their subjects, but have also trebled the number of their ships, masters and mariners.*

The greatest strength of this realm for defence and offence is the multitude of ships ready to assist the most stately and royal navy of Her Majesty, which by reason of this voyage shall have both increase and maintenance.

If our nation were once planted in North America, whereas we now fish for but two months of the year, we might then fish as long as we please.

All savages, so soon as they begin to taste of civilisation, will take marvellous delight in any garment – as a shirt, a gown, a cap, or such like. What a market for our English clothes will follow and great benefit to clothiers, woolmen, spinners, weavers, etc.

It will prove a general benefit unto our country, that a great number of men which do now live idly at home and are a burden, shall hereby be set to work, but also children of twelve or fourteen years of age, or older, may be kept from idleness, in making a thousand kinds of things which will be good merchandise. And, our idle women shall also be employed.

The savages shall have cause to bless the hour when this enterprise was undertaken. Firstly and chiefly, in respect of the most happy and gladsome tidings of the most glorious Gospel of our Saviour, Jesus Christ, whereby they may be brought from falsehood to truth. Being brought from brutish ignorance to civilisation and knowledge, and made to understand how the tenth part of their land may be so manured and worked, as it may yield more commodities [crops] as the whole now doth. But that is not all the benefit which they shall receive; they shall be reduced from unseemly customs to honest manners, from disordered riotous routs to a well governed COMMONWEALTH. ❞

How successful were the voyages of English seamen?

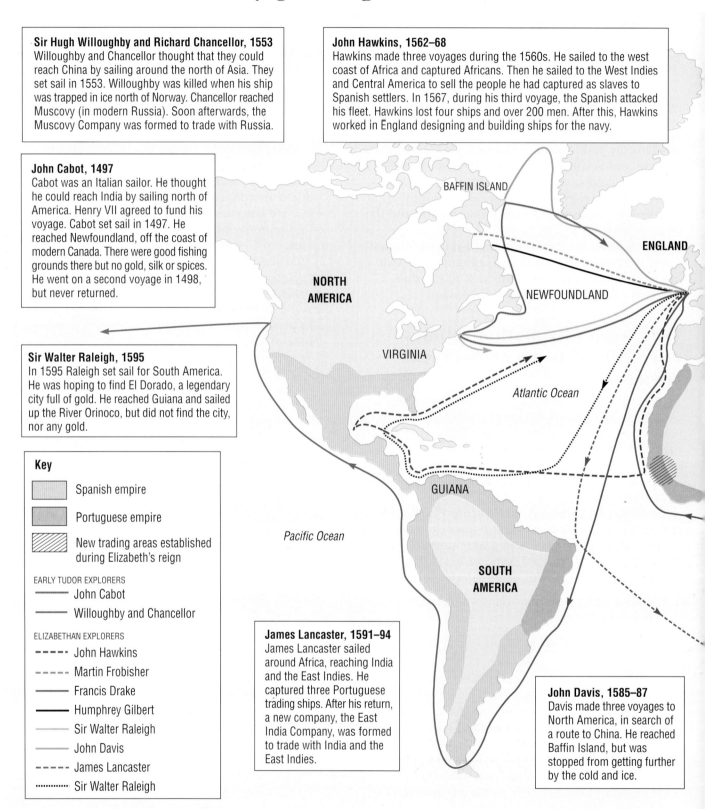

Sir Hugh Willoughby and Richard Chancellor, 1553
Willoughby and Chancellor thought that they could reach China by sailing around the north of Asia. They set sail in 1553. Willoughby was killed when his ship was trapped in ice north of Norway. Chancellor reached Muscovy (in modern Russia). Soon afterwards, the Muscovy Company was formed to trade with Russia.

John Hawkins, 1562–68
Hawkins made three voyages during the 1560s. He sailed to the west coast of Africa and captured Africans. Then he sailed to the West Indies and Central America to sell the people he had captured as slaves to Spanish settlers. In 1567, during his third voyage, the Spanish attacked his fleet. Hawkins lost four ships and over 200 men. After this, Hawkins worked in England designing and building ships for the navy.

John Cabot, 1497
Cabot was an Italian sailor. He thought he could reach India by sailing north of America. Henry VII agreed to fund his voyage. Cabot set sail in 1497. He reached Newfoundland, off the coast of modern Canada. There were good fishing grounds there but no gold, silk or spices. He went on a second voyage in 1498, but never returned.

Sir Walter Raleigh, 1595
In 1595 Raleigh set sail for South America. He was hoping to find El Dorado, a legendary city full of gold. He reached Guiana and sailed up the River Orinoco, but did not find the city, nor any gold.

Key

- Spanish empire
- Portuguese empire
- New trading areas established during Elizabeth's reign

EARLY TUDOR EXPLORERS
- John Cabot
- Willoughby and Chancellor

ELIZABETHAN EXPLORERS
- John Hawkins
- Martin Frobisher
- Francis Drake
- Humphrey Gilbert
- Sir Walter Raleigh
- John Davis
- James Lancaster
- Sir Walter Raleigh

James Lancaster, 1591–94
James Lancaster sailed around Africa, reaching India and the East Indies. He captured three Portuguese trading ships. After his return, a new company, the East India Company, was formed to trade with India and the East Indies.

John Davis, 1585–87
Davis made three voyages to North America, in search of a route to China. He reached Baffin Island, but was stopped from getting further by the cold and ice.

BAFFIN ISLAND
ENGLAND
NORTH AMERICA
NEWFOUNDLAND
VIRGINIA
Atlantic Ocean
GUIANA
Pacific Ocean
SOUTH AMERICA

SOURCE 3 English voyages of exploration in the sixteenth century

Martin Frobisher, 1576
Frobisher believed that it was possible to reach China by sailing around North America. In 1576, he reached Baffin Island in the Arctic. He found a black rock, which he hoped would contain gold – but he was wrong. He made two more voyages but each time was forced back by the cold and ice.

Francis Drake, 1577–80
In 1577 Francis Drake set sail to attack Spanish settlements in Central America. He sailed around South America and attacked Spanish towns in Mexico, capturing gold, silver and jewels. He returned to England by sailing across the Pacific and Indian Oceans and then up the west coast of Africa. Drake became the first Englishman to sail around the world. He made a large profit from the voyage.

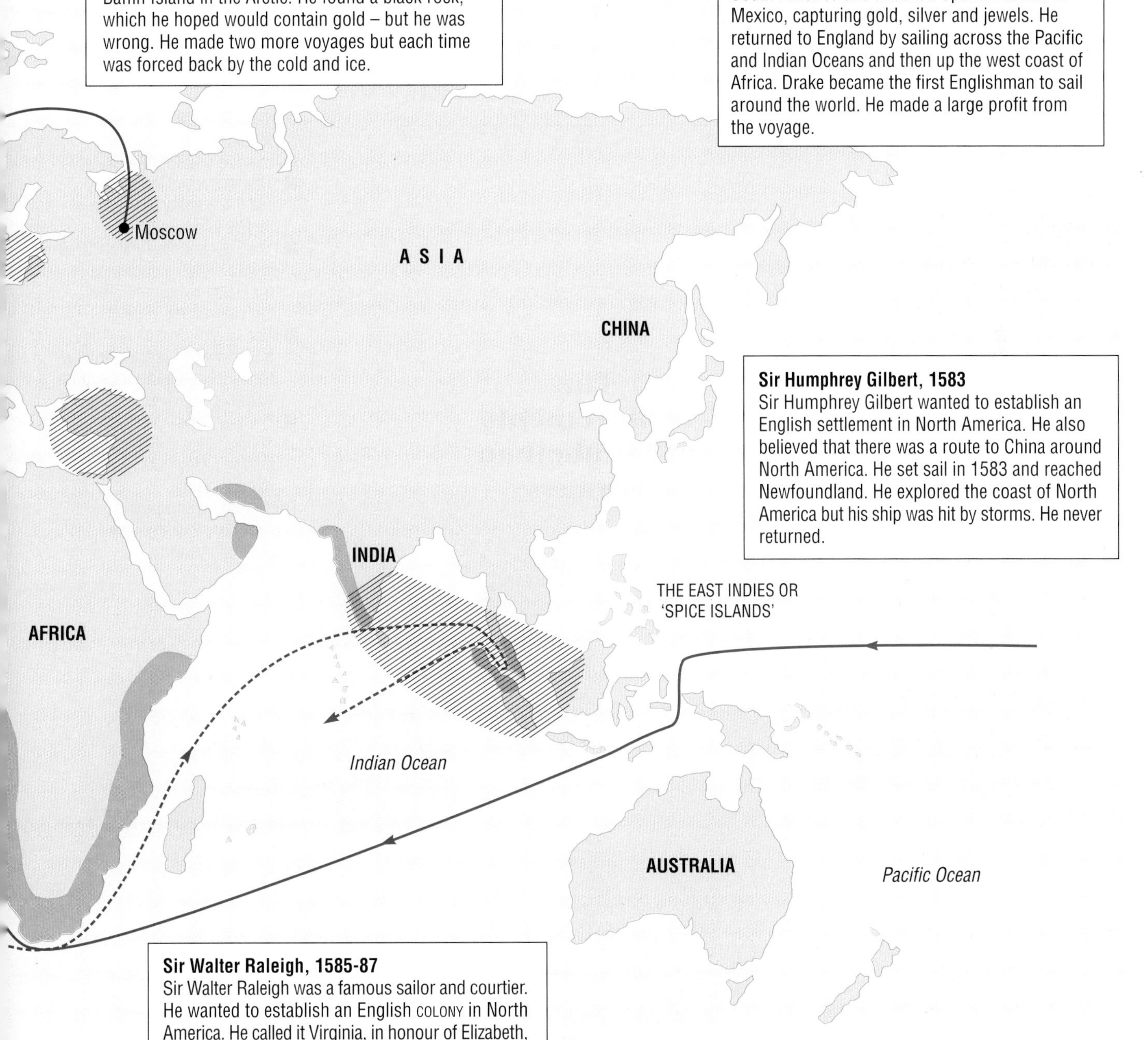

Moscow

A S I A

CHINA

Sir Humphrey Gilbert, 1583
Sir Humphrey Gilbert wanted to establish an English settlement in North America. He also believed that there was a route to China around North America. He set sail in 1583 and reached Newfoundland. He explored the coast of North America but his ship was hit by storms. He never returned.

INDIA

THE EAST INDIES OR 'SPICE ISLANDS'

AFRICA

Indian Ocean

AUSTRALIA

Pacific Ocean

Sir Walter Raleigh, 1585-87
Sir Walter Raleigh was a famous sailor and courtier. He wanted to establish an English COLONY in North America. He called it Virginia, in honour of Elizabeth, the Virgin Queen. He organised two expeditions to take settlers to the colony. The first settlers came home after one year. The second group were never seen again.

■ ACTIVITY

You are planning a long overseas voyage. As a class, make a list of all the different kinds of people, equipment and supplies you will need. Your teacher will help you.

As Source 3 on pages 116–117 shows, English seamen sailed all over the world during Elizabeth's reign. Many of their voyages were failures. They were expensive, and many sailors lost their lives. They also caused trouble with Spain, which eventually led to a long and costly war. So, were the voyages worth it? What did they achieve?

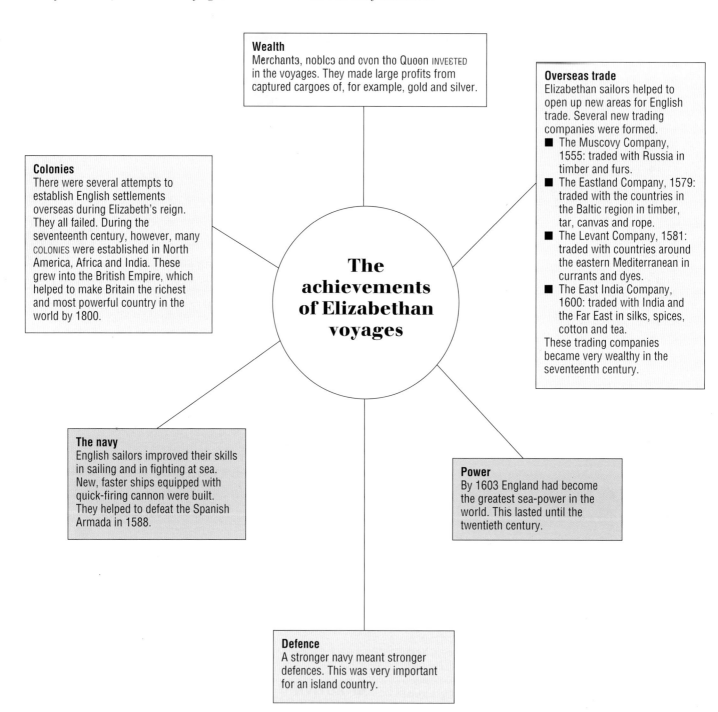

Wealth
Merchants, nobles and even the Queen INVESTED in the voyages. They made large profits from captured cargoes of, for example, gold and silver.

Overseas trade
Elizabethan sailors helped to open up new areas for English trade. Several new trading companies were formed.
- The Muscovy Company, 1555: traded with Russia in timber and furs.
- The Eastland Company, 1579: traded with the countries in the Baltic region in timber, tar, canvas and rope.
- The Levant Company, 1581: traded with countries around the eastern Mediterranean in currants and dyes.
- The East India Company, 1600: traded with India and the Far East in silks, spices, cotton and tea.
These trading companies became very wealthy in the seventeenth century.

Colonies
There were several attempts to establish English settlements overseas during Elizabeth's reign. They all failed. During the seventeenth century, however, many COLONIES were established in North America, Africa and India. These grew into the British Empire, which helped to make Britain the richest and most powerful country in the world by 1800.

The achievements of Elizabethan voyages

The navy
English sailors improved their skills in sailing and in fighting at sea. New, faster ships equipped with quick-firing cannon were built. They helped to defeat the Spanish Armada in 1588.

Power
By 1603 England had become the greatest sea-power in the world. This lasted until the twentieth century.

Defence
A stronger navy meant stronger defences. This was very important for an island country.

SOURCE 4 The achievements of Elizabethan voyages

■ ACTIVITY

It is 1603. Richard Hakluyt is planning an introduction for a new edition of his book (see Source 2, page 115). He has been thinking back over the overseas voyages of Elizabeth's reign. In the new introduction he will explain how satisfied he is with:

■ the number of voyages that were made
■ what these voyages achieved.

What will he write?

■ TASK

1. Study Source 3. Make a list of the difficulties and dangers sailors faced in making these voyages. Give one example for each item on your list.
2. Make a copy of the table below. Using the information in Source 3 complete the table by:

■ giving examples of each type of voyage
■ explaining how successful they were.

English voyages of exploration in the sixteenth century

Aims of the voyages	Examples	How successful the voyages were and why
To find a northerly sea route to India or China		
To trade and bring back riches		
To attack Spanish settlements in Central America		
To establish English settlements overseas (colonies)		

3. a) Which types of voyage were the most successful and why?
b) Which types of voyage were unsuccessful? What reasons can you suggest for their failure?
4. What do you think was the most important achievement of all these voyages? Explain the reasons for your answer.

Francis Drake: hero or villain?

> 66 *A brave and a brilliant sailor who almost singlehandedly challenged the might of Spain, the most powerful country in the world. One of the greatest figures in English history.* 99

> 66 *A pirate and a thief who should have been hanged for his crimes.* 99

THESE TWO DESCRIPTIONS seem to be about two very different men. In fact, they both refer to Francis Drake, the most famous seaman of Elizabeth's reign. In this enquiry we will try to uncover the truth about Drake and help you to reach your own conclusions about him. We will focus mainly on his world voyage of 1577–80. Was Francis Drake a hero or a villain? Why has his career been interpreted in such different ways?

SOURCE 1 A portrait of Francis Drake, painted in 1581 by Nicholas Hilliard

Drake's early career

Francis Drake was born in Devon in 1542. His father was a farmer and a strong Protestant. In 1549 there was a Catholic rebellion in Devon. Drake's family were threatened and decided to move. They settled in Gillingham, near a new dockyard on the River Medway in Kent. Drake became interested in sailing. He grew up as a Puritan who hated Catholics.

He went on his first voyage in 1566, with Captain John Lovell. They captured 90 Africans and then sailed to the West Indies (part of the Spanish Empire). There, they sold the Africans as slaves, even though the King of Spain did not allow foreigners to trade with his colonies.

Drake then sailed with his cousin, John Hawkins, to sell slaves to Spanish settlers. In 1568 their ships were attacked at San Juan de Ulua in Mexico. Hawkins lost four ships and over 300 men. Drake, Hawkins and about 70 men returned to England. Drake was thirsting for revenge.

Relations between England and Spain got worse (see pages 129–130). In 1572 Drake sailed to Central America with two ships and 100 sailors. He knew that Spanish ships were loaded with gold from Mexico and silver from Peru at a town called Nombre de Dios. Drake attacked and captured the town. He seized silver worth £20,000 (about £30 million today). About 40 of his men were killed. Drake returned to England a rich and famous man. Secretly, he began planning another voyage ...

SOURCE 2 The Spanish Empire in Central America

SOURCE 3 A Spanish view of Drake

> 66 *The master thief of the New World.* 99

1. Explain why Francis Drake:
a) became interested in sailing
b) hated Catholics
c) hated Spain.
2. How do you think Drake would have replied to the view expressed about him in Source 3?

Case study: Drake's world voyage, 1577–80

This case study focuses on Drake's longest and most famous voyage. You will be investigating why Drake went on it, what happened during the voyage and how successful it was. This study will also help you to understand the difficulties and dangers that sixteenth-century seamen faced when they went on long voyages.

Drake's motives

Drake's next voyage began in great secrecy. Even his sailors did not know where they were going. The Queen knew that Drake's activities were causing trouble with Spain; and she did not want a war. Even so, she and several courtiers invested in the voyage.

Drake appears to have had several aims.

■ He still wanted revenge for the Spanish attack on Hawkins' fleet in 1568. He planned to attack Spanish settlements in Central America from the Pacific Ocean, where the Spanish had few defences.

■ He wanted to capture gold, silver and other riches. He would become wealthier and make profits for the people who had financed the voyage.

■ As a Puritan, Drake wanted to cause damage to Spain because it was the most powerful Roman Catholic country in the world.

■ He hoped to find new lands to claim for the Queen. This would make the country more powerful and provide English merchants with new opportunities for trade. Several merchants helped to finance the voyage.

3. Why do you think Drake kept his plans so secret?
4. Why could Drake claim that he had the Queen's approval for the voyage?

SOURCE 4 An extract from an account given to the Spanish government after the voyage, by a Spaniard who had been captured by Drake

66 *Drake said 'The Queen ordered me to come to these parts. It is thus that I am acting. I am not going to stop until I have collected the two millions that my cousin, John Hawkins, lost at San Juan de Ulua.'* 99

How do we know about the voyage?

Our knowledge of past events depends on sources surviving from the time. Log-books are the most important source for finding out about sixteenth-century voyages. Sea captains wrote them rather like diaries – as accurate, detailed records of their voyages. Drake's log-book has not survived. The following people are our main sources for this voyage.

■ **John Drake** was Francis Drake's cousin. He went on the voyage but was later captured by the Spanish. They forced him to tell them about the voyage.

■ **John Cooke** sailed with the voyage. He wrote an account about it when he returned to England. He disliked Francis Drake.

■ **Sir Francis Drake** was Drake's nephew. He did not go on the voyage. He wrote a book called *The World Encompassed* for the Queen in 1592, although it was not published until 1628. His book was probably based on his uncle's notebook.

■ **Richard Hakluyt** (see page 115) wrote an account of the voyage in his book *Principal Navigations* (1589). He did not go on the voyage but he interviewed several sailors who did, and these probably included Drake himself.

■ **Spanish prisoners** who were captured by Drake during the voyage. When they returned to Spain they were interviewed by government officials.

■ TASK 1

Before historians reach their conclusions, they must consider how reliable their sources are. How reliable, do you think, are the sources about Drake's voyage? Make a copy of the table below to record your ideas.

Historians' sources for Drake's world voyage

Source	Good points	Bad points

■ TASK 2

Make a large copy of the table below. As you follow the story of the voyage, keep a record of the problems that Drake and his crew faced.

Drake's world voyage, 1577–80: difficulties and dangers

Problem	Examples		
	Date:	Place:	What happened:

What happened during the voyage?

In November 1577 Drake was ready to set sail. His fleet left Plymouth on 15 November. It soon ran into difficulties and returned to Plymouth. Drake set sail again on 13 December.

SOURCE 5 A sixteenth-century drawing of the *Pelican*, Drake's flagship. It was later renamed the *Golden Hind*

SOURCE 6 An extract from *The World Encompassed*, written by Drake's nephew, 1628

66 *He had fitted himself with 5 ships:*

1. *The* Pelican, *admiral, 80 tons, Captain-General Francis Drake*
2. *The* Elizabeth, *vice-admiral, 80 tons, Captain John Winter*
3. *The* Marigold, *a* BARK *of 30 tons, Captain John Thomas*
4. *The* Swan, *a* FLYBOAT *of 50 tons, Captain John Chester*
5. *The* Christopher, *a* PINNACE *of 15 tons, Captain Thomas Moore*

These ships he manned with 164 able and sufficient men, and furnished them also with such plentiful provision of all things necessary, as so long and dangerous a voyage did seem to require.

He set sail out of Plymouth about 5 o'clock in the afternoon, November 15. Running all that night south-west, by morning he came to the Lizard [Lizard Point in Cornwall]. The next day towards evening there arose a storm, continuing all that night and the following day with such violence that two of his ships, the admiral [Pelican] and the Marigold, *had their masts damaged. For the repairing of them, and many other damages in the tempest sustained, they bore back to Plymouth again.* 99

The coast of Africa and across the Atlantic, December 1577–April 1578

The fleet sailed south along the west coast of Africa to the Cape Verde Islands. There they captured a Portuguese ship and its cargo of wine. They took it with them across the Atlantic Ocean. As they approached the Equator they faced new problems and the crew began to quarrel.

SOURCE 7 An extract from an account by John Cooke, who sailed on the *Elizabeth*

66 *We met with adverse winds, unwelcome storms and less welcome calms. Being in the burning zone we felt the effects of sultry heat.* 99

The east coast of South America, April–August 1578

In April 1578 the fleet reached the coast of Brazil. As they sailed further south, more quarrels broke out. On 20 June the fleet anchored at Port St Julian. Some of the crew went ashore to trade. They were attacked by local people and two men were killed. The quarrels got worse. Drake's friend, Sir Thomas Doughty, was accused of MUTINY and put on trial. He was found guilty and executed.

Drake decided to put all his men and stores on to his three best ships. The others were burnt. Drake gave the *Pelican* a new name. He called it the *Golden Hind*, the emblem of Sir Christopher Hatton who had invested in the voyage. The fleet sailed on. On 21 August they entered the Strait of Magellan.

■ ACTIVITY

It is September 1578. The fleet has just sailed through the Strait of Magellan. Drake is alone in his cabin, thinking about how successful the voyage has been so far. Write his thoughts as an entry in his log-book.

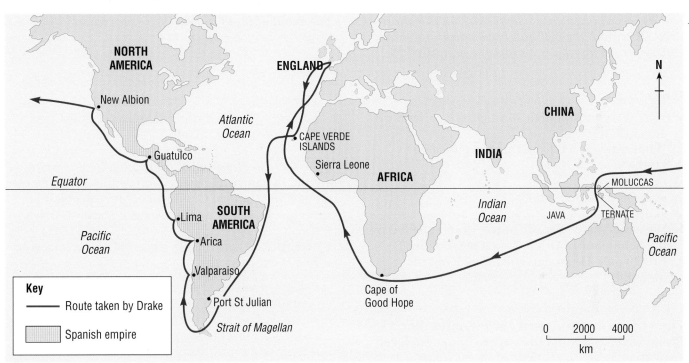

$\mathcal{S}$OURCE 8 Drake's world voyage, 1577–80

$\mathcal{S}$OURCE 9 An account by Pedro Sarmiento, a Spanish prisoner

&&*He went to the island of Mocha which is inhabited by Indians, and landed to get water. But the Indians attacked him and killed his pilot and surgeon and wounded nine or ten. The chief (Drake) was wounded by arrows, one of which entered his head, the other his face. There was one man who received twenty-five arrow wounds, another [received] twenty-three.*''

Attacking Spanish settlements, September 1578–April 1579

In early September 1578 the three surviving ships entered the Pacific Ocean. Then they were hit by bad storms which lasted for over one month. The *Marigold* sank. The *Elizabeth* got lost and sailed back to England. The *Golden Hind* was alone and short of food and water. It sailed north and landed on an island (see Source 9).

After treating the wounded, Drake sailed north. He attacked several Spanish settlements. Each time, the Spanish were taken by surprise. At Valparaiso, Drake's men captured supplies of wine, gold and Spanish coins. At Arica they seized 57 ingots (blocks) of silver. In February 1579 Drake reached Callao, the port that served Lima (the capital of Peru). He attacked twelve ships in the harbour, capturing large quantities of silk and Spanish coins. Then he heard that the *Cacafuego*, a Spanish treasure ship, had set sail a few days earlier. He chased after it and captured its valuable cargo (see the Source Investigation on page 126). Then he attacked Guatulco, capturing more silver, gold and jewels.

123

SOURCE 10 An account of Drake's attack on Guatulco, by the Alcade [Mayor] of Guatulco, 1580

❝ *In the month of April on Monday of Holy Week at about noon, two vessels entered the port. Twenty or twenty-five men came ashore. No one at this time knew who they were until a sailor cried out 'The English! The English!' More English jumped ashore with guns, swords and shields. No one remained with me so I went to the wood near the church. I stayed there for about three or four hours during which time the Englishmen sacked the port.*

Then I went to the church and found it robbed of all its sacred vestments. The picture on the altar was destroyed, the bell had been stolen and other offences and sacrileges had been committed. ❞

SOURCE 11 An extract from an interview with one of Drake's men, in Richard Hakluyt's *Principal Navigations*, 1589

❝ *When we set sail again we had a bad wind and we found the course very dangerous among the islands, so our ship and our lives were in great danger. On 9 January 1580 we ran suddenly upon a rock where we stuck fast from 8 at night until 4 the next afternoon, losing all hope. But our General, with his courage and hope in God, made us do our best to save ourselves. God blessed our efforts and the wind changed and the happy gale drove our ship off the rocks. So we cleared ourselves of the danger.* ❞

5. Why were the Spanish so surprised by Drake's attacks?
6. What can you tell from these events about Drake's:
   a) personality?
   b) skills as a commander?
   c) skills as a sailor?
7. Why was the writer of Source 10 so appalled by the behaviour of Drake's men at Guatulco?
8. How would Drake have justified what his men did?

9. According to the author of Source 11 how was the *Golden Hind* saved?

The *Golden Hind* sailed on to Java to take on more supplies. Then Drake sailed across the Indian Ocean and past the Cape of Good Hope. More problems arose as they sailed up the western coast of Africa.

SOURCE 12 John Drake's account of the journey around the African coast

❝ *They found themselves reduced to three pipes of water and half a pipe of wine. There were 59 persons on board. When they arrived in sight of Sierra Leone, all the water on board was portioned out and for every three men there was not more than half a pint remaining. If they had been delayed two or three days longer, they would have died of thirst.* ❞

The voyage home, April 1579–September 1580

Drake began planning the voyage home. He faced Spanish attacks if he sailed south, back towards the Strait of Magellan. He wanted to find a route back to England around North America. He landed his prisoners in Mexico and then sailed north.

In July 1579 the *Golden Hind* anchored in a bay, somewhere near the modern city of San Francisco. Drake claimed the land for Queen Elizabeth and called it 'New Albion'. The native peoples thought Drake was a god. They gave him gifts of feathers and tobacco. Drake took supplies of food and water on board and set sail across the Pacific Ocean.

Two months later they landed on the Molucca Islands. The local people were friendly and allowed Drake to take supplies of food and water on board. Then Drake sailed on to another island, Ternate, where spices grew. He made a treaty with the King which allowed English merchants to trade with the island. Seven tons of cloves, ginger and pepper were loaded on board. Soon after the *Golden Hind* set sail, disaster struck ...

After landing to take on water Drake sailed on. The *Golden Hind* landed at Plymouth on 26 September 1580. Drake asked if Queen Elizabeth was still alive.

■ **TASK 1**

Your teacher will give you a larger copy of the map on page 123. Find out when Drake reached each of the places shown on the map and what happened there. Write the date and a brief explanation of what happened in the boxes around the map.

S OURCE 13 A modern replica of the *Golden Hind*, built to commemorate the 400th anniversary of Drake's voyage. It sailed to California in 1975. The original ship rotted and was broken up in the seventeenth century

10. Which is the more useful source about the *Golden Hind* – Source 5 (page 122) or Source 13?

What were the results of the voyage?

Drake was now a national hero. He was the first Englishman to sail around the world. He had launched successful attacks on the Spanish Empire, and other sailors soon followed his example. He had brought back gold, silver and jewels worth about £140,000 (about £200 million today). Drake himself made £10,000. The rest was paid to his investors. They received £40 for every £1 they had lent him. Drake had claimed new lands for England and made valuable trading contacts with the Spice Islands.

Philip II of Spain was furious with Drake. Elizabeth was delighted. In 1581 she knighted him on board the *Golden Hind* in London. Soon afterwards she made him an admiral.

TASK 2

Drake had several aims when he set off on his voyage in 1577 (see page 121).

1. How successful was he in achieving each of his aims?
2. Did the voyage have any unexpected results?
3. Why was Elizabeth so pleased with the voyage?

S OURCE 14 A portrait of Sir Francis Drake, painted in the 1580s by Jodocus Hondius. His hand is on a knight's helmet and there is a globe in the background

11. Why has the artist shown a helmet and a globe in Source 14?
12. Do you think that the artist was English? Why?

■ SOURCE INVESTIGATION

The attack on the *Cacafuego*

SOURCE 15 John Drake's account of the attack

66 *We first saw the ship at a distance of about nine miles. Drake pretended not to chase her – so he could capture her more easily. He slowed down, lowered the sails and hid the ship's boat on the far side of the ship.*

At dusk, the Spanish ship came towards him. Drake made some of the Spanish prisoners call out 'This ship belongs to Miguel Angel'. Then San Juan de Anton [the Captain of the Cacafuego*] called out 'It can't be. That ship was left empty at Callao. Surrender in the name of the King of Spain.'*

Drake said 'You surrender in the name of the Queen of England!' And he fired a cannon shot which destroyed the mizzen [rear] mast. San Juan was wounded by an arrow and he surrendered. And so we captured the ship. We found a certain quantity of jewels and precious stones, thirteen chests of coins, 80 pounds weight of gold, 26 tons of silver and two very fair gilt silver drinking bowls. 99

SOURCE 16 An extract from the report of San Juan de Anton, the Captain of the *Cacafuego*, to the King of Spain

66 *About 9 o'clock the English ship crossed in front of us. I thought she was from Chile and so I went to the side of my ship. At that the English began to attack us, shouting 'We're English! Strike sail!' I answered, 'I won't take orders from Englishmen. Come and strike the sails yourselves.' Then they blew a whistle and a trumpet. They fired a volley from about 60 muskets and then a shower of arrows. A cannon fired shot which knocked out our mizzen mast and sails. The English fired another large gun. At the same time their boat came up with 40 archers. They climbed up the side of our ship. Men were swarming across from the English pirate ship.*

Our ship did not carry cannon or guns and so I could not resist. I was forced to surrender and was taken to the English ship. Here I saw the pirate Francis Drake who was taking off his helmet and armour. He greeted me and said 'Have patience. This sort of thing happens in war.' He ordered me to be locked up in his cabin which was guarded by twelve men. On the next calm days, Drake used the ship's boat to transfer all the ship's treasure. He kept all the Spanish prisoners in his own ship. 99

Caca Fogo.   Caca Plata.

SOURCE 17 A drawing of the *Golden Hind* attacking the *Cacafuego*, drawn in 1603. The *Golden Hind* is on the right

1. On what points do Sources 15 and 16 agree?
2. On what points do they disagree?
3. What details does John Drake (Source 15) include in his account that San Juan de Anton (Source 16) does not mention? Suggest the most likely reasons why Drake mentioned them and San Juan did not.
4. What details does the Spanish Captain include in his account that Drake does not mention? Suggest the most likely reasons for this.
5. Does Source 17 help your understanding of what happened?
6. Using evidence from these three sources, write your own account of the capture of the *Cacafuego* under these headings:

   ■ how the two ships met
   ■ how the attack began
   ■ the fighting
   ■ how the *Cacafuego* was captured
   ■ the results of its capture.

■ SOURCE INVESTIGATION

Was Drake a good captain?

Before we continue with our enquiry into Drake's career, we will investigate what kind of captain he was. Did he treat his men well? How did he treat his prisoners? Your answers to these questions will be important for your overall conclusions about him.

1. Choose words and phrases from the list below which best describe what Drake was like. Support each of your choices with evidence from Sources 18–20.

   brave; cowardly; strong; weak; tall; short; a good sailor; a bad sailor; kind; cruel; fair; strict; favoured his friends; treated everyone equally; popular; unpopular; honest; dishonest; greedy; generous; religious; not religious; arrogant; listened to his men's views; took no notice of his men's views.

2. Sources 19 and 20 are taken from accounts given by Drake's prisoners after the voyage.
   a) Are they good sources for finding out about Drake?
   b) Would accounts by Drake's sailors be more useful? Explain the reasons for your answers.

■ ACTIVITY

Write a job description for a sixteenth-century sea-captain. Think about what he would have to do and the kind of personal qualities he would need.

SOURCE 18 An extract from an account by Nuno de Silva, made in 1579 after he was captured by the Spanish. De Silva was a Portuguese pilot who had helped Drake

66 *The Englishman calls himself Francis Drake and is aged about 38. He is low in stature [not very tall], thickset [muscular] and very robust. He has a fine appearance, is ruddy of complexion [healthy-looking] and has a fair beard. He has the mark of an arrow in his right cheek and in one leg he has a musket-ball from when he was shot in the Indies. He is a great mariner.* 99

SOURCE 19 An account by Francisco de Zarate, a Spanish prisoner, 1579

66 *He treats his men with affection and they treat him with respect. Even the young sailors form part of his council which he calls together for even the most trivial matter. Although he takes advice from no one, he enjoys hearing what they say and afterwards issues his orders. He has no favourites. He shows his men great favour, but he punishes the least fault. I managed to find out whether the General was well liked, and his men said that they adored him.*

Drake sits at a table with a Portuguese pilot whom he brought from England, who spoke not a word all the time while I was on board. Drake is served on silver dishes with gold borders. He said many of these had been given to him by the Queen. Of that which belonged to me he took but little. Indeed he was quite courteous. Certain trifles [worthless things] of mine having taken his fancy, he had them brought to his ship and gave me in exchange a sword and a small silver tray. On his return to the vessel he asked me to pardon him for taking them, but they were for his wife. The next morning he gave back to some of the passengers their boxes and having called all our sailors together, he gave them each a handful of silver coins. He also gave the same to some other men who appeared to him to be the most needy. 99

SOURCE 20 An account by the Factor of Guatulco, another Spaniard captured by Drake, 1580

66 *Francis Drake had a table placed on deck and, at its head on the floor, a small box and an embroidered cushion. He then sent for a book of the lives of the saints, and nine Englishmen, with nine small books, joined him and seated themselves around the table. Then Drake crossed his hands and, kneeling on the cushions and small box, lifted his eyes to heaven for about a quarter of an hour. He then said to me and the other prisoners that if we wanted to recite the psalms according to his method we could stay, but if not, we could go to the prow [front of the ship]. As we stood up to go he said that we were to keep quiet. Then he began reading the psalms in the English language of which I understood nothing. This lasted for about an hour. Then they brought four viols and cried out and sang songs together. Then a boy danced and with that the service ended.* 99

What did Drake do after his world voyage?

War broke out between England and Spain in 1585. Elizabeth put Drake in charge of an expedition to attack the West Indies. He sailed with 30 ships and 2300 men. He captured two towns and returned home with £30,000 and nearly 250 Spanish cannon.

In 1587 he was ordered to attack the Spanish port of Cadiz. The Armada, a huge invasion fleet, was being prepared there. Drake attacked the harbour and destroyed 24 Spanish ships. He boasted that he had 'singed the King of Spain's beard'.

The Armada set sail to attack England in 1588. Drake was made Vice-Admiral of the English navy (see pages 131–143).

After 1588 Drake's career was not so successful. In 1589 he attacked Lisbon but he failed to capture the town or any riches, and 11,000 of his men died of disease. In 1595 the Queen ordered him to attack the West Indies again. The attack failed and Drake died of yellow fever in January 1596. He was 53 years old. His body was buried at sea in a lead coffin off the coast of Mexico.

SOURCE 21 A Spanish book illustration, 1598. Drake is shown as a dragon, Spain is represented by an eagle. The caption means: 'Finally the eagle wins'

■ **TALKING POINT**

Drake was in the news again in 1995. To mark the 400th anniversary of his death, a group of English people planned to recover his body and bury it in England. Other people protested. Why do you think this idea was controversial?

■ **ACTIVITY**

Work in groups of four and split into pairs. It is March 1596. The news of Drake's death has just reached Europe. You have been asked to write Drake's obituary. One pair should write it for an English newspaper; the other pair for a Spanish one. It must only be one page long and should contain:

■ a bold headline
■ an article containing facts and opinions about Drake's life
■ a picture, showing Drake as you think he should be remembered.

Each pair should read the obituary produced by the other pair. In what ways are they different and why?

■ **TASK**

Write an essay to answer this question: was Francis Drake a brave hero or a pirate and a villain?
  Write three detailed paragraphs:
a) what evidence is there to support the view that he was a villain?
b) what evidence is there to support the view that he was a hero?
c) why have there been such different views of Drake?

Then write a short conclusion to explain which of these views you agree with most.

Why did war break out with Spain?

IN THE SUMMER of 1588 the Spanish Armada – a huge invasion fleet – set sail for England. The most dangerous moment of Elizabeth's reign had arrived. If you had told anyone about this 30 years earlier they would have been astonished. England and Spain had been allies for most of the sixteenth century. Henry VIII's first wife, Catherine of Aragon, was a Spanish princess. Mary Tudor had married Prince Philip of Spain in 1554. During the early years of Elizabeth's reign England and Spain were on friendly terms.

In this enquiry we will investigate why two friendly countries became enemies and why war broke out between them.

The power of Spain

King Philip II was the ruler of the most powerful and wealthy country in the world. As well as being King of Spain, Philip II ruled the Netherlands, an important centre of European trade, and parts of Italy (see the map on pages 112–113). His army was the strongest in Europe. As you have seen, Spain also ruled an empire in the New World. Ships from the colonies in Central and South America set sail for Spain every year loaded with gold and silver. In 1580 Philip became the ruler of Portugal and its empire, too. He was determined to protect his empire. It brought great wealth to his country.

Philip was a strong Roman Catholic. He wanted every country in Europe to follow the Catholic religion and punished Protestants severely.

Friendship between England and Spain

In 1558 Philip wanted to be friendly with the new Queen of England. At first he hoped to marry Elizabeth. He was disappointed when she created a new Protestant Church, but still wanted to keep on good terms with her. There were two main reasons for this.

- Philip knew that if Elizabeth was overthrown, Mary, Queen of Scots, would be the new Queen of England. Mary would make England Roman Catholic again, but she was friendly with France, Spain's most dangerous enemy – so France, not Spain, would benefit.
- The Netherlands was the most valuable part of Philip's European empire. The easiest and cheapest route from Spain to the Netherlands was through the English Channel. If he remained friendly with Elizabeth, Spanish ships could continue to use this route without fear of attack from England.

Even when the Pope excommunicated Elizabeth in 1570, ordering Catholics to overthrow her, Philip did little. He did not want an expensive war with England if Spain had nothing to gain.

Elizabeth wanted to keep on good terms with Spain. She was short of money. She already had serious problems to deal with, such as Mary, Queen of Scots. Elizabeth could not afford a war against the most powerful country in the world.

So why did their attitudes change?

1. Why was Spain such a powerful country in the sixteenth century?
2. Why was Philip II keen to keep on friendly terms with Elizabeth?
3. Why did Elizabeth want to keep on friendly terms with Philip?
4. Which do you think was more important to Philip – his religion or his empire?

SOURCE 1 A portrait of Philip II, painted by Spanish artist Alonso Sanchez Coello in 1571

5. What impression of Philip II was this artist trying to give?

Why did England and Spain go to war?

During the early years of Elizabeth's reign, Catholic Spain and Protestant England remained friendly. Gradually, however, this friendship changed into rivalry. Tension grew between the two countries. Finally the tension snapped – and war broke out. Now you are going to investigate why.

Religious differences

King Philip II of Spain was a strong Roman Catholic. He wanted all Protestant countries to return to the Catholic Church. In 1559, however, Elizabeth broke away from the Catholic Church and created a Protestant Church of England.

Marriage

Philip had been married to Elizabeth's sister, Mary Tudor. In 1559 he offered to marry Elizabeth. Elizabeth rejected his offer and remained single.

Civil war in France

France was the traditional enemy of both England and Spain. In 1562 civil war broke out between Catholics and Protestants. It lasted, on and off, until 1598. France was no longer a threat to either England or Spain.

The Dutch Revolt

Protestants in the Netherlands began a revolt against Spanish rule in 1572. Philip sent a Spanish army to defeat them. The Dutch asked Elizabeth for help. She knew that their revolt would keep Spain too busy to threaten England. She was careful not to help them too openly, but allowed Dutch refugees to settle in England and Dutch ships to use English ports. She also secretly sent money and weapons to help the Dutch rebels.

English sailors

Spain did not allow foreign merchants to trade with their colonies in the New World. Trouble with English sailors soon occurred. In 1568 John Hawkins' fleet was attacked at San Juan de Ulua (see page 120). In the 1570s and 1580s Francis Drake and other English sailors attacked Spanish settlements and seized Spanish treasure. Philip II was furious about these attacks on his empire, but Elizabeth encouraged them. She knighted Drake and shared in the profits of the voyages.

Spanish help for Catholic plots

Mary, Queen of Scots, arrived in England in 1568 and Catholics began plotting to overthrow Elizabeth. Although Philip did not want Mary to become Queen of England, he was willing to stir up trouble for Elizabeth. The Spanish ambassador was involved in most of the Catholic plots in England in the 1570s and 1580s. Philip offered money to the plotters and promised to send Spanish troops to help them.

Elizabeth sent an army to the Netherlands

In 1578 Philip sent the Duke of Parma to defeat the Dutch rebels. In 1584 their leader, William of Orange, was assassinated. The Dutch now faced defeat. If that happened, Spanish armies would be free to threaten England. Elizabeth refused an offer to become Queen of the Dutch. But in 1585 she sent an English army to help them. It was led by the Earl of Leicester. England and Spain were now at war. Their armies were fighting against each other for the first time. Philip began planning to invade England.

■ TASK 1

1. Draw a timeline covering the years 1558–1603. Mark on it the main events you have studied in this enquiry. Then divide your timeline into three sections to show when England and Spain were:
a) friendly
b) rivals
c) at war.
2. a) What were the long-term causes of the war?
b) What were its short-term causes?
c) Did the war have a trigger cause?
3. Which played the more important role in causing the war: religious differences between the two countries, or trade and economic rivalry?

■ TASK 2

Write an essay to answer this question: why did war break out between England and Spain in 1585?

Use your answers to questions 2 and 3 in the previous Task to help you.

Why did the Armada fail?

ELIZABETH WAS EXPECTED to protect her people from invasion. By going to war with Spain, she exposed them to this danger. By the summer of 1588 Philip II's preparations for the invasion of England were complete. He had assembled the 'invincible' Armada – a huge fleet of 130 ships and nearly 30,000 men. It set sail in July 1588. The most dangerous crisis of Elizabeth's whole reign had begun ...

In this enquiry you will be finding out what happened in the summer of 1588. Was the Armada a serious threat to Elizabethan England? How close did it come to success? Why did it eventually fail?

Philip's plan to defeat England

Philip began planning the Armada in 1585. At first he wanted to send a force directly from Spain to invade England. His advisers told him that he would need over 500 ships and 50,000 men. This was much too expensive, even for the richest country in the world. A cheaper plan was agreed.

At last I will stop these English helping the Dutch rebels and attacking my treasure ships. My empire will be safe!

MY PLAN TO DEFEAT ENGLAND

■ The Armada will sail through the English Channel to Calais.

■ The Duke of Parma, my best general, will join the Armada at Calais with 20,000 troops from the Netherlands.

■ The Armada will protect Parma's men as they cross the Channel in barges.

■ They will land in Kent and then attack and capture London.

■ English Catholics will start a rebellion against Elizabeth to help us.

■ Elizabeth will have to surrender. After she is overthrown, the Roman Catholic religion will be restored in England.

SOURCE 1 Philip II's plan for the invasion of England

1. What benefits did Philip hope to gain by invading England?
2. Can you suggest any possible problems with Philip's plan? Were there any unpredictable factors which might affect its outcome?
3. Today we would expect information about a country's invasion force to be kept secret. In 1588 the Spanish government published full details about the Armada. Why do you think they did this?

The Spanish forces

Ships
130 ships: 64 battleships, including 22 huge GALLEONS, and 45 converted merchant ships. Other ships carried stores. The store-ships were slow, heavy and difficult to handle in rough seas.

Sailors and soldiers
30,000 men on board: 8000 experienced sailors, 19,000 well-trained soldiers and nearly 3000 servants, priests (including 180 monks and friars), and officials. Another 20,000 soldiers led by the Duke of Parma were waiting in the Netherlands.

Commander
The Duke of Medina Sidonia, a brave nobleman and good organiser, but with little experience of sailing. His commanders were experienced sea captains. He was appointed to command the Armada in February 1588, after the original commander had died.

Food supplies
Supplies of ship's biscuit, bacon, fish, cheese, rice, beans, wine, vinegar and water to last six months. They were stored in barrels long before the fleet set sail. This was plenty for the voyage but it would be difficult to get fresh supplies once the Armada set sail.

Philip's annual income
£3 million

Weapons
2000 cannon, mostly to fire heavy cannon-balls over a short distance. 125,000 cannon-balls. Bullets, pikes, swords, armour and gunpowder.

Tactics for fighting at sea
To get close enough to enemy ships for men to board them and then capture them.

SOURCE 2 Spain's forces in 1588 led by the Duke of Medina Sidonia

SOURCE 3 An extract from a letter written by the Duke of Medina Sidonia to King Philip II in February 1588

❝ I wish I possessed the talents and strength necessary to it. But Sir, I have not the health for the sea. I soon become seasick. It would not be right for a person like myself, possessing no experience of seafaring or war, to take charge of it. ❞

SOURCE 4 An extract from the Duke of Medina Sidonia's orders to his men before the Armada set sail, May 1588

❝ You must all know, from the highest to the lowest, that the principal reason which has moved His Majesty to undertake this enterprise is his desire to serve God, and to convert to His church many peoples and souls who are now oppressed by the heretical enemies of our holy Catholic faith, and are subjected to errors. ❞

SOURCE 5 An extract from a letter written by the Duke of Medina Sidonia to Philip II in June 1588, after the Armada had left Lisbon

❝ Your Majesty ordered me to fit out his Armada to take charge of it. When I accepted the task, I submitted to your Majesty many reasons, in the interest of your service, why it was better that I should not do so. This was not because I wished to refuse the work, but because I recognised that we were attacking a kingdom so powerful, and so warmly aided by its neighbours, that we should need a much larger force than your Majesty has collected. To undertake so great a task with an inferior force, as ours is now, with our men lacking in experience, would be unwise. The opportunity should be taken, and the difficulties avoided, by making some honourable terms with the enemy. ❞

4. What can you learn about the Duke of Medina Sidonia from Source 3?
5. How useful is Source 4 as evidence of the reasons why the Armada was sent?
6. Is Source 5 more or less reliable than Source 4?
7. Can you learn anything more about the Duke of Medina Sidonia from Source 5 than from Source 3?

■ TASK

1. Make a larger copy of this table. Use the information you have studied so far to help you complete it.

Spanish forces in 1588

Strengths	Weaknesses

2. 'It was inevitable that the Armada would be defeated.' Explain whether you agree or disagree with this statement.

How did Elizabeth prepare the country's defences?

By 1588 Elizabeth had known about Philip's plans for nearly two years. In the previous year she had sent Drake to attack Cadiz, where the Armada was being prepared. He had sunk 30 Spanish battleships and destroyed a lot of the Armada's supplies. This gave Elizabeth another year to prepare her defences. Her objective was straightforward – she had to stop the Spanish from landing.

Soldiers

Elizabeth did not have a full-time army. She ordered every county to provide soldiers. About 20,000 soldiers were gathered but they had little training and few weapons. Some only had bows and arrows.

Elizabeth's biggest problem was that she did not know where the Armada would land. Soldiers were needed all around the coast. She organised three main armies, one based in the north of England, another in Kent, and the third at Tilbury in Essex.

The navy

There were only 34 battleships in the navy. Private individuals like Drake provided another 20 battleships. Trading companies and the ports were ordered to make their trading ships available and these were quickly prepared for war. Charles Howard, Duke of Effingham, was appointed to command the fleet.

Other preparations

Warning beacons were set up on high land around the coast. When the Armada was sighted, these would be lit to spread the news around the country. Church bells would also be rung to warn people.

The government was worried that there might be a Catholic rebellion to help the Spanish invasion. JPs were ordered to punish anyone who spread rumours or tried to stir up trouble. Many Catholics were arrested.

How can I stop the Spanish forces from landing?

■ TASK

1. Make a larger copy of this table. Use the information above and Source 6 on the opposite page to complete it.

English forces in 1588

Strengths	Weaknesses

2. Compare this table with the table you made in the Task on page 133. Which side do you think was strongest:
   a) at sea?
   b) on land?
3. 'Elizabeth had every reason to be worried about the Spanish Armada.' Do you agree or disagree with this statement? Explain the reasons for your answer.

SOURCE 6 English forces in 1588 led by Lord Howard of Effingham

Commander
Lord Howard of Effingham, a noble who had little experience of fighting at sea. Drake and Hawkins, both experienced in fighting at sea, were his Vice-Admirals.

Ships
54 battleships which were strong, light and fast. Another 140 merchant ships were converted into battleships. In total, Elizabeth had about 200 ships.

Elizabeth's annual income
£300,000. Parliament also granted taxes to Elizabeth. Elizabeth was short of money in 1588.

Sailors
14,000 sailors. Many of them were experienced in sailing in the Atlantic and fighting against the Spanish. They had not been paid and many sailors were sick.

Tactics
To destroy enemy ships from a distance by firing cannon at them.

Soldiers
About 20,000 soldiers in England. Most of them had little training, few weapons and were spread around the coast. The main armies were in the north of England, Kent, and at Tilbury in Essex.

Weapons
Nearly 2000 cannon and smaller guns. English cannon were light and could be fired quickly, but they were not very effective over longer distances.

Food supplies
Food was supplied on a daily basis. English sailors' rations consisted of badly brewed beer, dry ship's biscuit, fish, cheese, butter, bacon and salted beef.

What happened in the summer of 1588?

The Armada left Lisbon on 28 May. Then it was hit by storms. On 19 June it sailed into the harbour at Corunna, a Spanish port. Repairs were quickly made. Supplies of food and water were taken on board. It finally set sail for England on 21 July.

The Armada was first sighted off Lizard Point in Cornwall on 29 July. Warning beacons were lit. The Spanish fleet sailed into the English Channel and moved into a crescent formation. The slow, unarmed store-ships were in the centre. The heavily armed galleons sailed on the outer edges.

The main part of the English fleet was based at Plymouth. It waited for a favourable tide and then sailed in pursuit of the Spanish ships. For the next week it followed the Armada, but the long-range guns of the English ships had little effect. They found it impossible to inflict any serious damage on the Spanish fleet. On 6 August, when the Armada sailed into the harbour at Calais, it had lost just two ships. One had blown up, probably by accident. The other was badly damaged when it collided with another Spanish ship.

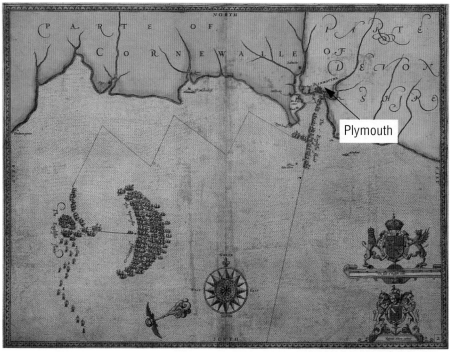

SOURCE 7 The Armada sailing towards Plymouth in July 1588. This is taken from a series of ten drawings of the Armada campaign by a Dutch artist, 1590

SOURCE 8 A traditional story about Sir Francis Drake's reaction when told that the Armada had been sighted

> *The English commanders were playing bowls in Plymouth when they heard that the Armada had been sighted. Drake said 'There is time to finish the game and beat the Spaniards too.' They finished the game before heading for their ships.*

8. What impression does Source 8 give of Sir Francis Drake?

9. Nobody today knows whether this story is true or not. If it is not true, why do you think it was made up?

SOURCE 9 An extract from the journal of Lord Howard, commander of the English fleet

> *For as much as [because] our powder and shot was well wasted, the Lord Admiral thought it was not good policy to attack them any more until they came near to Dover.*

■ ACTIVITY

It is 6 August 1588. The Armada has just anchored in Calais harbour.
a) You are the Duke of Medina Sidonia. Write a short letter to King Philip II to explain how well the Armada has done so far.
b) Now you are Lord Howard, the commander of the English fleet. Write a short account in your private journal to explain how well your fleet has done so far.
c) Your two accounts are both about the same events. Why are they so different?
d) Would you have written Lord Howard's account differently if it had been an official report to the Queen? Why?

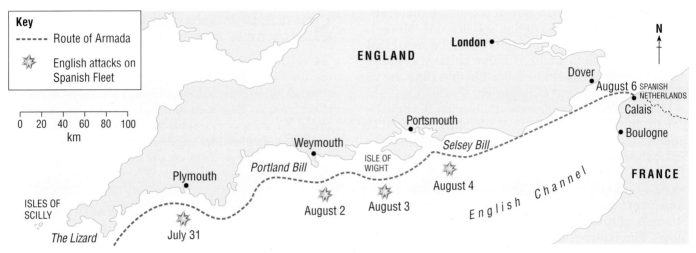

S OURCE 10 The Armada's route to Calais

Soon after reaching Calais, the Duke of Medina Sidonia received a message from the Duke of Parma. His troops were only 50 km away but they were being attacked by the Dutch. Parma said they could not reach Calais for at least a week.

Lord Howard did not know that Parma's troops had been delayed, but he decided to take action. Eight unmanned ships were filled with tar, gunpowder and other inflammable materials. Their cannon were loaded. Shortly after midnight on 7 August these eight fireships were set alight and let loose to drift into Calais harbour. The Spanish ships sailed in panic out of the harbour. None of them were damaged but their crescent formation was broken.

10. Was the message he received from the Duke of Parma good or bad news for Medina Sidonia?

S OURCE 11 An extract from the Duke of Medina Sidonia's report to King Philip II, 7 August 1588

66 *At midnight two fires were seen among the English fleet and these gradually increased to eight. They were eight vessels with sails set, which were drifting with the current directly towards our flagship and the rest of the Armada, all of them burning with great fury. When I saw them approaching, fearing that they might contain fire machines or mines, I ordered the flagship to let go the cables, the rest of the Armada receiving similar orders, with an indication that when the fires had passed they were to return to the same positions again. The current was so strong that most of the ships of the Armada were carried towards Dunkirk.* 99

11. Study Sources 11 and 12. Which do you think gives the more reliable evidence about the fireship attack?

S OURCE 12 A painting of the fireships attacking the Armada in Calais harbour. It was painted in the late sixteenth century by a Dutch artist

The Spanish fleet was blown towards dangerous sandbanks off the coast of the Netherlands. More English ships arrived from the River Thames. Lord Howard decided to attack. A fierce battle was fought near the port of Gravelines. For the first time the two fleets were fighting at close range.

The Battle of Gravelines took place on 8 August. Fought in rough seas and poor visibility, it lasted for nine hours. English cannon fire damaged many Spanish ships. One was sunk. Two others ran aground on the sandbanks. About 1000 Spaniards were killed and over 800 were wounded. No English ships were lost but 50 English sailors were killed. Spanish cannon caused little damage to English ships. The battle ended in the afternoon when the English fleet ran out of ammunition.

SOURCE 13 A drawing of the Battle of Gravelines, by Visscher, a Dutch artist, in about 1615

SOURCE 14 An account of the fighting at Gravelines by a Spanish sailor

66 *The enemy inflicted such damage on two of our ships that their guns were put out of action. Don Francisco de Toledo, commander of the* San Felipe, *shouted at the enemy to come to close quarters. They demanded that he should surrender and one Englishman called out 'Good soldiers that you are, surrender to the fair terms that we offer you'. But the only answer that he got was a musketball which brought him down in sight of everyone. Don Francisco then ordered that all the muskets be brought into action. The enemy then retreated and our men shouted to them that they were cowards and called them chicken.* 99

12. Use Sources 13 and 14 to describe the kind of fighting that took place during the Battle of Gravelines.

SOURCE 15 An extract from a letter by Lord Howard to Sir Francis Walsingham after the battle

66 *We have chased them in fight until late this evening, and distressed them much, but their fleet consists of mighty ships and great strength. Yet we doubt not, by God's good assistance, to defeat them. Their force is wonderful great and strong, and yet we pluck their feathers little by little. I pray to God that the powers on the land be strong enough to answer this force.* 99

13. Study Source 15. Did the fighting at Gravelines end the danger from the Armada?

On 9 August the wind changed direction. The Armada sailed into the North Sea. The English fleet chased after it until the Armada sailed past the Scottish border on 12 August. The English fleet then turned back. It was short of ammunition and food. Many sailors were sick and had not been paid.

SOURCE 16 An extract from Elizabeth's speech to her troops at Tilbury in Essex, 18 August 1588

66 *I am resolved in the midst and heat of battle to live and die amongst you all. I know that I have the body of a weak and feeble woman, but I have the heart and stomach of a King, and of a King of England too, and think foul scorn that Parma or Spain, or any other Prince of Europe should dare to invade the borders of my realm.* 99

SOURCE 17 An extract from a letter written by Lord Howard to the Privy Council on 20 August

66 *Sickness and mortality begins terribly to grow amongst us and it is a most pitiable sight to see, here at Margate, how the men having no place to receive them die in the streets. It would grieve any man's heart to see them that have served so valiantly, die so miserably.* 99

The Armada tried to sail home around Scotland and Ireland. Spanish sailors had never sailed around these coastlines before. They had no accurate maps. Many men were sick from polluted water and rotten food. About 44 ships were wrecked in storms. Thousands of sailors were drowned. Many sailors who reached dry land were hunted down and killed. About 80 ships reached Spain by the end of the year.

SOURCE 18 A Spanish official's report to Philip II on 1 October 1588

❝ There are over a thousand sick and if the men be disembarked at once, the hospital would be so overcrowded that, although there has been nothing contagious yet, I greatly fear that something of the sort will appear. I understand that there is a great deal of rotten foodstuff on the ships and I beg you to order it to be thrown overboard. If this be not done someone will be sure to buy it to grind up and mix it with the new biscuit, which will be enough to poison all the Armadas afloat. ❞

SOURCE 19 Losses of the two sides

	Spain	England
Ships lost	51 (5 captured or sunk by the English navy)	None
Casualties	20,000 men killed	About 100 sailors killed in battle; several thousand died of disease

SOURCE 20 A seventeenth-century English playing card

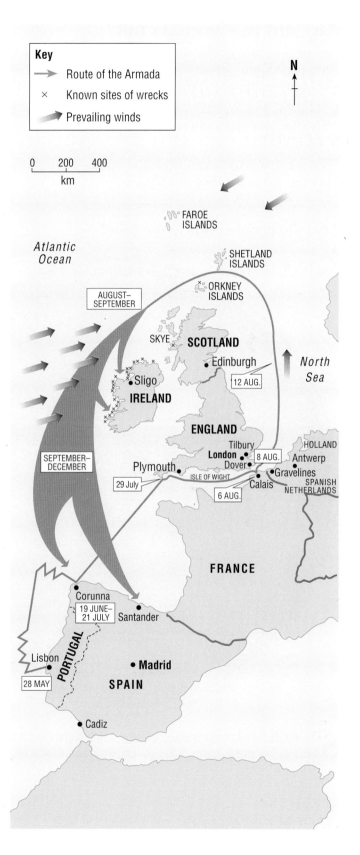

SOURCE 21 The route of the Armada in 1588

Why did the Armada fail?

Now we are going to investigate why the 'invincible' Armada failed in 1588. You should already have some ideas. First, we will examine what people thought at the time. Then we will see what recent historians have written.

■ ACTIVITY

From what you have studied so far, make a list of the reasons why you think the Armada failed in 1588.

What did people think at the time?

SOURCE 22 A medal made soon after 1588 to commemorate the defeat of the Armada. The words mean 'God blew and they were scattered'

SOURCE 23 A comment made by Philip II in 1588

66 I sent my fleet against men, not against the wind and waves. 99

SOURCE 24 An extract from Sir Walter Raleigh's *History of the World*, written in 1618. Raleigh was an English sailor but he did not take part in the campaign of 1588

66 To invade by sea on a perilous coast, being neither in possession of any port, nor with allies, may better fit a prince presuming on his fortune than enriched with understanding. 99

SOURCE 25 An extract from a report on the Armada's defeat, written in September 1588 by Francisco de Bobadilla, the general in charge of the Armada's soldiers

66 We found that many of the enemy's ships held great advantages over us in combat, both in the design, and in their guns, gunners and crews who could do with us as they wished. But in spite of this the Duke of Medina Sidonia managed to bring his fleet to anchor in Calais just several leagues from Dunkirk. If on the day that we arrived there, Parma had come out with his troops, we should have carried out the invasion. 99

■ TASK

1. Make a list of the reasons given in Sources 22–26 to explain the Armada's defeat.
2. Study Elizabeth's 'Armada Portrait' (Source 8 on page 31). What reasons for the Armada's defeat does it suggest?
3. Look again at all of these sources. Do you think that any of them might be unreliable? Explain your reasons.

SOURCE 26 A painting by Robert Stephenson in 1610 of the Armada's defeat. The Armada is shown as a huge dragon being defeated by a much smaller fleet

Historians' explanations

Many historians have investigated why the Armada failed. In some ways they have an advantage over people of the time:

■ there is less pressure on them to please their rulers
■ they can study English and Spanish documents
■ archaeologists have investigated the wrecks of Spanish ships which sank off the coast of Ireland in 1588.

As you examine these sources, bear in mind the evidence you have already studied.

SOURCE 27 An extract from *Spain under the Hapsburgs*, by John Lynch, 1964

❝ *The seamanship, discipline and fighting spirit of the Spaniards were superb. Keeping a tight formation, they moved slowly up the Channel for nine days, while the English fired their guns to no great purpose. The defeat of the Spanish Armada was not the fault of the Duke of Medina Sidonia, whose courage and leadership could hardly have been bettered.* ❞

SOURCE 28 The biggest ships in the two fleets

Ship	Country	Guns	Men	Tons
Triumph	English	67	500	1100
San Juan	Spanish	50	522	1050
Bear	English	80	500	1000
San Martín	Spanish	48	469	1000
Elizabeth Jonas	English	76	500	900
San Luis	Spanish	38	439	830
San Felipe	Spanish	40	439	800
Victory	English	64	400	800
Ark	English	–	425	800

SOURCE 29 An extract from *The Spanish Armada*, by Felipe Fernandez-Armesto, a Spanish historian, 1988

❝ *The English were overwhelmingly superior in long-range guns: 497 guns to 172. The English were able to use their huge superiority to fire at a safe distance.* ❞

141

SOURCE 30 Unused Spanish cannon-balls found on the wreck of a Spanish ship off the coast of Ireland

SOURCE 31 An extract from *The Spanish Armada*, by Colin Martin and Geoffrey Parker, 1988

66 *We now know for certain that the Spanish did not run out of shot. So here at last is a full explanation for the Armada's remarkable failure to inflict serious damage on the English fleet: the Spaniards simply did not fire their guns often enough – but why was this so? The design of Spanish gun-carriages suggests that it was impossible to reload them quickly. The cannon and cannon-balls came from all over Europe; some of the cannon were badly made and many cannon-balls did not fit the guns. The small wheels of the English gun carriages meant that firing could be done consecutively. It was not until Gravelines that this advantage was fully exploited by the English, and by then it was almost too late, for their ammunition stocks were almost exhausted.* 99

SOURCE 32 An extract from *Tudor Britain*, by Roger Lockyer and Dan O'Sullivan, 1997

66 *The Spanish ships were on the whole much slower and less manoeuvrable than the English. The Armada included many merchant ships to carry the necessary stores and equipment. Since the 1560s, John Hawkins had developed a new type of fighting galleon – faster, lower and more 'weatherly' [better able to withstand bad weather], than any in the Spanish fleet.* 99

SOURCE 33 An extract from *The Spanish Armada*, by Felipe Fernandez-Armesto

66 *The most widespread contemporary analysis of the Armada's failure – winds – seems justified. If there was a critical omission from the Spanish plan, it was probably the lack of a secure port in northern waters.* 99

■ TASK 1

1. Make a list of the reasons that are given in Sources 27–33 to explain the Armada's defeat.
2. a) Which of these reasons were **not** given in Sources 22-26?
   b) Does this mean that these reasons cannot be correct?

■ TASK 2

Why was the Armada defeated in 1588? Write an essay to answer this question. Cover the following factors in your answer and explain which you think were the most important causes of the Armada's defeat:

- Philip's plan
- the commanders
- supplies
- allies
- the weather
- ships and guns
- tactics.

Was the defeat of the Armada important?

In England there were celebrations at the news of the Armada's defeat. Church bells were rung all over the country. In November Elizabeth went to St Paul's Cathedral to celebrate the victory. She ordered a new portrait of herself (see Source 8 on page 31).

In Spain there was mourning. Philip II was bitterly disappointed by the Armada's failure but he was determined to continue the war. It continued for the rest of Elizabeth's reign. When it finally ended in 1604, neither side had really won.

> Was the defeat of the Armada important? There are two ways of answering this question.

> The first is to work out what would have happened if the Armada had succeeded.

> The second way is to see what actually happened afterwards.

- England would have been invaded.
- Elizabeth would have been overthrown.
- The Roman Catholic religion would have been restored and Protestants punished.
- England would have lost its independence and become part of the Spanish Empire.

- Within two years Philip had built another fleet of over 100 ships. He sent two more armadas to invade England but they were both driven back by storms.
- Elizabeth continued to help the Dutch rebels. They finally won their independence from Spain in 1609.
- English sailors carried on attacking Spanish treasure ships and ports.
- Philip continued stirring up trouble for Elizabeth. In 1595 he sent Spanish troops to Ireland to help an Irish rebellion against Elizabeth.

SOURCE 34 Was the defeat of the Armada important?

■ ACTIVITY

It is September 1588. The Armada campaign is over.

Work in groups. Design a newspaper front page to report the news of the Armada's defeat. Half the group are working for an English newspaper; the other half are working for a Spanish newspaper. Both front pages should include:

- a strong headline
- a report on the main events of the campaign and its results for your country
- an illustration.

Compare your two newspapers. How different are they and why?

■ TASK

1. Briefly explain what happened to the Armada on each of the following dates: 28 May; 19 June; 21 July; 29 July; 30 July–5 August; 6 August; 8 August; 12 August; August–September; September–December.
2. What do you think was the most important turning point in the campaign? Explain the reasons for your answer.
3. Study Source 16 on page 138. What impression did Elizabeth want this speech to give and why?
4. What were the short-term results of the Armada's defeat for:
a) England?
b) Spain?
5. What were the longer-term results of the Armada's defeat?

Did Elizabeth succeed in making England a great power?

IN THIS CHAPTER we have been investigating whether Elizabeth helped to make England more powerful. So far we have concentrated on her relations with Spain. But there were other countries that posed threats to England in 1558 (look back at pages 112–113). Before you reach your conclusions about Elizabeth's success, we need to examine how she dealt with these other threats.

FRANCE

1562: Civil war broke out between Catholics and Protestants. Elizabeth sent an army to help the Protestants.

1572: Many Protestants were killed in the St Bartholomew's Day Massacre.

1579: Elizabeth held marriage talks with the Duke of Alençon, the heir to the French throne.

1584: The Duke of Alençon died.

1587: French Catholics protested against the execution of Mary, Queen of Scots.

1589: Henry IV, a Protestant, became King of France. Elizabeth sent money and soldiers to help him.

1598: The civil wars ended.

1603: King Henry IV, now a Catholic, had a friendly relationship with England.

SCOTLAND

1559: Scottish Protestants rebelled against the country's Catholic rulers. Elizabeth sent help to the Protestants.

1560: The Protestants won the war. French troops left Scotland.

1561: Mary, Queen of Scots, returned to Scotland from France.

1567: Mary was overthrown and imprisoned.

1568: Mary escaped and fled to England, where Elizabeth held her prisoner. Protestant lords ruled Scotland.

1578: James VI, Mary's son, began ruling Scotland. He had been brought up as a Protestant.

1587: Mary, Queen of Scots, was executed. Elizabeth apologised to James VI.

1603: Scotland was a friendly Protestant country.

THE NETHERLANDS

1572: Dutch Protestants rebelled against Spanish rule. Elizabeth sent money to help them.

1578: The Duke of Parma was sent to defeat the Dutch rebels.

1584: William of Orange, the Dutch leader, was murdered.

1585: Elizabeth sent an English army, commanded by the Earl of Leicester, to help the Dutch.

1590s: Elizabeth continued to help Dutch Protestants. They won several victories against the Spanish.

1603: Dutch Protestants had won control of Holland. Spain was facing defeat.

IRELAND

1566: A Catholic rebellion was defeated by English troops.

1572: A rebellion in southern Ireland was defeated. The leader of the rebels, James Fitzgerald, an Irish Catholic, fled abroad.

1579: Fitzgerald invaded Ireland with Spanish and Italian soldiers.

1580: English soldiers defeated the invaders. Fitzgerald was killed. Elizabeth gave English settlers land in southern Ireland.

1594: The Earl of Tyrone led a rebellion. He soon won control of most of Ireland.

1599: Elizabeth sent the Earl of Essex to defeat the rebellion. Instead, he made peace with the rebels.

1600: Lord Mountjoy was sent to attack the rebels.

1603: Tyrone surrendered. England regained control of the area around Dublin. English settlers controlled other lands in Ireland but Irish Catholics hated them.

1. Why did Elizabeth dislike rebels?
2. What examples are there of her sending troops to defeat rebels?
3. What examples can you find of her sending troops to help rebels?
4. Explain why Elizabeth sometimes helped rebels even though she disliked them.

■ TASK

On pages 112–113 you found out about the problems with other countries that Elizabeth faced in 1558. Your teacher will give you a copy of this table. Complete the last column to show whether the situation was better or worse when Elizabeth died in 1603.

	The situation in 1558	The situation in 1603
Scotland	A hostile, Roman Catholic country, friendly with France. Mary, Queen of Scots, was married to a French prince and claimed the English throne.	
Ireland	Elizabeth claimed to rule all of Ireland, but only controlled a small area around Dublin. Most Irish people were Roman Catholic and hostile towards the English.	
France	France had been England's main enemy for centuries. France was Roman Catholic and had strong links with Scotland. In 1558 England and France were at war.	
Spain	Spain was the most powerful country in the world. It was Roman Catholic. England and Spain were friendly. King Philip II hoped to marry Elizabeth.	
The Netherlands	Ruled by Spain. Protestant ideas were spreading.	
Overseas trade, voyages and colonies	Most of England's trade was with Europe. There were few contacts with other parts of the world, few overseas voyages and no English colonies.	
Conclusion	England was a weak country.	

■ REVIEW TASK

So, did Elizabethan England become a more powerful country? Was it a 'Great Power' by 1603?

1. Rate Elizabeth's success for each of the criteria in the diagram. Your teacher will give you a sheet to help you.

2. Now write an essay to answer this question: how successful was Elizabeth in making England a more powerful country?

Organise your answer like this:

■ a short introduction describing England's situation in 1558

■ a paragraph explaining how successful Elizabeth was in her dealings with Scotland and Ireland

■ two paragraphs explaining how successful Elizabeth was in her dealings with Spain, France and the Netherlands

■ a paragraph explaining whether there were any English successes in other parts of the world (think about trade, overseas voyages and colonies)

■ your conclusion: was England a more powerful country by the end of Elizabeth's reign? If so, was this mainly the result of decisions taken by the Queen herself – or were other factors (such as other people's actions or just good luck) more important?

chapter 7

WERE ELIZABETH'S LAST YEARS A 'GOLDEN SUNSET'?

AFTER THE DEFEAT of the Armada, Elizabeth reigned for another fifteen years. This was a third of her reign. Elizabeth faced one big new problem during her last years – growing old. By 1600 she was 67 years old. Her leading advisers had died: Leicester in 1588, Walsingham in 1590 and William Cecil, Lord Burghley, in 1598. These were the men she had known well and trusted. Now there was a new generation of young, ambitious nobles who wanted power.

Could an ageing woman still be a strong ruler? Was Elizabeth a successful ruler in her final years; or did she lose her grip on the country? Were the last years of her reign a 'golden sunset' or were 'storm clouds' starting to appear – problems that would lead, 40 years later, to the English Civil War?

Government

Advisers: Ambitious young noblemen, eager for power, began competing to replace Elizabeth's old advisers. There were two main rivals. Robert Devereux, the Earl of Essex, quickly gained the Queen's favour. Eventually, however, she chose Robert Cecil, the son of William Cecil, as her chief minister. Essex led a rebellion in 1601. It failed and he was executed.

Finance: Elizabeth's biggest expense was the war with Spain. It continued for the rest of her reign. High taxes were essential, but even these were not enough to pay for the war. Elizabeth had to use other unpopular ways of raising money, such as monopolies. She left £350,000 of debts when she died.

Parliament: Elizabeth called four more Parliaments after 1588. Her MPs approved taxes for the war. But some of them challenged the Queen's authority. Some asked her to name her successor. She refused. Others complained about monopolies. Elizabeth said she would look into their complaints. MPs passed the Elizabethan Poor Law (see page 69) in 1601. Elizabeth gave her last speech to Parliament in 1601. This 'Golden Speech' (page 40) was very popular with her MPs.

Culture

New schools were opened. New houses were being built all over the country. Hardwick Hall, for example (see pages 52–53) was completed in 1597. The theatre was bursting into life. The Globe Theatre opened in 1599. Marlowe and Shakespeare were writing some of their greatest plays.

Religion

By 1600 Elizabeth's Church of England had been in existence for over 40 years. Most people supported it. Few of them could remember anything else.

The government continued to hunt down Roman Catholic priests and 53 were executed. But there were no more Catholic plots or rebellions. The number of Catholics fell.

The Puritans caused no more trouble after 1590 although Puritan ideas continued to spread. Their attempt to change the Church had failed.

Rich and poor

By 1603 England's population had reached four million. For some people this was a time of prosperity. Most people, however, faced serious hardship. High taxes, four terrible harvests (1594–97), rocketing food prices and outbreaks of plague caused a rise in poverty and crime. The government was worried about rebellions breaking out. The Elizabethan Poor Law (1601) provided help for the deserving poor. It remained in force until the nineteenth century.

Foreign affairs

More English sailors made overseas voyages to the Americas and the East Indies than ever before. New trading companies were formed, such as the East India Company in 1600.

France, weakened by years of civil war, and Scotland were now friendly with England. A serious rebellion in Ireland was put down in 1603.

The war with Spain continued but England was safe from invasion. In 1596 there was a successful English attack on Cadiz. The same year Drake died in an unsuccessful attack on Central America. By 1603 Dutch Protestants were winning their war against Spain.

SOURCE 1 An overview of the last years of Elizabeth's reign, 1588–1603

Case study: why did the Earl of Essex rebel in 1601?

THROUGHOUT HER LONG reign Elizabeth kept the loyalty of most of her nobles. In 1601, however, the Earl of Essex led a rebellion against her. It was the most dramatic event of Elizabeth's last years. In this case study we will investigate why it happened and why it failed. Does this rebellion show that Elizabeth was losing her grip?

SOURCE 1 A portrait of Robert Devereux, Earl of Essex. It was painted in 1597 by Dutch artist Marcus Gheeraerts, at the height of Essex's popularity

SOURCE 2 Robert Devereux's early life

1567: Robert Devereux, the son of the Earl of Essex, was born.
1576: His father died. Robert became Earl of Essex when he was nine years old.
1578: The Earl of Leicester married Robert's mother.
1584: Robert went to Court for the first time. He was a good-looking and ambitious young man who quickly won Elizabeth's favour. They spent a lot of time together.
1589: He joined Sir Francis Drake's expedition to Portugal against the Queen's wishes (see page 128).
1590: He secretly got married, without the Queen's permission. She was furious and refused to see him for two weeks.
1593: Essex became a Privy Councillor.
1596: He led an expedition to attack the Spanish port of Cadiz. He captured the town and destroyed many Spanish warships. When he returned to England he was a national hero.

1. Why do you think Essex won the Queen's favour so quickly?
2. Did Essex always act wisely?

Essex was 29 years old in 1596. A great future seemed to lie ahead. He wanted to be Elizabeth's most important minister, giving him power to rule the country as she grew older. The obstacles to his ambitions were William Cecil and his son Robert. While Essex was attacking Cadiz Elizabeth made Robert Cecil her new Secretary of State. Essex was furious.

Rivalry between Essex and the Cecils dominated life at Court for the next four years. In 1598 Essex asked Elizabeth to appoint one of his supporters as Lord Deputy of Ireland. She refused. Essex lost his temper, shouted out that 'her conditions are as crooked as her carcass' and rudely turned his back on her. Elizabeth punched him on the ear. Essex nearly drew his sword and then stormed out of the meeting.

Essex was banned from Court. He did not return until January 1599, after William Cecil's death. Elizabeth gave him another chance to impress her. A rebellion, led by the Earl of Tyrone, had broken out in Ireland. Essex was ordered to defeat the rebels. He landed at Dublin in April 1599 with 17,000 soldiers. Against the Queen's orders, Essex made peace with Tyrone. He also rewarded many of his supporters by making them knights. Elizabeth was furious and ordered him to attack and defeat the rebels. Then Essex heard that Robert Cecil had been given another important job in the government. He left Ireland. When Essex reached London he burst into the Queen's bedchamber.

The next day Essex was ordered to appear before the Privy Council. He was banned from Court and lost all his government jobs.

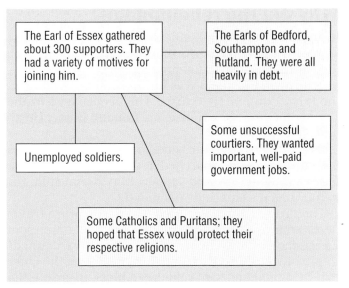

SOURCE 4 The supporters of Essex's rebellion

5. What did Essex's supporters hope to gain from the rebellion?
6. Did Essex have any powerful supporters?
7. Did he have enough supporters?

SOURCE 3 A description of Essex's return to Court in September 1599, by Rowland Whyte, an eyewitness

66 On 28 September, about 10 o'clock in the morning, my Lord of Essex made all haste up to the Queen's bedchamber, where he found the Queen newly up, her hair about her face; he kneeled unto her, kissed her hands, and had some private speech with her. It is much wondered at here that he went so boldly to her Majesty's presence, she not being ready, and he so full of dirt and mire that his very face was full of it. 99

3. Why was Elizabeth angry with Essex's behaviour:
a) at Court in 1598?
b) in Ireland?
c) when he returned to court in 1599?
4. Do these events reveal any weaknesses in Essex's character?

Essex's political career was now in ruins. He also had debts of £15,000. His monopoly on sweet wines was one of his most important sources of money. The monopoly ran out in September 1600. Elizabeth did not renew it.

Essex was desperate. He decided to seize power. He needed a plan and supporters to help him.

SOURCE 5 How Essex planned to win power

Why did the rebellion fail?

Rumours of a rebellion quickly spread. In February 1601 Essex's supporters put on a performance of Shakespeare's play *Richard II* at the Globe Theatre. It included a scene in which the king was overthrown. Elizabeth was furious and ordered Essex to appear before the Privy Council. He refused. On 8 February Elizabeth sent four Privy Councillors to Essex House, his London home. He arrested them and locked them up.

Essex then started the rebellion. He rode out of Essex House with his 300 supporters and marched to the centre of London. Essex hoped that many Londoners would support him. No one did. He decided to march to the Queen's palace in Whitehall.

The Privy Council declared that Essex was a traitor but anyone who deserted him would be pardoned. Some of his supporters surrendered. Essex decided to go home and use the Privy Councillors he had imprisoned as hostages to make a deal with the Queen. However, the Privy Council had sent soldiers to block his route. They closed the gates in the city walls.

After some fighting, Essex went to the river and returned home by boat. When he reached Essex House he found that the prisoners had already been released. Armed soldiers sent by the Privy Council quickly surrounded Essex House. He surrendered. His rebellion had lasted just twelve hours.

Essex and his supporters were put on trial and found guilty of treason. The Earl of Essex was executed at the Tower of London on 25 February 1601. He was 34 years old.

■ TASK

1. Explain how each of the following factors helped to cause Essex's rebellion:
a) weaknesses in Essex's character
b) military failures
c) political failures
d) financial problems
e) the performance of *Richard II*
f) Elizabeth's treatment of Essex.
2. What was most to blame for the rebellion: Elizabeth's decline or Essex's ambition? Explain the reasons for your answer.

■ ACTIVITY

Elizabeth is furious to hear about the rebellion. She orders a report about it. She particularly wants to know why it failed. You work for the government. The Privy Council chooses you to write the report. They want answers to the following questions:

■ was the rebellion well planned?
■ did it have enough support?
■ did the Privy Council handle the situation well?
■ what was the most important reason why the rebellion failed?

How did Elizabethan England end?

ELIZABETH LIVED FOR two more years after Essex's rebellion. By December 1602 she was becoming increasingly frail. The Privy Council ordered that news about her health should be kept secret.

> **S**OURCE 1 An extract from a letter written by Sir John Harington, Elizabeth's godson, to his wife in December 1602
>
> 66 *My royal godmother, and this country's natural mother, does now show human weakness too fast for that evil that we shall get by her death. And too slow for that good which we shall get from her release from her pains and misery.* 99

Elizabeth lost her appetite. She could not sleep. She became too weak to speak. Her doctors and astrologers could not save her. Even in her final days, Elizabeth refused to name her successor. However, Robert Cecil, her chief minister, secretly sent letters about the situation to King James VI of Scotland.

Queen Elizabeth I died in her sleep on 24 March 1603. She was 69 years old and had been Queen of England for 44 years. She was buried in Westminster Abbey four days later.

> **S**OURCE 2 William Camden's comments about Elizabeth's death, from his *History of the Most Renowned and Victorious Princess Elizabeth*, 1615
>
> 66 *On the 24 of March, she was called out of the prison of her earthly body to enjoy an everlasting country in heaven, peaceably and quietly leaving this life, having reigned 44 years, 4 months and in the seventieth year of her age; to which no king of England ever attained before.* 99

Immediately after her death a lone rider left London on horseback. Three days later, he reached Edinburgh, the capital of Scotland. He told King James VI – the son of Mary, Queen of Scots – that he was the new King of England. Elizabethan England – and the rule of the Tudors – had come to an end.

1. Why did the Privy Council refuse to release news about Elizabeth's health?
2. Why did Elizabeth refuse to name her successor?
3. Why did Robert Cecil write to the King of Scotland?
4. Why did James VI become King of England after Elizabeth's death? (Look at the family tree on page 19.)

■ REVIEW TASK

Your teacher will give you a larger copy of this diagram.

1. Make two lists:
   - ■ successes during Elizabeth's last years
   - ■ failures.

   Write them in the spaces on the diagram. Then decide where on the diagram the arrow should finally point.
2. 'Elizabeth's successes in her last years outweighed her failures.' Do you agree or disagree with this statement? Explain your answer fully, using information from your lists.

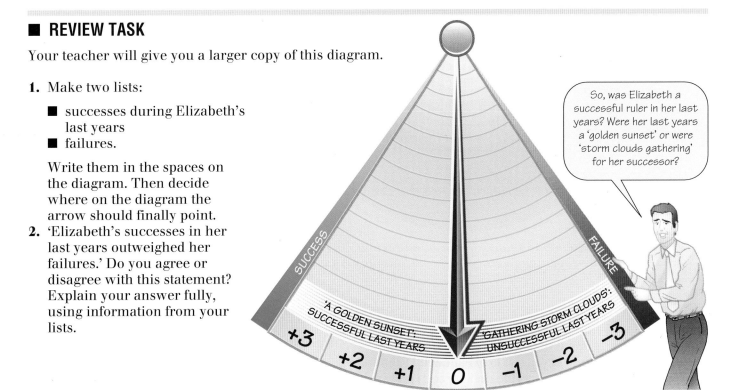

> So, was Elizabeth a successful ruler in her last years? Were her last years a 'golden sunset' or were 'storm clouds gathering' for her successor?

SUCCESS FAILURE

'A GOLDEN SUNSET': SUCCESSFUL LAST YEARS   'GATHERING STORM CLOUDS': UNSUCCESSFUL LAST YEARS

+3 +2 +1 0 –1 –2 –3

8 CONCLUSION: WAS ELIZABETH I A SUCCESSFUL RULER?

Your investigation of Elizabethan England has reached its last stage. You now know a lot more about Elizabeth's reign than you did a few months ago. The main purpose of this final chapter is to help you bring together all your ideas and conclusions about her reign. You will use them to work out your overall answer to the question 'Was Elizabeth I a successful ruler?' This will help you to:

■ remember what you have learned
■ begin revising your work for the GCSE examination.

Was Elizabeth popular with her people?

'GLORIANA', A STRONG, successful and popular Queen – this was the view of Elizabeth that was deliberately spread by the Queen and her councillors (see pages 28–33). But was it true?

It is not easy for us today to measure how popular Elizabeth really was. She ruled four million people. There were no opinion polls to ask them what they thought. There are many sources that say she was popular, but a lot of them were propaganda. Criticisms of her are much less common – it was very dangerous to criticise the Queen!

SOURCE 1 An extract from *The Faerie Queene*, written by the poet Edmund Spenser, 1589

❝ *O goddess heavenly bright,*
Mirror of grace and majesty divine,
Great lady of the greatest isle, whose light
Like Phoebus' lamp [the sun] throughout the world doth shine. ❞

SOURCE 2 An extract from *Elizabeth I*, by Christopher Haigh, 1988

❝ *In 1583 the Warwickshire Catholic John Somerville told his neighbours he was going to shoot Elizabeth, and set off for London – but he declared his intention to everyone he met on the way and was arrested.* ❞

1. Does Source 1 prove that Elizabeth was popular?
2. Does Source 2 prove that she was unpopular?
3. What reasons can you suggest to explain why Edmund Spenser (Source 1) and John Somerville (in Source 2) had such different views of Elizabeth?
4. Can historians decide how popular Elizabeth was simply by counting how many sources supported her and how many did not?

■ ACTIVITY

Work individually or in pairs. All the people shown here and over the page lived during Elizabeth's reign. Choose **one** of them. Decide how pleased he or she would have been with Elizabeth's rule – and why. (You will find the index useful for this activity.) Then explain your decision and reasons to the rest of the class.

The whole class should then discuss how to complete this short statement about Elizabeth I's popularity:

'Elizabeth I was a <u>very/quite/not very/completely un-</u> popular ruler with <u>all/most/some/a few/hardly any/none</u> of her people.'

William Cecil, Lord Burghley (see pages 36–37)

Robert Dudley, Earl of Leicester (see pages 42–44)

Sir Francis Walsingham (see pages 36–37)

Sir Francis Drake (see pages 120–128)

Robert Devereux, the Earl of Essex (see pages 148–150)

Edmund Campion, a Roman Catholic priest (see pages 89–91)

Bess of Hardwick (see pages 52–53)

William Shakespeare (see pages 104–108)

Thomas Howard, Duke of Norfolk (see page 82)

A beggar (see pages 66–69)

A farm labourer (see page 60)

A woman who spins wool (see page 61)

A yeoman farmer (see page 60)

A merchant who traded with other countries (see pages 114-119)

A Puritan (see pages 92–94)

A moderate Protestant (see pages 76–79)

A Roman Catholic (see pages 76–79)

■ TALKING POINT

Did sixteenth-century rulers need to be popular in order to be successful?

How has Elizabeth been remembered?

■ **TASK**

1. Study Sources 1–10. Which sources give a:

a) favourable

b) hostile

c) balanced

view of Elizabeth I?

2. Study each of the factors in Source 11 and find one example of a source that might have been affected by them. Record your findings in a larger copy of the table below. Make sure that your examples include different views of Elizabeth.

Reasons for different views about Elizabeth	Examples				
	Source	**Author**	**Date**	**View of Elizabeth: favourable, hostile or balanced?**	**Explanation**
Experiences					
Sources					
Times					
Background					
Purpose					
Audience					

3. 'Elizabeth I has usually been remembered as a very successful ruler. But recently this view has been challenged.' Do you agree or disagree with this statement?

ELIZABETH I DIED about 400 years ago. Since then many different kinds of people – including historians, politicians, artists, novelists, playwrights, film-makers and advertisers – have presented their views about her. Have they portrayed her as a successful ruler? Here is a small selection of their views...

SOURCE 1 An extract from *The History of the Most Renowned and Victorious Princess Elizabeth*, by William Camden, 1615. Camden, a JP, was asked by William Cecil to write this book, which was the first history of Elizabeth's reign

❝ *Those golden years. She maintained the dignity of England all her lifetime with peace, prosperity and glory. For never was a prince more beloved, obeyed or more admired abroad.* ❞

SOURCE 2 Gilbert Burnet, a Church of England bishop and historian, writing in 1680

❝ *It was wonderful that a virgin queen should rule for above 44 years with constant success and with such glory abroad.* ❞

SOURCE 3 James Froude, writing in the 1860s. He was the first historian to study the Cecil family's documents

❝ *It is more and more clear to me that Burghley [William Cecil] was the author of Elizabeth's and England's greatness.* ❞

SOURCE 4 Suggestions for school teachers, from *Modern Teaching*, by L. Court, 1928

❝ *Bring home clearly to children the fact that, by her love of country and wise ruling, Elizabeth raised England from a position of despair to one of greatness and glory.* ❞

SOURCE 5 An extract from *The First Queen Elizabeth*, by L. Du Garde Peach, 1958. This was a Ladybird book written for younger children during the early years of Elizabeth II's reign

When she came to the throne England was poor. When she died, England was rich, prosperous, united and happy.

Much of this was due to the character of Elizabeth herself. She never despaired and she never gave in.

SOURCE 6 An extract from *Elizabeth I*, by Christopher Haigh, a historian, 1988

Elizabeth died unloved and it was partly her own fault. She ended her days as an irascible [bad-tempered] old woman, presiding over war and failure abroad and poverty and factionalism [divisions] at home. Her reign had been thirty years of illusions, followed by fifteen of disillusion. The English never loved the real Elizabeth, they loved the image she created.

SOURCE 7 An extract from a school textbook, *England under the Tudors and Stuarts, 1485–1689*, written in 1965 by Michael Graves, a historian

No one can deny the greatness of Elizabeth. On the other hand, Elizabeth's rule was by no means perfect. Indeed some of her policies stored up great trouble for the future.

SOURCE 8 A scene from the 1970s BBC Television series *Elizabeth R*. Elizabeth, played by the actress Glenda Jackson, was portrayed as a strong ruler who eventually lost touch with her people

SOURCE 9 A painting of Elizabeth with members of her Court, by Frank Moss Bennett. It was painted in 1942, during the Second World War, when Britain was fighting against Germany

SOURCE 10 A poster advertising the film *Elizabeth*, 1998. Elizabeth is shown as a powerful, determined young Queen in troubled times. She has a passionate love affair with the Earl of Leicester. But at Court her other nobles and foreign ambassadors plot against each other to arrange her marriage. To stop their plans and win her people's support, Elizabeth invents the idea that she is a 'Virgin Queen'.

It was a very CONTROVERSIAL film. Critics praised it but historians complained that it contained too many inaccuracies. Shekhar Kapur, the film's director, said 'I don't mind turning history on its head'

Different times

People's views can be affected by the times in which they live. Someone living in a time of peace, prosperity and successful rulers might interpret past events very differently from someone who lives during a period of war, poverty and bad rulers.

Different backgrounds

People's views about the past can be influenced by their:

- political opinions
- religious beliefs
- country or culture.

Different purposes

Some people, like good historians, try to present the truth about the past. Other people have different purposes. They try:

- to persuade other people to accept their views (propaganda)
- to entertain other people
- to become famous
- to make money.

Different audiences

People usually 'aim' their views at a specific audience. These could be:

- the general public
- people who read a particular newspaper or watch a particular TV channel
- young children
- older students
- specialists, such as other historians.

Different experiences

Events usually affect people in different ways. Some people might gain from them but others might lose or suffer.

Different sources

Some people base their views on what they have heard. Others work like historians, using sources to reach their conclusions. But:

- they can only use the sources that have survived. Historical evidence is always incomplete. This leaves room for people to reach different views about the past.
- there are usually so many sources that people have to make decisions about which ones to use. Some choose a good, balanced range of sources. Others might use a narrow, one-sided selection.
- new sources are often found. These can contain important new evidence about the past. This leads people to revise or abandon earlier ideas.

SOURCE 11 Reasons for different interpretations of past people and events

■ ACTIVITY

The student in Source 11 is confused. He needs help. Draw up a list of questions to help him tell the difference between reliable and unreliable views about the past.

Finishing your investigation: was Elizabeth I a successful ruler?

YOU HAVE STUDIED other people's views about Elizabeth I. Now it is your turn. Was she a successful ruler? Remember – you will need evidence to support your conclusions. You first tried to answer this question several months ago. In Task 1 on page 11 you were asked to write an 'initial hypothesis'. Look at it again. Is it still a good answer?

■ TASK

Was the country stronger in 1603, when Elizabeth died, than it was in 1558, when she became Queen?

One way of deciding whether Elizabeth was a successful ruler is to answer this question. You will need to follow three steps.

1. Look again at the situation when Elizabeth became Queen in 1558 (see Source 2 on page 24). How serious were the problems she faced?
2. Look at the situation when Elizabeth died in 1603 (see Chapter 7, especially Source 1). How serious were the problems she left?
3. Decide whether the problems she left behind in 1603 were more, less or just as serious as the problems she faced in 1558.

Your teacher will give you a sheet to help you plan your answer.

SOURCE 1 One of the few paintings showing Elizabeth as an old woman. It was painted in the 1620s, after her death

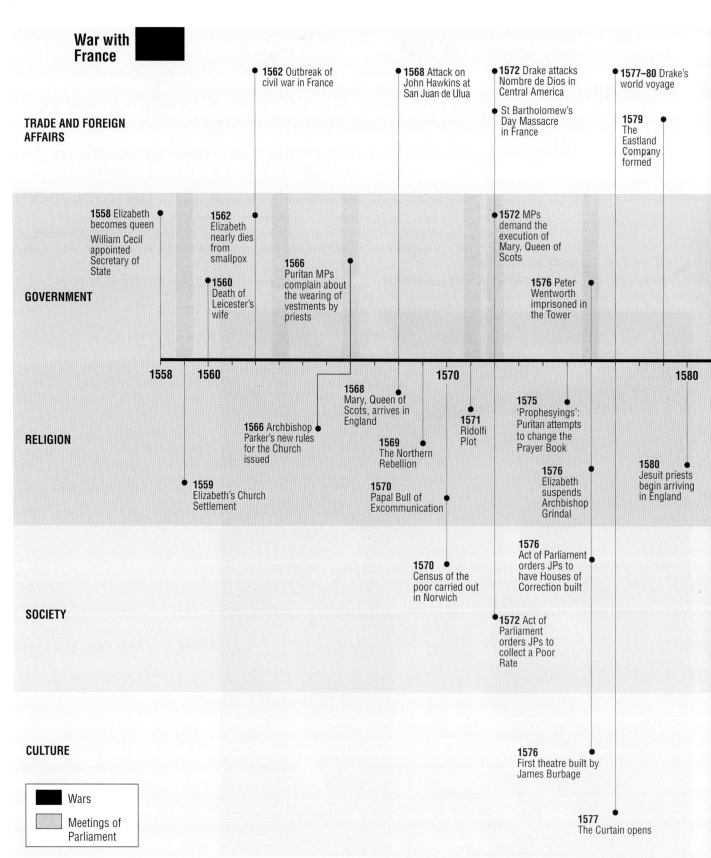

War with France

TRADE AND FOREIGN AFFAIRS

1562 Outbreak of civil war in France

1568 Attack on John Hawkins at San Juan de Ulua

1572 Drake attacks Nombre de Dios in Central America

St Bartholomew's Day Massacre in France

1577–80 Drake's world voyage

1579 The Eastland Company formed

GOVERNMENT

1558 Elizabeth becomes queen

William Cecil appointed Secretary of State

1562 Elizabeth nearly dies from smallpox

1560 Death of Leicester's wife

1566 Puritan MPs complain about the wearing of vestments by priests

1572 MPs demand the execution of Mary, Queen of Scots

1576 Peter Wentworth imprisoned in the Tower

1558   1560   1570   1580

RELIGION

1566 Archbishop Parker's new rules for the Church issued

1568 Mary, Queen of Scots, arrives in England

1569 The Northern Rebellion

1571 Ridolfi Plot

1575 'Prophesyings': Puritan attempts to change the Prayer Book

1559 Elizabeth's Church Settlement

1570 Papal Bull of Excommunication

1576 Elizabeth suspends Archbishop Grindal

1580 Jesuit priests begin arriving in England

1570 Census of the poor carried out in Norwich

1576 Act of Parliament orders JPs to have Houses of Correction built

SOCIETY

1572 Act of Parliament orders JPs to collect a Poor Rate

CULTURE

1576 First theatre built by James Burbage

1577 The Curtain opens

■ Wars

▨ Meetings of Parliament

SOURCE 2   A timeline 1558–1603. It summarises the main events and issues you have investigated in your Depth Study of Elizabethan England

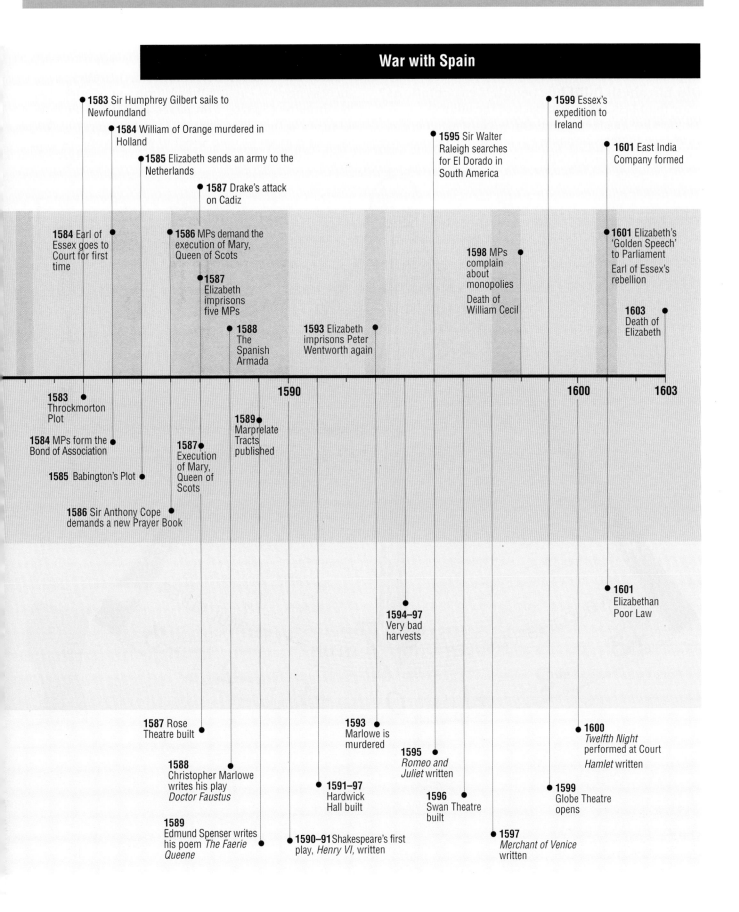

War with Spain

1583 Sir Humphrey Gilbert sails to Newfoundland

1584 William of Orange murdered in Holland

1585 Elizabeth sends an army to the Netherlands

1587 Drake's attack on Cadiz

1599 Essex's expedition to Ireland

1595 Sir Walter Raleigh searches for El Dorado in South America

1601 East India Company formed

1584 Earl of Essex goes to Court for first time

1586 MPs demand the execution of Mary, Queen of Scots

1587 Elizabeth imprisons five MPs

1588 The Spanish Armada

1593 Elizabeth imprisons Peter Wentworth again

1598 MPs complain about monopolies

Death of William Cecil

1601 Elizabeth's 'Golden Speech' to Parliament

Earl of Essex's rebellion

1603 Death of Elizabeth

1590

1600

1603

1583 Throckmorton Plot

1584 MPs form the Bond of Association

1585 Babington's Plot

1587 Execution of Mary, Queen of Scots

1589 Marprelate Tracts published

1586 Sir Anthony Cope demands a new Prayer Book

1601 Elizabethan Poor Law

1594–97 Very bad harvests

1587 Rose Theatre built

1593 Marlowe is murdered

1588 Christopher Marlowe writes his play *Doctor Faustus*

1591–97 Hardwick Hall built

1595 *Romeo and Juliet* written

1596 Swan Theatre built

1600 *Twelfth Night* performed at Court

Hamlet written

1599 Globe Theatre opens

1589 Edmund Spenser writes his poem *The Faerie Queene*

1590–91 Shakespeare's first play, *Henry VI*, written

1597 *Merchant of Venice* written

■ REVIEW TASK

Did Elizabeth fulfil her people's expectations?
Your final task takes you back to the advice Elizabeth was given when she became Queen in 1558 (see Source 2 on page 17). How successful was she in fulfilling her people's expectations?

Study the diagram below and rate Elizabeth's success against each of the criteria in the table. Use the timeline (Source 2 on pages 160–161) and your answers to the other Review Tasks to help you. Your teacher will give you a sheet to record your conclusions.

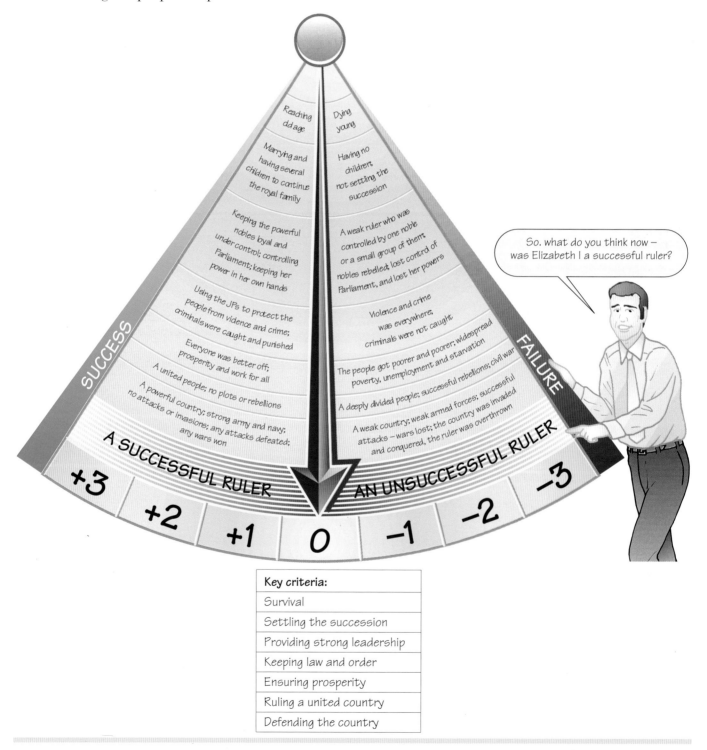

Key criteria:
Survival
Settling the succession
Providing strong leadership
Keeping law and order
Ensuring prosperity
Ruling a united country
Defending the country

Glossary

Act of Parliament   a law approved by the monarch and both Houses of Parliament.

almanacs   booklets written by astrologers which contained calendars and predictions. They were very popular.

alms   charity given to the poor.

almshouse   a house for the poor, paid for by charity.

ambassador   the official representative of a foreign ruler.

apprenticeship   the period a young person (called an apprentice) spent with a craftsman, learning a trade. Apprenticeships usually lasted for seven years.

Armada   the fleet of 130 Spanish ships which sailed to attack England in 1588 (Armada is the Spanish word for fleet).

astrologer   someone who makes predictions about events by studying the movements of the stars and planets.

bark   a small ship with three masts.

bill   a proposed law that has not yet been approved by the monarch and Parliament.

Bridewell   a House of Correction or prison for persistent beggars.

bull   a declaration by the Pope, which all Catholics were expected to obey.

bullion   bars of gold or silver.

Catholics   *see* Roman Catholics (below).

civil war   a war fought between different groups inside the same country.

colony   land or settlement outside a country's borders, which belongs to it. Colonies were usually seized or conquered.

commonwealth   a group of people united by a common interest; often used in the sixteenth century to mean the people of England.

controversial   ideas or beliefs about which people disagree and argue; sometimes controversy over an idea can lead to violence.

empire   a group of colonies belonging to, and ruled by, one country.

enclosure   the division of land (often including the village common land) into separate fields with hedges or fences between them. Enclosure was often carried out by landlords so that they could change to sheep farming.

excommunication   expelling someone from the Roman Catholic Church. This meant that the offender could not be married or buried in a church. Churchgoers were not allowed to help them or have anything to do with them. It was the most serious punishment the Roman Catholic Church could give.

exports   goods that are sold abroad.

fly-boat   a small, fast sailing boat.

galleon   a large battleship with several decks.

heir   the next in line to the throne.

heretic   someone whose beliefs went against the teachings of the Church. Heretics were severely punished.

hierarchical   organised into layers or groups. The people in each layer are more wealthy and powerful than, and require the obedience of, everyone below them.

House of Correction   a prison for beggars who refused to work. Also known as Bridewells.

illegitimate   the child of unmarried parents. The illegitimate child of a king or queen had no right to inherit the throne.

impotency   weakness. People who were unable to work were known as the impotent poor.

inflation   rising prices.

inn-yard   the yard of an inn or tavern which was used for performing plays.

inventory   a list of someone's possessions, usually made as part of a will.

invested   lent money to a business, in the hope of making a profit later.

Jesuit   Roman Catholic missionary priests.

martyr   someone who is prepared to die for his or her beliefs.

monopoly   a royal licence which gave individuals the sole right to sell or manufacture a product. Many people disliked monopolies because it was thought that they led to an increase in prices.

mutiny   a rebellion in the army or navy.

New World   a sixteenth-century term for North and South America.

night-watchman   someone who patrolled the streets at night, looking out for criminals.

patronage   the practice of using wealth and power to help people, by protecting them, giving them money or getting them a job.

pewter   a metal made from a mixture of tin and lead.

pinnace   a small ship with oars and sails.

Privy Councillors   members of the Privy Council, the committee of ministers appointed by Elizabeth to advise her.

propaganda   material issued, usually by governments, to persuade people to think or behave in a particular way.

Protestant   someone who rejects the authority of the Pope and most of the Catholic Church's teachings and ceremonies.

Puritan   an extreme Protestant who wanted churches to be very plain, without decoration, and wanted simple services, with no music.

purveyance   the monarch's right to buy cheap supplies, such as food for the army, in wartime.

rack-renting   the raising of rents by a greedy landowner.

recusant   someone, usually a Roman Catholic, who refused to go to church services. Punishments for not attending church were increased during Elizabeth's reign.

Renaissance   a period of 'rebirth', a renewed interest in the culture and achievements of the Ancient Greeks and Romans. It began in Europe in about 1450 and spread to England in the sixteenth century. It led to new ideas and changes in art, literature, music, architecture and science.

Roman Catholics   Christians whose religious leader is the Pope. Before the sixteenth century nearly everyone in western Europe belonged to the Roman Catholic Church and believed the Pope to be God's representative on Earth, with greater authority than a monarch.

stocks   a medieval punishment, still used in the sixteenth century. Criminals had their legs locked in a wooden frame and were left in a public place so that local people could see them.

sturdy beggars   the name given to people who were believed to be fit enough to work, but chose to beg instead.

traitor   someone who is guilty of treason.

treason   the crime of plotting against a monarch, the punishment for which was execution. During Elizabeth's reign the treason law was extended to include anyone who said that she was not the rightful Queen.

vagabond   a wandering beggar who often turned to crime. Vagabonds were seen as a serious threat to the social order and were severely punished.

Index

Acknowledgements

The Publishers would like to thank the following for permission to reproduce copyright material:

Pictures:
p.10 © BBC; **p.13** The Royal Collection © Her Majesty The Queen; **p.25** The Royal Collection © Her Majesty The Queen; **p.28** *t* By courtesy of the National Portrait Gallery, London, *b* The British Library (Eger. 3320 f.5); **p.29** Private Collection/Bridgeman Art Library, London; **p.30** The British Museum; **p.31** Woburn Abbey, Bedfordshire/Bridgeman Art Library, London; **p.32** Fotomas Index, Collection of Marquis of Salisbury at Hatfield House; **p.33** By courtesy of the National Portrait Gallery, London; **p.38** Hulton Getty; **p.43** By courtesy of the National Portrait Gallery, London; **p.46** Fotomas Index; **p.52** *t* National Trust Photographic Library/John Bethell, *bl* National Trust Photographic Library/Geoff Morgan, *br* National Trust Photographic Library/Andreas von Einsiedel; **p.53** *t* National Trust Photographic Library/Andreas von Einsiedel, *b* National Trust Photographic Library/Graham Challifour; **p.54** *t* English Life Publications Ltd., *b* National Trust Photographic Library/Rupert Truman; **p.55** *t* A. Harmsworth, *b* National Trust Photographic Library/Alan North; **p.60** *t & b* Hulton Getty; **p.62** Andrew Moore/Rex Features; **p.71** *t* The Fotomas Index, *bl & br* Mary Evans Picture Library; **p.72** *t & b* Mary Evans Picture Library; **p.80** Victoria & Albert Museum, London/Bridgeman Art Library, London; **p.81** Scottish National Portrait Gallery; **p.84** The British Library (Add. 48027 f.650); **p.88** *t* E + E Picture Library, *b* Mary Evans Picture Library; **p.96** The Shakespeare Centre Library, Stratford-upon-Avon; **p.97** Mary Evans Picture Library; **p.99** The British Museum; **p.105** Mary Evans Picture Library; **p.107** Hulton Getty; **p.120** By courtesy of the National Portrait Gallery, London; **p.122** E.T. Archive; **p.125** *l* Golden Hinde Ltd, *r* By courtesy of the National Portrait Gallery, London; **p.126** Mary Evans Picture Library; **p.128** Weidenfeld & Nicolson Archives; **p.129** Glasgow Museums: The Stirling Maxwell Collection, Pollock House; **p.132** Institut Amatller d'Art Hispanic; **p.135** By courtesy of the National Portrait Gallery, London; **p.136** © National Maritime Museum Picture Library (D.3292); **p.137** © National Maritime Museum Picture Library (BHC0263); **p.138** © National Maritime Museum Picture Library (A3683); **p.139** © National Maritime Museum Picture Library (A8122(8)); **p.140** The British Museum; **p.141** Private Collection; **p.142** © Colin Martin; **p.148** By courtesy of the National Portrait Gallery, London; **p.156** *t* © BBC, *b* Private Collection/Bridgeman Art Library, London; **p.157** © 1998 Polygram Filmed Entertainment, All Rights Reserved/Working Title Productions; **p.159** Corsham Court Collection.

Written sources:
p.28 Paul Johnson, *Elizabeth 1, A Study in Power and Intellect*, Orion Publishing Group Ltd., 1974; **p.41** Christopher Haig, *Elizabeth 1*, Addison Wesley Longman Ltd., 1988; **p.60** adapted from a figure in Yvonne Griffiths, *A New History of England 1485-1688*, Chatto & Windus, 1967; **p.141** John Lynch, *Spain under the Hapsburgs*, Blackwell Publishers, 1964; Felipe Fernandez-Armesto, *The Spanish Armada*, Oxford University Press, 1988; **p.142** Colin Martin and Geoffrey Parker, *The Spanish Armada*, Manchester University Press, 1988; Roger Lockyer and Dan O'Sullivan, *Tudor Britain*, Addison Wesley Longman Ltd., 1997; Felipe Fernandez-Armesto, *The Spanish Armada*, Oxford University Press, 1988; **p.152** Christopher Haig, *Elizabeth 1*, Addison Wesley Longman Ltd., 1988; **p.155** L. Court, *Modern Teaching*, The Home Library Book Company, 1928; **p.156** Extract adapted from L. Du Garde Peach, *The First Queen Elizabeth*, (Ladybird, 1958) © Ladybird Books, 1958; Christopher Haig, *Elizabeth I*, Addison Wesley Longman Ltd., 1988; Michael Graves, *England under the Tudors and Stuarts, 1485-1689*, G Bell and Sons, 1965.

Every effort has been made to trace all copyright holders, but if any have been inadvertently overlooked the publishers will be pleased to make the necessary arrangement at the first opportunity.